NO RETURN FROM DEMOCRACY

NO RETURN FROM DEMOCRACY

A Survey of Interviews with Fethullah Gülen

Faruk Mercan

NEW JERSEY • LONDON • FRANKFURT • CAIRO • JAKARTA

Published by Blue Dome Press

335 Clifton Ave.

Clifton, NJ, 07011, USA

www.bluedomepress.com

Printed in Canada by Marquis

Contents

Introduction

This book was first published in Turkish in February, 2016. The purpose was to reflect Fethullah Gülen's views on diverse topics, including Islam and democracy, politics, terrorism, jihad, Western civilization, women, and human rights in Islam. What did Gülen say on some of the crucial issues in interviews that have spanned more than two decades? The book was supposed to present a survey of his thoughts and highlight their importance to the time in which he voiced his ideas.

Five months after the book was published, a coup attempt took place in Turkey, on the night of July 15, 2016. Only three hours after the incident started, President Recep Tayyip Erdoğan claimed it was Gülen who was behind the coup. The next day, Fethullah Gülen had a press conference in Pennsylvania and answered questions from members of the press, representing by the *New York Times*, Reuters, *The Guardian*, and the *Financial Times*. On July 17, he spoke to CNN and CBS, followed by an interview with the BBC. In the following days he had interviews with CNN's Fareed Zakaria and with Kamran Safiarian, from German public broadcaster ZDF. In his op-eds for the *New York Times* and *Le Monde,* and in interviews with *Die Zeit* in Germany, El Pais in Spain, and Al Ahram in Egypt, Gülen answered claims about the coup and explained the background to his dispute with Erdoğan. He asked for an international committee to investigate who was really behind this coup attempt. He said he would comply with the decision of such a committee. Gülen said he had been harmed by all four military coups in Turkey's past, and that he always stood against such interventions.

In 1994, when Gülen had said that there was no going back from democracy, political Islamists targeted him, to the point of excommunicating him from Islam. Erdoğan's political Islamist supporters did the same when Gülen met with the Pope in 1998 and asked the Pope's support for Turkey's bid of European Union accession. In the same period, when Erdoğan was the mayor of Istanbul, he openly opposed the European Union, and said, "Democracy is like a streetcar. When we come to our stop, we get off. Democracy is not a purpose; it is an instrument."[1]

Yet in 2017, Erdoğan is accusing Gülen of toppling democracy.

---

1 Interview with Erdoğan on July 14, 1996, *Milliyet* newspaper.

Who is right?

Gülen has said that Erdoğan does not believe in democracy, destroyed all democratic progress in Turkey, and staged this coup to consolidate his oppressive regime in Turkey. In his interview with Fareed Zakaria, Gülen reminded viewers that Erdoğan defined the coup attempt as "a gift of God":

"It looks more like a Hollywood movie than a military coup. It seems something like a staged scenario. It is understood from what it is seen that they have prepared the ground to realize what they have already planned."

Gülen also told Fareed Zakaria of his firm stance against military interventions:

"In every coup d'état, I have been adversely affected. I have always been against coups, since I have spent my entire life with coups and pressures. I have the opinion that nothing good will come out of coups. Coups will divide, separate, disintegrate and make people the enemy of each other. This animosity will also affect future generations, just like it is in Turkey now. In this regard, as common sense requires, I have always been against coups, and I curse them. I would curse people who resort to coups against democracy, liberty, the republic. This is my general opinion" (CNN, July 31, 2016).

In almost all of his interviews, Gülen was asked about his past relationship with Erdoğan: "You were allies with Erdoğan in the past. Why did you fall apart?"

Gülen responded to this question with an anecdote:

"Before he established his party, Erdoğan came to me to ask for advice. As he was leaving, he said to his friend in the elevator, 'We first have to get rid of them.' This was perhaps 20 years ago. He said he could not tolerate any movement other than his own. It seems he has kept all these feelings inside" (July 16, 2016).[2]

---

2   As of April, 2017, more than 130,000 public servants have been dismissed and 50,000 individuals have been arrested in Turkey. Among the detainees are even the wives and daughters of these public servants or civilians who were arrested. Under the state of emergency declared after the coup attempt, Erdoğan purged thousands of people through the use of executive orders signed by himself. He extended detention periods to 30 days and lifted restrictions on torture. Since hundreds of lawyers have also been ar-

He was asked by a *Politico* journalist, "Is it true that you and President Erdoğan were once friends and allies? If so, what caused the tensions between you that have led to this situation today?"

Gülen's response was as follows:

"Many observers called our relationship an alliance, but in truth, we were never very close. I met him two or three times, all before he ran for elections. When his party ran for elections I was already here, so I could not vote anyway, but Hizmet sympathizers supported his party through their votes and their voices in the media. The reason for this support is not complicated. In going into elections in 2002 they [Erdoğan's Justice and Development Party] promised moving Turkey forward in its bid for European Union membership by implementing democratic reforms; enhancing human rights and freedoms; better integrating Turkey with the world; ending public corruption and the government's political profiling of people and their discriminatory measures. I and my friends supported them for these promises. Leading into the elections in 2011, they promised a democratic constitution that would be drafted by civilians without fear of military generals. But after winning that election they began to reverse every democratic reform they implemented before. The democratic constitution was first conditioned upon the inclusion of an executive presidency and then completely forgotten" (September 9, 2016, *Politico*, "Fethullah Gülen: 'I don't have any regrets'").

Gülen emphasized that a major reason behind the dispute has been Erdoğan's aspirations to become the Caliph of the Islamic world. In his interview with German broadcaster ZDF on September 23, 2016, Gülen said that Erdoğan demanded support for this aspiration:

"What really mattered for them is to have everything under their tutelage. Behind all these atrocities lies this: He wanted to be leader of the Muslims in the Islamic world and he wanted to use the schools in 170 countries for this purpose. If this potential was to be used in this direction, he would not do anything. This was what he really cared about. But he could not see the reality of these schools. 'What is their worth if

---

rested, there is a huge shortage of legal professionals who can defend the detainees. Over 2,000 schools, dormitories, and foundations, as well as 17 universities, 35 hospitals, and numerous media outlets, have been shut down. Erdoğan also confiscated the companies and properties of around 800 business people. Their worth totals billions of dollars.

not under my control; if of no use to Tayyibism or Erdoğanism, then let these movements be cursed, even if they lead to Paradise.' Those who are familiar with Germany in the 1940s would recognize what this mentality means. Up until yesterday, this man [Erdoğan] was living in a shack. Then, he landed in palaces, villas, fleets, and ships. He has money worth billions that he carried to various places in the world. When these were revealed, he placed the blame on me and those who were sympathetic to me. He saw himself as the leader of all Muslims. He thought he was a devout Muslim. So, he developed a severe animosity [towards me]. Then, he plotted this coup scenario."

Erdoğan's project for a Caliphate was triggered by the Arab Spring in 2011. He supported the Muslim Brotherhood and Muhammad Morsi in Egypt. Then he initiated the project to topple Bashar Al-Assad in Syria. Yet, he was unable to attain what he wanted in both of these countries. For Gülen, these were risky ventures, and he was critical of them. He told his views to both the Turkish Minister of Foreign Affairs and the government spokesman who Erdoğan sent to Pennsylvania to meet Gülen in 2013. Erdoğan ignored Gülen's advice on these matters.

In congruence with his self-assumed role as the "leader" of the Islamic world, Erdoğan has always kept tensions with Israel very high. He sent a resistance ship, the Mavi Marmara, to join the Gaza Freedom Flotilla, which aimed to break the Israeli blockade. The Israeli army raided the ships, and ten civilians on the Mavi Marmara were killed. Those who organized this ship planned everything with Erdoğan. Although the Israeli government warned that they would launch an operation, the Erdoğan government did not stop the ship. After the tragedy, Gülen said in his interview with the *Wall Street Journal* that necessary permissions should have been taken. Turkish relief organizations, Kızılay (Red Crescent) and Kimse Yok Mu, were already bringing in humanitarian aid to Gaza after obtaining proper permissions ("Reclusive Turkish Imam Criticizes Gaza Flotilla," June 4, 2010, *Wall Street Journal*).

Gülen's criticism did not please Erdoğan. Erdoğan said many times at his rallies, "He [Gülen] considers the state of Israel as the authority. If I am the authority, it was me who gave that permission." Erdoğan went as far as to say that Gülen cooperated with the "country in the south" to topple his administration. By the "country in the south," he was referring to Israel. He accused Gülen and the Hizmet Movement of being servants to Israel and working with MOSSAD, Israel's intelligence agency. He was holding Israel responsible for the overthrow of Morsi in Egypt. He said, "We have evidence; Israel is behind the incidents in Egypt" (August 20, 2013).[3]

In his interview with *Politico*, Gülen pointed to another major reason for the dispute with Erdoğan: the executive presidency. For Gülen, this was something like a "sultan's regime."

"In the past, I did support the idea of a presidential system if it was to be modeled after the U.S. or France or other countries where there are checks and balances against the president. But Erdoğan's proposal was akin to a sultan's regime. I could not support such a system with a clear conscience. Erdoğan put pressure on me and Hizmet sympathizers to publicly support his idea of a presidential system. He increased the pressure by supporting government-funded alternatives to Hizmet institutions and then began threatening to close them down. If we complied with his demand and became loyalists, we would be enjoying the Turkish government's favors now. But we declined and we have been facing their wrath for the last three years. This might be called the price of independence. It is a heavy price indeed but I don't have any regrets and I don't believe any of my friends have any regrets. My only sorrow is that the country continues to suffer because nobody can stand against his uninhibited ambitions" (September 9, 2016, *Politico*, "Fethullah Gülen: 'I don't have any regrets'").

Erdoğan's U-turn from democracy was perhaps best illustrated on the cover of *The Economist* (June 8, 2013), which featured Erdoğan wearing the robe of a Sultan and the title "Democrat or Sultan?" Those were the days when a huge protest was underway against Erdoğan and his government's plan to build a shopping center on one of the symbolic parks in the very heart of Istanbul, a space known as Gezi Park. The brutal police intervention left behind 6 dead and thousands wounded. 5,000 people were detained. The following lines from *The Economist* heralded what was going to happen in today's Turkey:

---

3 Later, Erdoğan pulled back all of his claims to reach an agreement with Israel. With the support of Jewish institutions he met in March, 2016, in the US and with President Barack Obama's mediation, Erdoğan agreed to resume relations with Israel. Erdoğan, who had said on July 17, 2014, "We were the authority, we gave permission to the ship," then said on June 30, 2016, "Did you ask me at all to send the humanitarian aid?"

"Broken heads, tear gas, water-cannons: it must be Cairo, Tripoli or some other capital of a brutal dictatorship. Yet this is not Tahrir but Taksim Square, in Istanbul, Europe's biggest city and the business capital of democratic Turkey. The protests are a sign of rising dissatisfaction with Recep Tayyip Erdogan... The rioting spread like wildfire across the country. The spark of protest was a plan to redevelop Gezi Park, one of the last green spots in central Istanbul. Resentment has been smouldering over the government's big construction projects, ranging from a third bridge over the Bosporus to a crazy canal from the Black Sea... A local dispute turned national because its elements serve as an extreme example of the authoritarian way Erdogan now runs his country. For some observers, Turkey's upheaval provides new evidence that Islam and democracy cannot coexist."[4]

Fethullah Gülen criticized this brutality, as well as Erdoğan's supporters' calling protestors "looters." Gülen wrote in his *New York Times* piece on July 25, 2016, that the plurality Erdoğan was trying to destroy in Turkey is the main philosophy of the Hizmet Movement:

"My philosophy [is] inclusive and pluralist Islam, dedicated to service to human beings from every faith... For more than 40 years, the participants in the movement that I am associated with — called Hizmet, the Turkish word for 'service' — have advocated for, and demonstrated their commitment to, a form of government that derives its legitimacy from the will of the people and that respects the rights of all citizens regardless of their religious views, political affiliations, or ethnic origins. Entrepreneurs and volunteers inspired by Hizmet's values have invested in modern education and community service in more than 150 countries..."

Gülen repeated his call for an international committee to investigate the coup attempt in Turkey in his op-ed in *Le Monde* on August 10, 2016:

"The Turkish judiciary has been politicized and controlled by the government since 2014 and, consequently, the possibility of a fair trial is very small. For this reason, I have advocated several times for the establishment of an international commission to investigate the coup attempt and I have expressed my commitment to abide by the findings of such a

---

4   Four years later, on April 15, 2017, The Economist was published with a new cover: "Turkey's slide into dictatorship." Sultan Erdoğan was on his path to becoming a dictator.

commission. Hizmet movement participants have not been involved in one single violent incident throughout [the Movement's] 50-year history. They haven't even taken to the streets to confront Turkish security forces while they have been suffering under the government's 'witch hunt,' to use Mr. Erdoğan's own words, for the last three years."

Erdoğan did not respond to this call, but responses came from the international community. Bruno Kahl, Germany's intelligence chief, said in an interview in *Der Spiegel* in March, 2017, "We are not convinced that Gülen was behind the coup. Turkey tried to convince us through different channels, but we are not."

Devin Nunes, the chairman of the House Intelligence Committee in the US, said on TV it is "hard to believe" that Gülen was involved in the failed coup attempt, and added "I haven't seen evidence for that" (Fox News, March 18, 2017).

A third response came from the United Kingdom. The Foreign Affairs Committee said in their report on the UK's relations with Turkey that "there is a relative lack of hard, publicly–available evidence to prove that the Gülenists as an organisation were responsible for the coup attempt in Turkey." While preparing this report, the 11-member Committee spoke with Erdoğan in Turkey (March 25, 2017, BBC).

Another response came from Belgium. A report prepared by Intcen, the EU's intelligence-sharing unit, noted, "It is unlikely that Gülen himself played a role" (January 17, 2017, *The Times*).

It appears that the international community has been comparing both Gülen's and Erdoğan's track records on democracy. When in the 1990s political Islamists considered discussions of democracy forbidden, Gülen argued that Islam and democracy were compatible, and there was no return from democracy. Gülen's consistency in his views over time certainly must be a positive effect on his record.

The schools, universities, hospitals, and cultural centers that have been opened in more than 170 countries since 1992 by people inspired from Gülen have shown his philosophy to the entire world. Erdoğan has been using all his energy and the privileges of the state to have these schools shut down abroad. He was able to do so only in certain countries which do not rank high well in regards to democracy.

It has been revealed that Erdoğan formed a wide network of spies against the followers of Gülen outside Turkey. Countries like Germany,

Belgium, the Netherlands, Denmark, and Sweden started investigations into this spy network. Even worse was a plan to kidnap Gülen and attempt to assassinate him. James Woolsey, the former CIA Director, told the *Wall Street Journal* that this plan was discussed in a meeting he was invited to participate in New York City on September 19, 2016. This meeting was organized by Mike Flynn, who was lobbying for Erdoğan in the US. Participants to the meeting were the Foreign Minister of Turkey and Erdoğan's son-in-law, who is also the Minister of Energy ("Ex-CIA Director: Mike Flynn and Turkish Officials Discussed Removal of Erdogan Foe from US," March 24, 2017, Wall Street Journal). 20 days after this meeting, the *Huffington Post* reported about an assassination plan against Gülen ("Turkey Mulling attack on US Based Cleric," October 5, 2016, the *Huffington Post*).

Gülen's views on Islam and democracy are the cornerstone of the book in your hands. Other topics discussed portray his thoughts on modernity and secularism, Western civilization and values, politics, fundamental human rights and freedoms, Islam and women, dialogue and coexistence, terrorism and jihad, the Kurdish issue, Alevi-Sunni divide, and minorities and their rights. In the Appendix, you will find some of his recent articles on Turkey, the coup attempt, and terrorist activities.

Gülen's comments around these topics also shed light on two things:

1) What kind of a world does Gülen desire? 2) Why does Erdoğan want to annihilate Gülen and the Hizmet Movement he represents?

In 1997, Gülen expressed his views on religion and politics: "The politicization of religion is dangerous, but it is much more dangerous for religion than it is for the regime, as it means sullying the spirit of religion."

After the devastating terrorist attacks of September 11, 2001, when many looked to the Islamic world for a voice of peace, Gülen said, "A Muslim cannot be a terrorist and a terrorist cannot be a Muslim. A person cannot go to heaven by killing a person."

This book invites the reader to journey through the horizons of all that Gülen has said in relation to these issues over more than two decades.

Faruk Mercan
June 20, 2017

CHAPTER 1

ISLAM AND DEMOCRACY

Islam and Democracy

Can Islam and democracy be reconciled? Can a Muslim also be a democrat? Can Muslims fully practice their religion in a democratic order? What kind of regime does Islam envisage? Does a theocratic regime exist in Islam? What is meant by an "Islamic order"? Many more questions can be asked about the relationship between Islam and democracy.

Islam does not envision a theocratic state, nor does it impose a certain type of government on the state. This is one of the key issues radical Islamists are mistaken about.

As an Islamic scholar, Gülen has brought serious attention to this grievous error in interpretation and judgment. This was why he has always been a target of radical Islamists.

Gülen has argued that for him, a republican regime is in harmony with Islam at its core and that Islam does not have any problems with democracy. He thinks democracy and a republican system are the best forms of government and ensure the most convenient institutional setting for Muslims to practice their faith. The general principles of Islam do not contradict democracy, nor does what Islam prescribes for lawful administration.

Islam holds the individual at its center; thus, individual experience of faith is its top priority. A vast majority of Qur'anic teachings concern a believer's personal practice of Islam. There is no definitive form of government that is strictly prescribed. Types of administration are to be determined according to the needs of the time. The human experience today reveals democracy and republican governments as the most suitable administrations for our times.

Radical Islamists considers the Qur'an as the constitution of Muslims. They reject modern legal systems. For Gülen, however, the Holy Qur'an is a manual, teaching us how to practice faith in the most ideal way. Thus, Islam and Muslims have no trouble with modern constitutions, as long as they are democratic and ensure freedoms for Muslims to practice their religion.

Let us recall Fethullah Gülen's speech on June 29, 1994, at the Istanbul Dedeman Hotel, celebrating the establishment of the Journalists and Writers Foundation. In his speech on the night, he gave three strong messages to Turkey and the world:

1. *There is no turning back from democracy.*

2. *The practicing believers are being treated as if they do not deserve even one- tenth of democratic rights as non-believers.*

3. *State administration during the Rashidun period could easily be called a Republic.*

Those who claim that "religion and democracy are irreconcilable" are wrong.

The July 2005 edition of *The Muslim World* journal, published in the United States, was a special issue devoted specifically to Fethullah Gülen and the Hizmet movement. The issue included an extensive interview with Gülen conducted by Professor Zeki Sarıtoprak and author Ali Ünal.

Gülen was asked, "Is it possible to reconcile Islam with democracy? How do you see the lack of democracy in many Muslim countries, and do you see this lack of democracy as a deficit for Muslim nations?"

Gülen offered a lengthy answer. An excerpt from this response is below:

"Yes, in the Islamic world and particularly in my country, Turkey, it is painful to see how those who speak on Islam and democracy and claim to pronounce in the name of religion have come to the understanding that Islam and democracy cannot be reconciled. This perception of mutual incompatibility extends to some pro-democracy people as well. The argument that is presented is based on the idea that the religion of Islam is based on the rule of God, while democracy is based on the view of humans, which opposes it. In my understanding, however, there is another idea that has become a victim of such a superficial comparison between Islam and democracy. The phrase, 'Sovereignty belongs to the nation unconditionally,' does not mean that sovereignty has been taken from God and given to humans. On the contrary, it means that sovereignty is entrusted to humans *by* God; that is to say, it has been taken from individual oppressors and dictators and given to the community members. To a certain extent, the era of the Rightly-Guided Caliphs of Islam illustrates the application of this democratic norm of democracy.

"Cosmologically speaking, there is no doubt that God is the sovereign of everything in the universe. Our thoughts and plans are always under the control of the power of such an Omnipotent. However, this does not mean that we have no will, inclination or choice. Humans are free to make choices in their personal lives. They are also free to make choices with regard to their social and political actions. Some may hold different types of elections to choose lawmakers and executives. There is not only one way to hold an election; as we can see, this was true even for the Era of Bliss, the time of the Prophet of Islam, and during the time of the Four Caliphs. The election of the first Caliph, Abu Bakr, was different than that of the second Caliph, 'Umar. 'Uthman's election was different from that of 'Ali, the fourth Caliph. God only knows the right method of election."

Islam is conducive to democracy

Seven years after this interview, German journalist Rainer Hermann, author of the book *Where Is Turkey Headed: Culture Battles in Turkey*, interviewed Gülen.

A part of this interview was published in the German daily Frankfurter Allgemeine Zeitung, on December 6, 2012. One of the questions Hermann put to Gülen was as follows:

"Are such basic attainments as democracy, pluralism and human rights only things invented by the West, or can they be accepted as universal values and applied in Muslim societies?"

In his answer to this question, Gülen made mention of the concept, "religious democracy":

"Important advances in such matters as democracy, pluralism, and human rights have of course been made in our day. But none of these are values that emerged only in the West and in modern times. We see that in its process of development, democracy has many different applications and that it underwent many modifications and revisions. More often than not in our day, another term, such as social, liberal, Christian, or radical, is added to democracy as a prefix. In some cases, even one of these forms of democracy may not consider the other as democracy.

"The principles and form of government that form the basis of democracy are compatible with Islamic values. Consultation, justice, freedom of religion, protection of the rights of individuals and minorities, the people's say in the election of those who will govern them and the latter being held accountable for their actions, and prevention of the oppression of the majority or minority, can be cited as examples of the values and principles espoused by both Islam and democracy. I can easily say that just as the general principles of Islam concerning government do not prevent the implementation of democracy in a Muslim society, they constitute an appropriate basis for the implementation of democracy."

The next question to come from the German journalist was the following: "But these have for the most part not been applied in Islamic history. What is the reason for this?" Let us look again at Gülen's response:

"Another issue that should be incorporated into democracy," Gülen said, "ought to be preparing a suitable ground for a human being to meet their needs concerning the humanity's needs in the afterlife, whether they believe or not. This is preparing the ground for their prayer, their fasting, and their going to church or to a synagogue to worship. Democracy should allocate a place for this within it, for it to be universal. Otherwise, it will become a system that functions only according to the whims and wishes of certain people. And this would narrow down the issue considerably. When democracy acquires such breadth, everyone will find a place for themselves within it. Maybe one day Muslims too will speak of a 'Muslim democracy' and 'religious democracy.' For the human being has been created for eternity. They cannot be satisfied with anything other than it. There may be those who do not believe as such, but the sentiments of people who do believe should be taken into account and be met with respect."

There is no need to establish a religious state if we can practice our religion

"Do you believe Islam should be given more room in the public sphere and in politics?"

In responding to this question asked in the interview with *Asharq Al-Awsat*, Gülen stated that in a country in which there is freedom of religious practice, first and foremost, and basic rights and freedoms, efforts to establish an Islamic state are redundant:

"Islam, as a religion, is a set of principles and practices based on divine revelation which guides human beings to absolute goodness through their own free will and shows them how to strive to become a 'perfect person.' People can live their religion in any way they please in a democratic country which allows people to enjoy their religious beliefs freely. In such a country, free elections are held in compliance with democratic principles and universal human rights and freedoms [are respected], and people freely voice their demands of their representatives.

"They do this by casting their votes at the elections and through using other democratic rights available to them. They can do this individually or collectively by participating in the activities of civil society groups. I always reject the idea of treating religion as a political ideology. In my opinion, a Muslim should continue to act as a Muslim in social life and as well as in the private, public, civilian, and bureaucratic spheres. In other words, a Muslim is supposed to stick to Islam's moral and ethical values everywhere and at all times. Theft, bribery, looting, graft, lying, gossip, backbiting, adultery, and moral lowness are sins and are illegitimate in every context. These sins cannot be committed for political or other purposes and no one can issue a fatwa allowing their commission. At the same time, these acts of corruption are generally deemed by universally accepted norms as criminal offences. If an individual has lost his or her moral integrity in these respects, what is the use of this individual assuming a role within a public body or within a political faction? Like anyone else, I would like to see these ethical positions adopted by all people who hold public office, whether as a civil servant or as a politician.

"Indeed, the aforementioned afflictions are the main source of complaints about public bodies and political structures everywhere around the world. Let me put it blatantly: if Muslims can freely cherish their religion, perform their religious duties and rituals, establish institutions defined by their religion, teach their religious values to their children or other aspirants, speak their mind about their religion in public debates, and make religious demands in compliance with laws and democracy, then they do not have to try to establish a religious or 'Islamic' state. We know from history that rebellions, revolutions, uprisings and other violent incidents that have the potential to drag a country into chaos and anarchy will eventually make us lose our democratic and human rights achievements and lead to irreparable damage to the country. As a matter of fact, if a country's administration is forcibly seized and people are forced to become religious, it would turn them into hypocrites.

"These people will pretend to be pious at home, but when they go abroad, they will indulge in the most extreme forms of sin and irreverent and irreligious acts. In such a country, respect for the rule of law diminishes and hypocrisy increases. If you look closely at diverse experiences in different countries, you will realize that my seemingly abstract words rely on concrete cases and observations" (March 24, 2014, *Asharq Al-Awsat*).

Turkey's transition to democracy occurred during the Ottoman era

Asharq Al-Awsat's following question was directly related to the connection between the Islam-democracy relationship and Turkey's experience: "Do you think Islam can be reconciled with democracy in Turkey? How could a successful reconciliation of the two affect Turkey's European Union membership bid?"

In his response, Gülen reaffirmed his belief that democracy is the system that is most suited to Islam's administrative principles:

"Turkey has been governed by democratic rule, despite its shortcomings, since the 1950s. The preliminary moves to transition of our country's administration to democracy was made by the Ottoman sultans, who were caliphs at the same time. In 1876, non-Muslim deputies constituted one-third of the first democratically elected parliament.

"It is wrong to see Islam as conflicting with democracy and vice versa. Perhaps it can be argued that democracy is a system that fits well with Islam's governance-related principles, both in terms of its allowing the rulers to be accountable to the ruled and its being the opposite of despotism, which is defined by Islam as an evil form of governance. Islam is readily compatible with human rights, democratic elections, accountability, the supremacy of law, and other basic principles.

"When I said, 'There will be no turning back from democracy; it is not perfect, but the best system we have,' in 1994, certain groups raised objections to my assertion. But there are numerous implementations and types of democracy. We can hardly say it is a perfect form of governance. It is still going through a process of perfection. A country where life and mind, as well as property, family, and religious freedoms are protected, and where individual rights and freedoms are not restricted save for in exceptional cases such as war, where minorities are treated as equal citizens and do not face any discrimination, and people are allowed to freely discuss and implement their personal, social, and political views—this would be a country which is suitable for Islam. If people can freely express their views and beliefs, cherish their religion, perform their religious duties and rituals, and have freedoms such as freely acquiring property, neither Muslims nor practitioners of other religions are supposed to change the regime in that country.

"In countries where they cannot enjoy these liberties, they should try to obtain them through democratic means, but never by resorting to violence. I believe that Islam and democracy can coexist peacefully not only in Turkey, but also in Muslim countries or, more precisely, in predominantly Muslim countries. We sadly observe that in countries where democracy is demonized, human rights violations, moral and legal turmoil, and religious and ethnic disputes and conflicts abound. Currently, democracy is evolving to become a common asset and custom, as it were, of the entire human race...."

As evidence that Islam and democracy are compatible, Gülen said, "In countries that comply with the EU standards, Muslims are entitled to cherish, implement, represent, and even promote and teach their religion.

"Both as individuals and as a community, our essential duty is to cherish and represent our religion. Turkey is not described as a full-fledged democracy. Practicing Muslims who were oppressed in the past, such as Muslim female students who were banned from wearing headscarves on university campuses, have attained many rights as a result of the country's EU bid. In this respect, the EU accession process has brought a number of benefits to Turkey. As part of this process, serious democratic reforms have been introduced to the country. If these reforms are maintained and Turkey's democratic system can attain the EU standards regarding the rule of law and respect for human rights and freedoms, then I think Turkey's Muslim identity will not be seen as a roadblock to its full membership.

"Even if anti-Islam fanatics block Turkey's EU membership, the gains Turkey makes during its attempt at becoming a full member are still important wins for Turkey's democracy. However, Turkey has recently started to backpedal from the EU's democratic standards" (*Asharq Al-Awsat*, March 24, 2014).

Perfect democracy is possible with Islamic ethics

When Gülen was interviewed by the correspondent of the French *Le Monde*, on April 28, 1998, he was asked, "What do you have to say about Islam and democracy?"

After indicating that Islam does not have a problem with democracy and to a large extent secularism, Gülen drew attention to a very important point, saying, "Democracy can be reconciled perfectly with the virtuous people who are well learned in the ethics of Islam."

Gülen: "Islam holds a pivotal place in this country [Turkey]. Muslims can speak of democracy, of secularism, according to their own understanding. Whatever the form of administration, even if it be the most perfect form of democracy, what is more important than this is the matter of being a good person. It is the matter of the existence of morally excellent and *virtuous* human beings. Scholars like the author of *Utopia* (Sir Thomas More) and Al-Farabi (Alpharabius) brought to the fore the virtuous cities, taking the matter a step further.

"But, what should always be given priority is the humanity. The city, civilization, the country, and the town should follow behind the human. For democracy, the existence of the meritorious, virtuous human beings are very important. In my opinion, Islam offers a very good democratic education and training. Democracy can be reconciled perfectly with the virtuous people who have gone through Islamic moral training. Now, just as you look at different parts of the world and question how many kinds of Islam exist on the basis of application, there are many varieties of democratic praxis. The conception of democracy and its implementation in France is different from the conception of democracy and its implementation in England or Germany.

"Islam has no problem with democracy. Even to a great measure, if you look at the codified non-canonical laws of the Ottomans, many people talk about the Ottoman period as one of secularism; as long as they were not contradicting the basic rules about faith and worship, new innovations took place in making laws in legislation... These are not explicit in the Qur'an, the Sunna, and the primary sources. Over time, as new issues arose, and if nothing could be found with a clear stipulation in the basic sources, then a new legislation was being produced with an effort not to contradict these sources... When viewed from this perspective, Islam has no problem with democracy and with secularism [as long as it is not repressive].

"Although secularism basically involves legal discipline, if you … try to exclude religion, if you try to enforce a type of secularism that would force individuals to leave their religion behind, you will cause conflicts in the society. Then so you will create many anti-secular and anti-democratic people. It is incumbent upon us to point to the fault of the people who cause this disruption as much as those who do the disrupting."

Whenever Gülen has been asked about whether or not Islam can be reconciled with democracy, he has often begun with a definition of religion and Islam. He has mentioned the phases democracy has undergone throughout history, and eventually discussed a democracy that is not closed to Islamic values. This is a democracy with a metaphysical dimension, taking into account not only a person's worldly life, but also their life in the Hereafter. This is a democracy that doesn't turn its back on religious values. A typical answer, which appeared in the *Muslim World* journal, is below:

"On the issue of Islam and democracy, one should remember that the former is a divine and heavenly religion, while the latter is a form of government developed by humans. The main purposes of religion are such universal subjects like faith [*iman*], servanthood to God [*ubudiyyah*], knowledge of God [*ma'rifa*], and beautiful actions [*ihsan*]. The Qur'an, in its hundreds of verses, invites people to the faith and worship of the True (al-Haqq). It also asks people to deepen their servanthood to God in a way that they may gain the consciousness of *ihsan*. 'To believe and do good deeds,' is among the subjects that the Qur'an emphatically stresses. It also frequently reminds people that they must develop a conscious relationship with God and act as if they see God, or as if they are seen by God.

"Such an introduction of Islam may play an important role in the Muslim world through enriching local forms of democracy and extending it in such a way that helps humans develop an understanding of the relationship between the spiritual and material worlds. I believe that Islam would also enrich democracy by answering the deep needs of humans, such as spiritual satisfaction, which cannot be fulfilled except through the remembrance of the Eternal One" (July 2005 issue of *Muslim World*).

What does Gülen mean when he says he expects democracy to solve the problems pertaining to the life in the hereafter? Gülen here points to freedom of worship. According to Islam, a pleasurable life after death is possible if one lives a virtuous life and can offer his or her observances to God.

Throughout history, freedom of worship has been one of the major problems for believers of any religious tradition. Often, they have had to conceal their prayers; if caught practicing their faith, they could be tortured or even killed. Among other freedoms, democratic societies protect freedom of worship as a fundamental human right.

Gülen had offered these views before, including in an interview with *Zaman* in the United States in March of 2004:

"What we call democracy can be interpreted differently. There are many different democracies in the world. During the times when Communism existed, they were calling it democracy as well. America calls itself a democracy, but so do England and Belgium. Many different types of democracy exist around the world. There are Christian Democrats, Buddhist Democrats, and even Jewish Democrats. People can be both a democrat and also own an understanding, a belief, a philosophy at the same time. There are no drawbacks to blending Islamic traditions and customs with democracy. In my opinion, such democracy could exist.

"The following can even be added to democracy: The needs of a person are not solely made up of worldly needs. Let me have the benefits of freedom of thought, freedom of earning, but, let me also have another side open to eternity. I am created for eternity. I am not satisfied with anything but eternity. If democracy is to be a full-fledged democracy, it needs to include things that help to fulfill my desire and it needs to give support to this. That means, democracy requires a metaphysical dimension. It also needs a side that is open to our accounts for the other world, to our unfulfilled accounts. Why not have such a democracy?" (*Zaman*, March 24, 2004).

The following statements are from Gülen's 2010 interview with the *New York Times*:

"... consideration should definitely be given to the richness that Islam can contribute to democracy. In our times, democracy is still trying to perfect itself. We should try to develop a democracy that is going to be able to respond to all the demands of humanity—a humanity that will not find fulfillment in anything other than God's favor and the promise of eternity.

"This issue should be put out on the table and opened up for discussion. I think that democracy should be encompassing enough to fulfill humanity's material and spiritual longings. Human beings should be able to live freely in accordance with what they believe, and democracy has to prepare such an environment for them" (A section of this interview by Brian Knowlton was published in the *New York Times* on June 11, 2010).

Islam's first era was a republic

Gülen also stressed that the era of the Rightly Guided Caliphs, the first era in Islam's history, was actually a republic and an unacknowledged democracy. In the case of Caliphs that served as the leaders of an Islamic state in earlier periods, it was essential to have popular consent and be elected to the position. This was how Abu Bakr became the first Caliph after the Prophet (pbuh). The successive three Caliphs also assumed the office with the approval of the community, which is the essence of democracy and a republic. Succession from father to son, as in dynasties, is not what Islam prescribes. Yet, these administrations emerged later in Islamic history and they hardly represent the true spirit of Islamic government. For Gülen and other scholars, the period of the first four caliphs reflects a much more accurate type of Islamic administration.

Responding to the questions of Yalçın Doğan for Kanal D on April 16, 1997, he explained:

"Democracy is a rule by the people. It is a profound form of 'republic.' It is [the republic's] soul; it is the more humane dimension of it. For this reason, in a sense ... it always existed in the past, although it was not named. We can even talk about a republic and the existence of a democracy without a name during the era of the Rightly Guided Caliphs. ... Maybe between the systems there is an overlap. It is possible to reconcile them. For this reason, it could be thought that a republic and democracy might make a proper ground for Islam, Islamic thought, and the possibility of practicing Islam. Considering them as against Islam, in my opinion, is a wrong interpretation, a wrong approach..."

In an interview broadcast on TRT (Turkish Radio and Television, the national public broadcaster of Turkey), on June 2, 1995, Gülen said, "Islam in its early period was a republic. It cannot be claimed otherwise."

On February 27, 1998, Gülen appeared on an NTV program jointly-presented by Taha Akyol and Cengiz Çandar. During the program, Çandar asked, "What can you say about democracy and Islam? Currently, there seems to be a consensus that Turkey is going through a troubled political period. How do you assess Turkey's current situation and immediate future? What kind of suggestions can you offer?"

Gülen's reply was long and thoughtful:

"I have never seen democracy as being opposed to the spirit of Islam. I even said at the very beginning (in a talk dated June 29, 1994), that this is a process, one than has been set in motion and a return from which is impossible... Democracy is of different kinds. There are social democrats, Christian democrats and liberal democrats in the world....

"I would like democracy to develop some day to such an extent that in that process of development, a setting is prepared in which all of the needs of individuals, material as well as spiritual, worldly and other worldly, can be met. That is to say, just as it responds to my needs until the grave, and provides me with opportunities that will not harm others, it ought to facilitate my comfortable passage through the grave and the intermediate realm. It should even prepare the ground for my entry into Paradise, through the opportunities with which it provides.

"When I shared these thoughts with an American academic, he noted them as an excellent definition of democracy. Given these considerations, where are we in terms of democracy? I think it is wrong to pass judgement on the basis of any one understanding."

Political Islam or the politicization of Islam

Taha Akyol asked Gülen specifically about political Islam and democracy:

"You represent an Islam which is rooted in these lands. As I understand it, you do not have an ideological connection with, let alone a sympathy for, movements collectively labelled as radical Islam, political Islam, or fundamentalist Islam; groups, such as Hamas, or activities like [so-called] Islamic jihad, which emerged in the Middle East, especially after the collapse of socialism. Your terminology is not the terminology of the Middle Eastern radicalism that is referred to as political Islam."

Gülen gave the following answer:

"Islam emerged in the Arabian Peninsula, moved to the Asian steppes where it became concentrated in feeling and thought, thereafter curving once again all the way to Anatolia, Asia Minor, which assumed the role of a mother and bequeathed certain things to Asia Major that would allow it to one day fulfil its legacy... Islam essentially developed in Asia with respect to jurisprudence, law, theology, and Sufi thought; from Asia, it spread out to all corners of the globe... We are the heirs to a rich cultural legacy; so rich that we do not have to feel any need for certain tiny currents that have formed here and there at the present time.

"I used this expression, and have referred to Hamas' inconsistent actions – and even some discouraging behaviors in this regard – on the basis of the Prophetic expression, 'Make things easy for the people and do not make things difficult; endear them (with glad tidings) and do not drive them away.'

"Ismail Hami Danishmend stated that the Turks entered Islam all the way back, during the time of Prophet Abraham; and that because the principles with which Abraham came were the principles of *tawhid*, this was the same source from which God's Messenger was nourished; as such, they came from the same source.

"I concur with such an opinion. It seems to me that this rich, deep-rooted thought and current leaves no need for any other current anywhere else in the world. Our task is to evaluate and reevaluate it, to bring it to new heights via new synthesis and analysis, and to express it loud and clear in platforms where it can gain recognition for the benefit of all humanity."

Politicizing religion is as damaging as hostility to religion

Political Islam, or the politicization of Islam, is one of the focal points in debates about Islam and democracy. Gülen has been a consistent voice in this debate: He does not believe religion should be politicized. He offers the following response to *Le Monde* correspondent Nicole Pope's question, "What do you think about political Islam?"

"Ninety-eight percent of Islam encompasses individual and family life, and the basic moral and spiritual values that can be espoused by society. Only two percent concerns affairs of the state. Ignoring the 98 percent without referring to this as Islam, only to present the 2 percent as Islam at a time when politics is in the foreground... is both wrong and a disservice to the 98 percent.

"The 98 percent includes such tenets of faith as belief in God, belief in the Resurrection, belief in the Books, belief in the Prophets, and belief in the angels, and such pillars of Islam as the prayer, the prescribed alms, fasting, and pilgrimage, followed by all moral principles; all of these are carried out in [Turkey]. Moreover, included in this are the many matters we share in common with other religions. Each individual or family can practice these on their own and no one can say anything regarding their doing so.

"But the remaining 2 percent concerns governance. Disregarding the 98 percent to present the 2 percent as Islam on the basis of those who perceive Islam as a political system, and then talking about political Islam, contradicts the reality of Islam.

"The expression political Islam was not used by Muslims wanting to make Islam a base for their national liberation and independence movements and who perceived it in this respect as an ideology more than as a religion. The expression was propounded either by the Western media who had to find a name for the movements of these Muslims, or by other circles. For all that, Muslims still approached the matter within the framework of religion or the *shari'a*. If what they imply by '*shari'a*' is the 2 percent I mentioned, they are making a mistake. Those taking shari'a to mean the same 2 percent are also mistaken.

"Whereas even when speaking here, the fact that my tone and manner of speaking needs to be respectful and never hurtful, rude or offensive, is a rule of the *shari'a*, and is fastidiously stressed in the Qur'an. Respecting people, being hospitable to guests, so much so that it even includes, as stated by the Prophet Muhammad, looking at another person's face with a smile, even drawing water from a well and giving it to a thirsty human being or animal, or emptying it into the bucket of the person next to you, or removing harmful obstacles from the path of travelers or pedestrians... All of these are requirements of the *shari'a*, of the religion of Islam. And we do all these in a spirit of worship, in the consciousness and exhilaration of fulfilling the religion's commands. These are the actual aspects of religion that need to be seen and shown because religion, as a whole, is a compendium of goodness and virtue. Whatever has beauty is from the religion, and whatever is repugnant has nothing to do with religion. The Messenger of God said, 'I have been sent to perfect noble character.' He is addressed in the Qur'an with the words, 'You are surely of a sublime character, and do act by a sublime pattern of conduct,' and 'We have not sent you but as an unequalled mercy for all the worlds.'

"When this is what religion actually is, constantly and somewhat deliberately presenting the 2 percent as the religion on the basis of the wrongs of some people is tantamount to politicizing the whole religion and seeing it as a political ideology, and this would be the greatest disservice to the religion. In this regard, we have long been against the politicization of religion, and have considered it just as harmful as hostility to religion."

For a full democracy in the Western sense

Canadian journalist-author Fred A. Reed met with Fethullah Gülen on November 30, 1999. In this meeting, Gülen underscored several points. Gülen indicated that religiously-minded people have a duty to show the whole world that Islam does not conflict with democracy:

"If democracy provides the favorable conditions for Muslims and others to live in harmony, then we should encourage ourselves to establish democracy and exert every effort to achieve a full democracy in the Western sense in our nation. This is critical and essential for two reasons:

"First, so that we can live out our creed and beliefs in peace, and second, so that new generations can live out their lives and worldviews in peace. If Islam is a religion of belief, worship, and morality, then no one in any democratic country can object to such a system. But ignoring this system and taking Islam to be just as a form of governance and administration and, as such, standing for certain political positions and enterprises, is nothing more than the misinterpretation of Islam. I mean, we need to present Islam to the wider segments of society as a phenomenon that is largely related to belief, praxis, and morality. And we must demonstrate that Islam does not contradict or conflict with democracy.

"In order to achieve just this, people need to be altruistic and giving. In order for future generations to live in peace and tranquility, people ought to be able to give up their own personal pleasures and comfort... Our aim will be to take the genuine interpretations of Islam to the people, to establish democracy in its entirety and with everyone's approval, and to work against the politicization of Islam."

Politicization darkens the soul of religion

In an interview with Kanal D television on April 16, 1997, Gülen pointed to an inherent danger within politics. Recalling that politicians have the ability to instrumentalize anything for political interests, Gülen maintained his views that politicians' coming forward with a claim as if they are the exclusive representatives of religion is the instrumentalization of religion, and that the flaws of politics thus infect the religion:

. "They say religion is politicized. Accepting such a maxim means some circles are politicizing religion. Politicization of religion is more dangerous for religion than it is for the regime. In fact, it means darkening the soul of religion, because religion is everybody's religion; it is the name of something everyone respects, through which everyone finds worldly tranquility and happiness. It is the name of everyone's connection with God.

"The politicization of religion means the endangering of religion. This is because those who lay claim to religion with political considerations seek to instrumentalize everything for their politics, their political views, and their political goals. While politicians exploit everything in the name of their politics, religion simultaneously darkens under their representation.

"In other words, if they pursue the matter with such notions as, 'We are religious, we will represent religion, we will carry religion to practice, we will make it prevail in life,' their mistakes will be ascribed to the spirit of that universal religion. The religion would have been darkened. This is another danger" (Kanal D, April 16, 1997).

There is no single form of government in Islam

In his interview published in the *Muslim World* journal in 2005, Gülen was asked, "In a time when political Islam has become very popular, what are your thoughts on the relationship between Islam and politics?"

He touched on two points in his answer:

1. Islam does not foresee a uniform state structure and many very different state systems can be encountered in the history of Islam.

2. Referring to the Qur'an purely for the purpose of finding material for political discourse is irreverence to the Qur'an. Thanks to the wise politicians the Qur'an inspires, and through its enrichment of the human soul, politics ceases to be merely a gamble, a game of chess.

Gülen elucidated on these points:

"In my opinion, people have either gone too far or not far enough with regard to understanding the relationship between Islam and politics. Some have said that the religion of Islam has no relationship with politics; others have perceived the religion as politics itself, ignoring the varied and rich aspects of religion.

"In the holy Qur'an, there are verses concerning administration and politics. The Prophet's practices also occupy an important place in this regard. For example, the Qur'anic terms '*ulu al-amr*' (those who rule), '*ita'at*' (obedience to the rulers), '*shura*' (consultation), '*harb*' (war), and '*sulh*' (peace), are all examples of some Qur'anic references with regard to political and legal decisions. In addition, there are Qur'anic verses related to legal institutions and also some that point to politics and governing.

"However, in Islam it is not possible to limit the concept of governance and politics into a single paradigm, unlike the principles of faith and the pillars of Islam. History shows us that in the Islamic world, since the time of the Prophet, there have been many types of states.

"It would not be a correct understanding of Islam to claim that politics is a vital principle of religion and among its well-established pillars. While some Qur'anic verses are related to politics, the structure of the state, and the forms of ruling, people who have connected the import of the Qur'anic message with such issues may have caused a misunderstanding. This misunderstanding is the result of their Islamic zeal, their limitations of their consideration solely of over-reliance on historical experiences, and their thinking that the problems of Islamic communities can be solved more easily through politics and ruling. All of these approaches within their own contexts are meaningful. However, the truth does not lie in these approaches alone.

"Although one cannot ignore the effects of ruling and administration in regulating communal relationships between individuals, families, and societies, yet these, within the framework of Qur'anic values, are considered secondary issues. That is because the values that we call major principles (*ummuhat*), such as faith (*iman*), submission (*islam*), doing what is beautiful (*ihsan*), and the acceptance of divine morals by the community, are references that form the essence of administrative, economic, and political issues.

"The Qur'an is a translation of the book of the universe, which comes from the Divine commands of creation, an interpretation of the world of the unseen, of the visible and invisible. It is an explanation of the reflections of the Divine names on earth and in the heavens. It is a prescription for the various problems of the Islamic world. It is a unique guide for bliss in this life and in the life to come. It is a great guide for the travelers in this world moving towards the Hereafter. It is an inexhaustible source of wisdom. Such a book should not be reduced to the level of political discourse, nor should it be considered a book about political theories or forms of state. To consider the Qur'an as an instrument of political discourse is a great disrespect for the Holy Book and is an obstacle that prevents people from benefiting from this deep source of divine grace. There is no doubt that the holy Qur'an, through its enrichment of the human soul, is able to inspire wise politicians and through them to prevent politics from being like gambling or merely a game of chess."

With respect to approaching the Qur'an as a political ideology, the following sentences from Gülen's article for the *Financial Times* are telling:

"The reductionist view of seeking political power in the name of a religion contradicts the spirit of Islam. When religion and politics are mixed, both suffer – religion most of all." (March 10, 2014, *Financial Times*).

Renewal in Islam

One of the issues coming up in discussions on the relationship between Islam and democracy is that of "reform in religion." Is Islam in need of a reform, or can it be subject to reform? Nicole Pope from *Le Monde* addressed this in 1998: "There are reform debates in Turkey and elsewhere in the Muslim world. The debate on whether or not Islam, like Christianity, can undergo reform."

In response, Gülen stated that Islam has not undergone a process of deformation that would require its reform, but that there is renewal in Islam:

"A reform was made one thousand five hundred years after the Messiah (Prophet Jesus). Researchers like Maurice Bucaille, even Christian researchers themselves, for instance, publications including the Catholic Encyclopedia, draw attention to some differences between the Gospels. Some ascribe these differences to the fact that the Gospels were penned a certain period of time after Jesus. They refer to a process in a sense like the gathering and codification of the hadith in the history of Islam.

"Personally, I would feel uncomfortable with these matters being approached in such a way, out of my respect for the Messiah and the Gospels as a Divine scripture. As a separate point, the role of the Church in Christianity is also very important. It is because of this role that the opinions of the church carry religious weight. Developments taking place over time led to different approaches among Christians on this point also and reform movements were seen in countries such as Germany and England. As is known, a stance was taken against certain applications such as indulgence, and some expressions and phrases in the Sacred Scripture were subjected to criticism within the framework of the developing sciences.

"In Islam, differing views gradually developed in relation to matters of second or third degree importance, on issues that were the subject-matter of jurisprudence, and different legal schools emerged; however, none of these were able to shake the foundations of Islam due to the Qur'an's transfer without change or alteration, and the recording of the Prophetic Practice in the early period. The greater part of basic Islamic principles thus remained unchanged.

"There is, however, *tajdid*, or renewal in Islam. Certain mistakes emerging over time were corrected by great figures known as *mujaddid*, with the basic principles preserved. If there were deviations, eventually a return back to these basic principles was ensured, and new interpretations necessitated by the age and prevailing conditions were offered for those aspects of Islam that were open to interpretation.

"But these are not reforms, because reform comes after a deformation. It cannot be said that a deformation requiring reform has been experienced in Islam."

In an interview published in the *Hürriyet* daily in 1995, Gülen said, "A deformation is not in question in Islam, for Islam has been able to protect its origins, and a reform, therefore, [in the sense of restructuring from nil] is irrelevant" (Hürriyet, January 26, 1995).

To German journalist Rainer Hermann's question, "Can Islam be modern, or is it a question of the Islamization of the modern world, as critics have claimed?" Gülen replies:

"The issue beyond dispute is that as can be seen in modernity's concept of democracy, there is no one-dimensional definition due to its different political, sociological, philosophical, and cultural interpretations and applications. The sources on modernity make mention of such principles as the importance of reason and science, individuals shaking off the power of others or the state, freedom of belief and thought, the protection of human rights, rule of law, and democratic governance.

"None of these pose a contradiction to Islamic values. Muslims' implementation of these principles on the individual and governmental plane does not mean that Islam is being modernized in this way. Rather, these implementations are efforts to interpret those aspects of Islam that are open to interpretation in line with the principles which are a product of modernity and which do not contradict the basic principles of Islam.

"On the other hand, we cannot act on the assumption that Islam approves of each and every demand of modernity encountered in its interpretations and applications. Examples include approaching the human being and the universe from a completely materialist perspective, the application of secularism as imposing disbelief, absolute freedoms with no sense of limitation, or claims about the end of religion or its substitution by reason and science.

"Conversely, Muslims' lending their own color to modernity and developing their own interpretations on particular issues cannot be called the 'Islamization of modernity'" (Interview conducted by Rainer Hermann on December 6, 2012).

Religious rulings vary over time

The question of whether or not legal rules change according to the needs of the time is one of most debated topics within the framework of Islam and democracy. Gülen discussed this issue at length in his interview with a Dutch television program:

"With the rule in the *Majalla,* or Ottoman Civil Code, religious rulings change with the changing times.

"There are things that can change. In the Ottoman legal system, there are decrees which constitute a majority concerning these customs and traditions, in matters for which there are no clear Qur'anic rulings, and in issues where there are no transmissions from the Prophet's Companions. These were set forth by the Shayks al-Islam of the period and by great Muslim scholars.

"But there are other issues which, although they are not even customs or traditions, were accepted by Islam, and perhaps we may have imported them from another nation and silently accepted them. These may be subject to change at any time.

"A case in point is dress and clothing. There is no need for it to be exactly as it was during the era of God's Messenger. These were the traditions of that society. They wore mantles without buttons. Their garments did not cover their chests… There were not the robes that we wear today. There was no such thing as the overcoats, the sack coats that we wear. Those who wish to do so can emulate them. There is no harm in doing so. But if you enforce this dress as a part of Islam, then you would have made things difficult and put people off.

"These cannot even be called secondary matters of the religion. These are customs and traditions. In fact, according to some, it can even be said that the turban is also one. For example, the turban used to be worn among Muslims during the Era of Happiness, and the Messenger of God used to wear a turban also. Despite its prevalence, there is nothing on the turban in such works as Bukhari, Muslim, and Tirmidhi. Reference to the turban in Abu Dawud's *Sunan* is that during the Messenger's entry in Mecca on the day of its conquest, there was a turban on his helmet. We cannot know its benefits.

"Perhaps it is something like the helmet we wear when riding a motorbike today, and was done with such intention. And there are some who say that this was indeed the case. Now if you say that these are necessary to be a Muslim, then you would have made things difficult. You would have brought the details before the fundamentals. Moreover, it is declared in the Qur'an, in the chapter al-Hajj, that venerating the public symbols and rituals set up by God are surely because of the true piety and God-consciousness of hearts. That is to say, the things that God deems great should be seen as great and acknowledged, while those things that God regards as small, does not mention, or to which He does not ascribe much importance while mentioning them should be left within their own context. Otherwise, if you place a matter that is not given much importance or emphasis by God's Messenger – like establishing a state – above the religious obligations, above belief, worship, prayer, fasting, the prescribed alms, pilgrimage, acting humanely, and loving and embracing other human beings, then you would have disrupted the Divinely-established balance.

"Just as disruption of the ecological balance is a handicap, disrupting the balance of religion, which regulates the lives of human beings, is also such a handicap. In this respect, giving precedence to the matters that can be called the details, the secondary issues, amounts to destroying the balance, the harmony in the religion. This should not be allowed for. Details must remain as such, and fundamentals must be adopted as just that – as fundamentals.

"The main methodology (*usul*) of Islam is to testify that there is no deity but God, and Muhammad is His messenger. Abu Hanifa considers a person who says this testimony religion believer in his *Fiqh al-Akbar*. This person can enter Paradise, and that is that. For that matter, it has been presented with such expansiveness that if God so wills, He will admit into Paradise those people who, as according to the Maturidi creed, believe in a Creator. [He will also admit] those to whom, according to the Ash'ari creed, a Messenger has not been sent, or if the Messenger's message has not been duly communicated to those people. Instead of condemning people and rendering damning judgments, I would think that it would be more appropriate as regards Islam to approach matters in terms of God's infinite mercy" (Interview with Dutch television on October 19, 1995).

Sarıtoprak and Ünal, in their 2005 *Muslim World* interview, asked a more in-depth question in the same vein:

"The subject of *ijtihad* (independent reasoning) has been debated in the Muslim world for a long time. Some thought that the door of *ijtihad* was closed, and of course this caused a stagnation of reasoning. What might be the criteria to use the methodology of *ijtihad*?"

Gülen's response:

"Islam, being the last and universal religion, is the epitome of solutions to humanity's problems, for all time and for all locations. These solutions are based on the limited texts of the Qur'an and the Sunnah, which address the unlimited problems of humans. This blessed activity started in the era of the Prophet and developed in the third and fourth centuries under the names of *ijtihad*, *ra'y* (subjective legal opinion), *istidlal* (inference), *qiyas* (analogy), and *istinbat* (deduction). It has remained alive within the practice of the dynamic systems of Islam and has been highly fruitful.

"This rich and original legal culture, unique to the Islamic world, has been fading for reasons such as the active Islamic system of life being excluded from the public sphere, the absence of active minds similar to those of the early Islamic period of Islam, the lack of inspired spirits, and the deficiency of superior intellects, and knowledge of the Qur'an and the Sunnah. Such brilliant minds have been replaced by some who lack reasoning with insufficient intelligence, and are very behind in their knowledge of the Qur'an and Sunnah, and closed to inspiration. Since these types of people have risen to power in religious circles, the fertile institution of *ijtihad* has been replaced by unquestioning adoption (*taqlid*), memorization, and copying.

"One can see several reasons why the spirit of *ijtihad* was lost and the door was closed: political oppression, inner struggles, the misuse of the institution of *ijtihad*, an extreme trust in the present legal system, the denial of reform, the blindness caused by the dominant monotonous present system of the time. All of these are among the reasons for this loss. Furthermore, the believers who were eligible to perform *ijtihad* based on their intelligence and abilities were at times included mistakenly among the groups of heretics who misused *ijtihad*.

"The door, in fact, has never been closed by anyone. However, some *ulama* had the inclination to close the door of *ijtihad* against those who would like to promote their own desires and interpretations as guidance. The door was closed automatically in the face of those who were not eligible to make *ijtihad*. As long as society does not have quality scholars who can perform *ijtihad*, it is not possible to ignore the argument of those who are against *ijtihad*.

"Today, people commonly think of the worldly life. The ideas and hearts of today's people are greatly disparate and the minds are estranged

from immaterial things. Religion and religiosity are not the essential issues for people, as was the case in the time of the early Muslims. On the
contrary, people are neutral to religiosity or religion; that is to say, being
religious or not being religious is the same thing. Many are highly disin-
terested in matters of faith and many essentials of religion are ignored. The
pillars of Islam and the principles of faith are viewed with doubt. Religion,
for many Muslims, has collapsed. Many make no effort to live their lives
within the framework of Islam. Under such circumstances, one can hardly
see that this dynamic aspect of Islam, *ijtihad*, will be used properly.

"Despite all of this, there has been a great revival of religion and
religiosity in the Islamic world today. I hope—God willing—this development will result in the rise of those who are eligible to open the door of
ijtihad in the near future. It is my conviction that when the proper season
comes, such gushing spirits and ingenious intellects will create groups
comprised of specialists and that they will have a sense of responsibility
to undertake *ijtihad*. I hope that through such consultation, these groups
will bridge the gap that has been created since the loss of the spirit of
ijtihad" (*Muslim World*, July 2005 issue).

What is meant by *shari'a*?

"*Shari'a*" is undoubtedly one of the most-debated concepts regarding Islam's relationship with democracy. For years *shari'a* evoked the idea of a
"religious state." In fact, *shari'a* was frequently used interchangeably with
"religious state."

New York Times reporter Brian Knowlton asked a question to
Gülen in his 2010 interview about this topic: "Should a Muslim-gov-
erned state be based on Shari'a law?"

Gülen: "If a country grants freedom of religion, equal rights for people
to live as they wish, learn, and manage their affairs according to their own
conscience, then it is in no way contrary to the teachings of the Qur'an.

"And if there is such a state, there is no need to come up with
an alternative system. And if the system does not provide full human
rights and freedoms, just as in some so-called democratic countries
today, it should be reviewed, renewed, and reformed according to the
norms of universal laws and human rights by [the country's] legislative
and executive organs.

"In Turkey, too, for example, simply as a result of democracy, people have asked for the opportunity to live freely according to their beliefs, in the schools and elsewhere. The people have asked for the right to be who they truly are—and this is the fundamental right of every human being" (Part of this interview was published in the *New York Times* on June 12, 2010).

Le Monde correspondent Nicole Pope also inquired about the issue, asking, "The word *shari'a* is another very sensitive word in Turkey. What is the *shari'a*?"

Gülen:

"*Shari'a* is a word that is actually synonymous with religion. All the essentials of belief, and all other moral principles, are to be found in the *shari'a*. *Shari'a* is not the part of religion concerning governance, which makes up only two percent of all religion. Those who understand it to be thus are greatly mistaken. Such an understanding engenders antipathy and discomfort in some [other] people towards the term.

"*Shari'a* is not unique to Islam. There is also a Jewish *shari'a*, and a Christian *shari'a*. These are contained in the scriptures. In Jesus' words, 'I have not come to abolish the Law but to fulfill it.' These are mentioned in the Gospels. *Shari'a* is a form of religious praxis, it is religion itself, and is, in a sense, akin to its sociological definition. But as I mentioned earlier, issues concerning administration and governance directly make up only 2 percent of the *shari'a*, and this concerns executives primarily. They do not concern each member of society."

The state system established by the Prophet

What kind of state system did the Prophet Muhammad establish? This question was asked by German journalist Rainer Hermann to Gülen with a comparison with Jesus:

"In the West, people argue that the Prophet Muhammad established a state, while Jesus stayed away from politics and rendered unto Caesar the things that are Caesar's. Is achieving world domination among the teachings of Islam?"

In responding to this question, Gülen elucidated the basic principles on which a Muslim state must rest:

"If there is to be an administration in Islam, there is nothing wrong with its being established in line with the Islamic disciplines, [including] Islamic morality and principles. Jesus and his disciples did not have the chance to establish a state. Had such an opportunity presented itself, he would have established an order like David and Solomon before him. They established a state in the era of the kings mentioned in the Old Testament. Moses and Joshua established a system. There is a kinship between Jesus, Zachariah, and John in this sense.

"They did not get such an opportunity. But later, when Roman Emperor Constantine the Great accepted Christianity as the dominant religion of the Roman Empire, he governed by the rule of Christianity.

"Yes, the Messenger of God set up a system of government in his time, but the system itself essentially became established during the era of the Rightly Guided Caliphs. As their name implies, they were most upright and on the straight path. But the same cannot be said for the Umayyads and the 'Abbasids in their entirety, or for the Ottomans and the Muslim states in Asia. We can't say that fairness, justice, uprightness, and social justice were implemented equally for all people. .

"Some rulers succumbed to their emotion and perpetrated certain injustices and cruelties, hiding behind Islam. Sometimes, murders were committed in the name of Islam because of errors in judgment and reasoning.

"More brutal forms of violence are being committed in our time. Suicide bombers and suicide attacks... It is innocent people who suffer. The Qur'an declares, 'But if you endure patiently, that is better for you.' Al-Qaeda and Hezbollah do nothing but blacken the pure countenance of Islam. All this stems from not knowing the Qur'an" (*Frankfurter Allgemeine Zeitung*, December 6, 2012).

In his 2005 interview with *Milliyet*, Gülen was asked: *"Should the state be an objective for a Muslim?"*

His answer emphasized on one point in particular. He explained the different ways in which the four Caliphs were elected to office and the larger implications of this:

"I also think that people can live 95%, or maybe 97%, of their religion without causing any worry, providing that the framework drawn by democracy is maintained and the fields of activity have not been narrowed by such things as 'public domain,' for religion assumes a role at certain times in social life, as well as in administration. However, these issues have diverse characteristics and historical aspects.

"For instance, there is no particular model for either the method of elections or the systems of administration. When we look into the historical development of the Islamic system of government, Abu Bakr was elected by the public, but 'Umar was elected after he was nominated by Abu Bakr. 'Uthman was elected after 'Umar indicated the group of *ashara al-mubashshara* (ten persons who had been given glad-tidings for Paradise), one of whom was 'Uthman. There was some opposition to Ali's election, and another administration was formed in Damascus, with an opportunity being born for Mu'awiya. During the Umayyad reign, rule began to be passed down from father to son, a practice which continued with the Ottomans.

"All this shows that the religion has certain commandments with a definite methodology; these have never been touched. Outside of this is a territory of relative truths that are open to interpretation (*ijtihad*) and judgmental inference (*istinbat*), so that the conditions and needs of the time should be duly evaluated" (January 16, 2005, *Milliyet*).

Can the Caliphate return?

In 1924, the Turkish parliament passed a law abolishing the institution of the Caliphate. But from time to time, it comes up in debates on Islam and democracy. In the interview published in *Muslim World*, Gülen was asked about the Caliphate:

"After the abolishment of the Caliphate (Khilafah) in Turkey, many new movements to restore this institution arose, especially in India. Thinking of the fast development in our world, do you think that the Caliphate could be re-established? Or is the Caliphate an unattainable utopia?"

Gülen's answer was as follows:

"When the institution of the Caliphate was abolished there were many views articulated either for or against it. A contemporary Turkish sociologist, Ziya Gökalp, and those following his line of thought had the following approach: 'The institution of the Khilafah, which draws its power from the Turkish Grand National assembly, has an honorable place among Muslims. If there is no such institution, the world of Islam will be similar to a rosary which has no center (imamah); all the beads would fall off.'

"Thinkers like Seyyid Bey (An islamic scholar, a member of Turkish parliament during 1923-25, and Justice Minister of Turkey during 1923-24), believed that, 'the Khilafah (the Caliphate) has a wise purpose and it is the issue of the nation itself and it follows the requirements of the time. When the Prophet died, he did not mention anything about Khilafah (the succession) to his Companions. In fact, even in the Qur'an there is no verse to this effect.' Seyyid Bey emphasized the importance of consultation and obedience to the rulers, as mentioned in the Qur'an. These two aspects are related to administration and politics.

"He believed that with the Caliphate of 'Ali, the fourth caliph in Islamic history, in the thirtieth year of the Islamic calendar, the Caliphate came to an end. In this regard, he mentioned the opinions of scholars of Islamic law and Islamic thought. He spoke of the historicity of Khilafah, in one sense, and suggested that one should benefit from this experience and understand the goal and the aim of Khilafah. According to Seyyid Bey, the rulers who came after the first four Caliphs were not real Caliphs; in appearance they were Caliphs, but in quality they did not follow the previous Caliphs. With this opinion, he supported the abolishment of Khilafah as found in the following statement by the Turkish parliament: 'The Caliph has been deposed. The institution of Khilafah is abolished since the meaning and the context of this institution has been absorbed into the government and the republic.'

"Long before these scholars, Ibn Khaldun, writing in his *Muqaddimah,* presented the following thought: 'With regard to Khilafah, there are three different views. The first is that Khilafah is a Divine institution and necessary. Secondly, Khilafah is based on needs. Thirdly, as some Kharijites defended, there is no need for the Caliphate.'

"Today, those who believe that there is no need for a Caliphate say this because of the establishment of nation states and the development of ideas like independence. For these reasons, some people believe that the Khilafah has lost its effectiveness. There are some people who believe in the dynamics of Khilafah, since it is a means of unity among Muslims and facilitates cooperation between Muslim nations through exchanging their skills and opportunities. The possibility of rallying the masses can easily coalesce around the religious term, Caliphate/Khilafah.

"Having said this, I believe that the revival of the Caliphate would be very difficult and making Muslims accept such a revived Khilafah would be impossible.

In an interview published in the *Milliyet* newspaper the same year, Gülen was asked, "What do you think about the subject of reviving the Caliphate?"

He responded: "When the Caliphate was to be abolished in 1924, İsmet İnönü [the second president of Turkey] opposed it, whereas Seyit (Seyyid) Bey, member of Parliament from Izmir, a teacher of the Islamic jurisprudence methodology, did not. He even prepared a booklet relating the history of the Caliphate, based on the verse 'I will create a caliph (vicegerent) on the Earth.' In this booklet, he emphasized that it was a title given by Muslims to the leader of the state. After having underlined that each of the Rightly Guided Caliphs (the first four) were elected in different ways, he said how it would be impossible to turn the method of election back to a single system; he called them the 'true Caliphs,' for they had carried out their duty within the criteria of justice and righteousness.

"He said that the real caliphate was represented by them. So, in a way he said that the ones who followed represented what could be called a 'relative caliphate.' Also, the Prophet said, 'the Caliphate will last for 30 years after me.' This duration was completed with the Caliphate of Hasan, which lasted for six months. Another weak narration says, 'If you are upon a straight path, the Caliphate will last for 70 years.' Then he [the Prophet] stated, 'Kingdom and monarchy will follow,' adding, 'tyrants will lead the people.' In other words, what Seyit Bey said was: if there is no caliph elected by a majority or by the *ashab al-ray* (scholars of opinion), and one who maintains the ideal of the Caliphate, fulfilling the duty of a real Caliph, then whether or not there is a Caliphate is relative.

"The Caliphate was abolished, and was regarded as being maintained within the existence of the parliament. No one rejected this claim. What matters is the meticulous practice of Islam. It would not be correct to emphasize historical subjects that are of secondary importance in order to cause polemics; these are always open to debate. If some fellow Muslims put an emphasis on this issue, I don't know who they are incited by. Can you say that there was a Caliphate in the real sense of the word during the era of the Umayyads and Abbasids? Did Yazid or Walid represent the Caliphate so properly that it is being demanded now? De-liberately or not, the creation of such debates can be something done by those who don't practice Islam in order to cover up their own flaws.

"If this issue (caliphate) is put forth in Turkey, Pakistan, Indonesia, or another country, the other countries will oppose it. This is because nation states have been established, and everybody has declared their independence" (*Milliyet*, January 24, 2005).

Fundamentalism, religious fanaticism, and secularist fanaticism

Fundamentalism is another concept that features in debates on Islam and democracy. In his interview with *Le Monde* correspondent Nicole Pope in 1998, Gülen associates fundamentalism in religion with other forms of decay in the society: "When the Ottoman Empire was declining, many other institutions, like the Sufi orders, dervish lodges, and the religious schools had their share from this decay, too. They became incapable of performing their real functions. The same thing was experienced in the army, as well. The Janissaries reacted to all the innovations and reforms, even sometimes taking along with them the religious schools. In short, all the institutions had their share from the general decline of the Otto-mans: the military, the academics, religious groups, which were once the driving forces behind the state's rise. The same thing can happen today. As the decay is experienced in the Sufi orders, and as we witness, it could be experienced in the schools for civil servants, and in some other vital institutions."

In stressing religious fundamentalism, Gülen also recalls the exis-tence of fanaticism against religion: " It can be said that some fanaticism was experienced in the country after a certain period. Just as there were those who engaged in religious bigotry, there have also been those who have engaged in bigotry against religion" (July 21, 1997, *Yeni Yüzyıl*).

Finally, let us look at Gülen's response to an important question concerning Turkey in his 2010 *New York Times* interview:

"The issue of developing a democracy responsive to man's spiri-tual needs, a spirit that would be satisfied with nothing other than the consent of the Almighty and the promise of eternity, should also be dis-cussed. If you like, you can call this 'democracy with a spiritual dimen-sion.' This means a democracy that includes respect toward the rights and freedoms of human beings and that ensures freedom of religion and at the same time prepares an environment where people can practice their beliefs freely and pursue a life of their own conscience.

"Furthermore, this means a democracy that assists people in fulfilling their desires concerning an eternal life. We should search for ways to expand and humanize democracy in these ways. An ideal democracy should promise to fulfill a human being's needs related to eternity as much as it promises to solve the issues of today and tomorrow. Only a democracy like that could develop into an ideal democracy, but unfortunately, humanity hasn't reached that horizon yet" (Interview by *New York Times* reporter Brian Knowlton, a section of which was published in the newspaper on June 12, 2010).

CHAPTER 2

MODERNITY AND SECULARISM

Modernity and Secularism

D uring the Ottoman period, there were different religious groups and sects who were free to practice their faiths as they liked. The Ottoman Empire was not a theocracy; yet, there was no absolute separation of the church from the state, either.

After the Empire collapsed, the first constitution of the Turkish Republic had an article which read, "The official religion of the state is Islam." This article was later removed in 1924, to be replaced by the principle of laicism. The Turkish version of laicism, however, has always been hotly debated. The Turkish model adopted the French-type laicism, which excludes religion in all its forms from state institutions. The Turkish Republic also copied many of its laws from France.

This oppressive laicism became a tool of persecution against religious individuals, who pointed to other types of secularism, as in the United States, where religion is not completely excluded from public life.

Fethullah Gülen is perhaps the first scholar in the Islamic world to argue that Muslims do not have any problem with modernity and laicism. For him, the form of laicism in Turkey is oppressing to the faithful and violates their basic rights. But he also said that believers are quite pleased with laicism that does not intervene with religious freedoms, as in the US and Germany.

On May 30, 1997, Fethullah Gülen gave an interview to *Time* magazine regarding the political situation in Turkey. Henry Muller of *Time* magazine asked:

"Do you think that the majority of Muslims in Turkey want to live in a democratic and secular state? Do Muslims wish to see changes in the republic's governing secular institutions? In other words, do they want a review of, for instance, the headscarf, Islamic dress, or Islamic education? Is it possible for democracy and Islam be reconciled in Turkey? If so, can Turkey serve as an example for the rest of the world?"

In his lengthy response to the question, Gülen indicated that secularism was once understood in Turkey as "divesting religion of the right to exist," and that democracy was not practiced in a manner which recognized "the freedom of worship and belief":

"Democracy and secularism have existed in Turkey for years. It can even be said that they partially existed during the Ottoman period and that the founders of the Republic took inspiration from the Ottomans, adopting and developing the notion of secularism. In later years, it became a concept featuring directly in the constitution. Nevertheless, not much has been said about the definition and the framework of it. The information was not provided. For this reason, the problem has stemmed from the ambiguity of the framework of the concept of 'secularism.' It is not unease with the concepts of democracy or secularism.

"For instance, when some stood for secularism, they did not recognize a place for religion. Of course, they could not say so to the Christians or the Jews in Turkey, because there was the USA behind them, there was Europe, there was the world. There was no one to defend the rights of the poor, wretched Muslims...

"Secularism in Turkey was understood to mean irreligiousness; it was this that caused unease. Democracy was perceived as restraining people's individual, social, or family lives. It had to do with matters related to worship and worldly transactions. The state did not allow them unhampered freedom of choice and action in accordance with their personal wishes, beliefs, and views. This was the cause of unease. Our nation has a good mannered-culture that it had inherited from the past. For this reason, we never witnessed, until today, the uprising of those groups who are anti-democrats or anti-secularists."

Secularism existed during the Ottoman period

In an interview with *Yeni Yüzyıl* daily on July 21, 1997, Gülen stated:
"A great number of laws were issued during the Ottoman period. As these were aimed at worldly benefits, the matter was approached from a secularist perspective. When considered from the perspective of a lack of interference in people's religion and worship, secularism comes into question. Look at the articles of the Constitution; there is no interference in anybody's religion. The Qur'an declares, 'You have your religion, and I have my religion.' The basic spirit of religion is its embracing everyone. The Ottomans may have their flaws, but their ability to govern tens of millions of people across such a vast territory, and comprised of so many different nationalities, religions and cultures, is precisely because of this profound tolerance."

Referring to arguments concerning the existence, in a sense, of secularism in the Ottoman period, and stating the views of many intellectuals who posit that secularism is not fully applied in Turkey, Gülen suggested that the problem stems from confounding laicism with secularism:

"Those considering the matter from this perspective assert that laicism, in a sense, existed in the Ottoman period. Laicism is also in question in our day. And many intellectuals state that laicism is not completely practiced in Turkey. Westerners say the same. This suggests a shortcoming, although not to the degree Westerners suggest. The matter is relative. In other words, it existed in that period also. It was present in the Constitutional Monarchy Era to a certain extent, and it was taken a little further with the founding of the Republic. The State adopted it as a very vital principle for the sake of its own existence and insisted upon it, placing it immutably in the very first articles of the Constitution.

"I am not well versed in the law, but I have roughly expressed my interpretations of laicism meaning that Religious Affairs does not meddle in worldly life, the administration does not interfere in religious life, and everyone is free to practice their belief in their own personal world.

"On the contrary, secularism is all too often confused with laicism in Turkey. Secularism is worldliness. Today there is even discussion about this worldliness perhaps existing in the Seljuk period, which predates the Ottoman period" (From an interview broadcast on Samanyolu TV on March 29, 1997).

Definition of a perfect democracy

At precisely this juncture, Gülen offered a definition of the "perfect democracy." For him, a perfect democracy is a democracy responding not only to people's worldly needs, but to their demands concerning the hereafter also:

"Those who take laicism to mean secularism approach the matter entirely in terms of worldliness. So, they say, let there be no spiritual dimension in our administration, no conception of a Hereafter. However, were democracy to be designed as a comprehensive system meeting all the needs of human beings – whether this were possible or not – and just as it is of service to me until the grave, I would very much want to see it answering my problems beyond the grave. I would want it to shoulder my problems on the Day of Judgement.

"I hope the highly democratized individuals of the future, those who will have democracy established upon a firm foundation, will think about the future. For we are not comprised merely of a [material] body. We have a spiritual dimension also. We have a metaphysical aspect in addition to the physical aspect, otherworldliness alongside worldliness. To be able to fulfill the human needs as a whole, we need to consider them with all their aspects. This is how we can internalize the peace promised by democracy. I am of the view that a perfect democracy needs to meet all the material and metaphysical needs of human beings" (From an interview broadcast on Samanyolu TV on March 29, 1997).

Democracy has not yet reached perfection

Gülen consolidated his views on "perfect democracy" eight years after the above interview. This was in an interview, which spanned 22 days, with *Milliyet*, Gülen said the following concerning this "perfect democracy" in the fifteenth part of the interview, published on January 17, 2005:

"Today there are many different forms of democracy: the Christian democrats, social democrats, liberal democrats... Why should not there be a democracy which has a place for Islamic sensibilities? We are human beings and we have certain needs. We have a feeling of eternity; we do not want to vanish. I cannot be satisfied with anything but God and the eternal life He promised. If I were not to think that there is an eternal life after this one and if I were to know that I simply vanish when I die, I would permanently suffer from anxiety and depression. I am able to breathe because I have a feeling for eternity and a meeting with God again.

"If a humane democracy is to exist, it should embrace me with all my being and should be developed to meet my needs. Humanity should be cared for in every way. If people are in need of metaphysics, then they should be provided with guidance, via education, on how to meet this need. No area should be left unattended; the school, the street, the place of worship, and the family should hold the hands of the people. In my opinion, in a developed democracy the opportunity should exist to live comfortably as a secular person – but it should also exist to live as a person of the Hereafter. Whoever wants to live like the Companions of the Prophet should be given that chance.

"Democracy is also going through a process of evolution. For instance, we have lived in a democracy for a long time now, but the Copenhagen criteria[5] made us aware of the proportion of our shortcomings. Our process will mature by development.

"I believe that one day circumstances will be such that we will fulfill all our needs, spiritual and intellectual, under the umbrella of democracy; I can see that we are heading in that direction. I believe the tension between the secularists and Islamists—I would like to say that I have never liked these terms—will be tempered. Educated people are supposed to save themselves from false fears that arise from suspicions and they need to be understanding toward each other."

Religious life can be lived freely in a secular system

In an interview broadcast on TRT (Turkish Radio and Television, the national public broadcaster of Turkey) on July 3, 1995, Gülen was asked the following question:

"I will ask in a concrete way: Do you hold a personal belief in secularism, are you secularist, and would you describe yourself as secular?"

Gülen: "I don't know if individuals can be secular. This may sound like boasting, but I am a person striving to live my religion to the smallest detail. Even if I were to pray until the early hours of the morning, I would still think I have not prayed enough; I would still feel it not as worthy as a single person's testimony of faith. I would wish that I had offered one thousand units of prayer. I strive to constantly be in a state of ablution. This is the kind of Muslim I strive to be.

"But secularism was adopted during a certain period for the sake of the system. It is a constituent element of a system allowing everyone

---

5   Laid down in 1993 in Copenhagen, these criteria are the rules a candidate country is required to fulfill to be eligible to join the European Union. These rules are used to determine whether the country has established institutions for a stable democratic governance, protection of human rights, and free market economy, in addition to other obligations to enter EU.

the right and opportunity to live out their own sensibilities and religious views. In my opinion, everyone can easily express, as well as practice, their religious feelings and religious views within such a system."

When presenter Reha Muhtar asked, "Within this system?" Gülen responded, "Yes, within this system."

The host then asked, *"Within the secular system?"*

"Yes," Gülen answered, and he continued:

"This is about whether secularism can be wholly implemented. And it should be considered that secularism might have certain defective aspects of its own. Democracy is a system in which virtually everyone has the opportunity to plant their feelings and thoughts in the form of seeds and eventually reap a harvest. If this system proves, or will one day prove insufficient, then this is a matter for consideration by those who think it is not enough. I am trying to make assessments for our present day."

Laicism and irreligiousness

Almost two years after this program, Gülen was asked pretty much the same questions by *Hürriyet* writer Yalçın Doğan on a program aired on *Kanal D* on April 16, 1997. Let us look at Gülen's answers to Doğan's questions:

"What is your understanding of laicism? Can religion and laicism coexist? Or not?"

Gülen responded with the following:

"An understanding of laicism needs to be sought in its own definition. Laicism signifies separation of state and religion, the state's neutrality in this regard, and even as expressed by the majority of our politicians, laicism denotes protecting religion in its own right. It means not allowing leeway for the abuse of religion with false interpretations. Differences may arise in an understanding of political laicism in accordance with the personal views of individuals. But it seems to me that laicism in Turkey has taken on a different interpretation altogether...

"As Ali Fuat Başgil touches upon in his book, *Din ve Laiklik* [Religion and Laicism], laicism has been somewhat construed as secularism (i.e. a total absence of religion in all aspects of life)[6] here.

---

6   Laicism and secularism are often confused, and this is more true in the Turkish con-

"When laicism first made its way into Turkey, its first Turkish commentators referred to it as *la dini*, or non-religious, to mean that there was no religion in the system. The system is the system, and is in any event a legal entity, a corporate personality. There does not have to be religion.

"But many criticized this interpretation. Asserting that it was not right to say so, they tried to reposition the matter by indicating that the separation between religion and state was more reasonable. But often, when our writers and thinkers propounded on the notion of laicism, it [the state] constantly communicated secularism to us. Or, rather, worldliness. Worldliness, and not a religion-state separation, is another facet of the discussion. Modern commentators thus reconciled laicism with certain Qur'anic principles, positing that laicism actually existed in ancient times, but without a name. It even existed during the Ottoman period.

"The Qur'an declares, 'There is no compulsion in the Religion. The right way stands there clearly distinguished from the false [i.e. those who wish can choose it, the right path, while those who do not can choose another way].' As such, a set of principles were established in the very early period concerning freedom of conscience. There are those who posit that the Seljuks and later the Ottomans were secular to a certain extent.

"Saying 'I am laicist' is different than believing in it or prescribing it. For some, it is even possible to reconcile laicism with our values, with certain understandings pertaining to Islam, and even with some of the ordinances of the Qur'an, including verses from its shorter chapters such as, 'You have your religion, and I have my religion' (109:6). As such I think that this is not something that should be blown out of proportion. If this is to be understood as the state's protection of religion without interfering with its practice, and others do not interfere with it either, and the faithful do not interfere with others while practicing their own beliefs, and if the state is to maintain the matter with a serious impartial-

---

text. In principle, both terms refer to the separation of church and state; but, laicism is more about a total absence of religion in government; in fact, in its most extreme forms, as has happened in Turkey, it leads to the removal and suppression of all that is religious from public space. This has happened in Turkey in the past.

ity, then there is no problem whatsoever. But it seems to me that some circles are creating artificial problems."

"So do you see laicism to be currently in danger?"

"I do not think that laicism is, or will be, in danger, because the greater majority in Turkey are happy as they are. Anti-laicists are but a handful of people. If people are not taking to the streets and rallying against it, if the fundamental principles of the state are not displeased with, and if there is no abuse of religion for some economic, political, or cultural objectives, then this means that everyone can practice their faith freely and that laicism is not much of a concern for anybody."

Religion and *shari'a*

In the same interview on TRT, Gülen was asked about the concept of "*shari'a.*" Although *shari'a* is law, over time, many have started using it synonymously with the terms "religious state" or "theocratic state." However, Islam does not stipulate any form of government, nor does it enjoin upon Muslims an indispensable duty to establish a religious state. Historically, there is also no such tradition of clergymen ruling over the state:

"The debate of whether or not religion is the same as *shari'a* has surfaced recently. The debate flared with women's demonstrations against the *shari'a.* These were followed by an Ankara State Security Court (DGM) decision which stated that the *shari'a* was not the same as religion but a state regime and rule of law based on religious principles. What is *shari'a*? Is *shari'a* a religion?"

Gülen responded:

"*Shari'a,* religion, and Islam are interchangeable terms. There are however some nuances; for example, *shari'a* as a word appears only once in the Qur'an and it denotes a path, a system, a road. Islam is the term signifying submission to God, obedience to His commands, and entrusting one's affairs to Him. The word 'religion,' one facet of which pertains to the Hereafter, is a path also, a method which eventually relates to the Hereafter, such as is expressed in the opening chapter of the Qur'an: Māliki yawmi l-dīn, 'The Master of the Day of Judgment.' It is a system in the world, but one which is to culminate in the Hereafter.

"It is a codification that will satisfy the never-ending desires of the human being, who will not be satisfied with anything other than infinity and the Infinite One. They describe all this under the term 'religion' – or 'din,' which has a long definition in Arabic, which is based on the Qur'an and the Prophetic Tradition.

"Religion is described as the compendium leading human beings with their own will and volition to that objective which is essentially very pleasing – they refer to this as glorious (*mahmudan*) 'in and of itself.' This description applies for both the *shari'a* and Islam also. That is, what we call a creed is a part of *shari'a*, a part of religion, a part of belief. All of these fall under *shari'a*; the fundamentals of the faith in which we believe fall under all *shari'a*. Even reading the universe as a book for the sake of belief's essentials, and its being beheld like the place of the Supreme Gathering, fall under it. Our prayer, our fast, our pilgrimage, our charity all fall under it. Some of our individual and familial dealings fall under it. Everything that falls into our individual and domestic dealings comprises 95 percent of religion, Islam, and the *shari'a*. There is nothing preventing people from doing this 95 percent, these things that God has imposed upon human beings. A person is not faced with any obstacle in relation to these. The 4 or 5 percent has to do with governance, administration and the legal system; this dimension does not concern individuals separately, but concerns administrators.

"Vociferous demonstrations in the name of *shari'a* are to me as disrespectful as cursing and cussing and demonstrating against laicism and democracy, as such things offend the feelings of so many people. Nobody knows what [*shari'a*] really means."

Religion is life, and it survives as long as it is lived

One of the chief subjects of debate about laicism and Islam is the role of religion in a secular system, especially when religion encompasses all facets of life.

This was one of the questions put to Gülen in an interview with *Milliyet* newspaper in January of 2005. In the section of the interview dated January 17, he was asked:

"Radical Islamists, as well as some secularists, argue that Islam covers all aspects of life. For this reason, the Court of Constitution, for instance, claims that we (Turkey) cannot have a liberal secularity as in the West. For the very same reason, radical Islamists are against secularism, demanding that Islam covers the State. What does Islam cover; what does it leave to the individuals, and to the mind?"

Gülen replied:

"At the level humanity has reached now, one of the things considered important is to recognize the right to believe and to be able to practice what one believes. Other attitudes might have been applied in the past, during a certain period, in order to establish the system; but today democracy has been adopted in Turkey. 10 years ago when [I] said 'Democracy is a process with no return,' [this argument] was interrogated [Gülen is referring to his speech in 1994 at the gathering for the opening of the Journalists and Writers Foundation]. Whereas now, everyone speaks of democracy in one way or another, so some solutions can be found within democracy."

Within a secular system, according to Gülen, a person with belief needs to be given the opportunity to live their life as they wish in personal and familial matters. Moreover, the believing person, given this opportunity, should not give precedence to the 5 percent of religion which looks to the state, over and above the 95 percent which looks to the individual:

"Religion is life, and it survives as long as it is lived. There are things that need to be given precedence when 'living' religion. For instance, the basic essentials of the religion, which we call *muhkamat* (the foundations), have a priority and no one can compromise them. Secondly, a Muslim should be allowed to observe the commandments of the Qur'an and Sunnah that are related to the life of the individual or the family in the way that they understand them; the extent of life should not be narrowed by imposing limitations. On the other hand, those who are trying to live like a Muslim should exert a maximum effort not to confuse certain issues.

"Secondary things in the religion are being made to seem like primary essentials. For instance, daily prayers, and fasting during Ramadan are two of the foundations of the religion which are observed individually. Those who seem to be at extremes, who oppose secularism, need to look into their sensitivity in observing the individual and familial commandments of the religion. Can we really observe them at an ideal level? If we missed one of the daily prayers, or did not fast one day, then we must think first before we make other claims and we must be ashamed before God.

"These are things that cannot be compromised. Those who neglect Islam's essentials, like the daily prayers, giving to charity, and fasting during Ramadan, are in a serious deficit. Those who slander, or speak in the absence of others (*ghiyba*), even if they are writing in representation of Muslims, are in great error. The Messenger of God says *ghiyba* is a greater sin than adultery; he says slander is unforgivable.

"If we are occupied with such errors, it would be disrespectful to the religion to argue about the wholeness of the religion. For the sake of God, let's complete our religion first in our personal lives, in the morality of our children, in our intellectual and spiritual lives. We have to save ourselves from the contradiction of being in conflict with others while we are lacking in the personal dimension of our religion and are committing major sins.

"This is our fault. After accomplishing this we can say, 'Our conscience is not confident since we cannot fully observe this or that commandment of our religion. You must avoid basing your judgments on possibilities. Let's find a solution by staying within the limits of mercy.'"

The State should prepare the ground for the practice of religion

Let us return to Gülen's *Milliyet* interview. Gülen gave the following response to the question, "The State needs the power of religion; in what proportion does religion need the State, and the State need the religion?":

"In order for the people to live their religion in peace, there is a need for the State to spread its wings of mercy and prepare the convenient environment for it. The State, on the other hand, needs the invincible power of religion to help individuals attain perfection, to put families and society in order, to guide the conscience and open the gates to the heart, thereby preventing many evils. The State has to be backed by this power, which is achieved through a quality education in religion. Human beings are not creatures of this world only; there are many other-worldly features that we possess and it is not possible for us to earn the qualities we need by the secular approach; these are possible through religion."

Modernity and secularism has been one of the most important themes of the Abant Meetings organized by the Journalists and Writers Foundation (GYV), of which Fethullah Gülen is Honorary President.

According to journalist and writer Taha Akyol, the Abant Platform was the first scholarly meeting in Islam's history which upheld political laicism from the perspective of Islamic creed (Taha Akyol's article published in Milliyet newspaper on June 25, 1999).

Fethullah Gülen has always believed in the benefit of bringing together scholars and intellectuals with different viewpoints to discuss the nation's problems. Abant Platform was established under the Journalists and Writers Foundation to do just that. The meetings of the platform were convened at a resort near the Abant Lake, three hours to the east of Istanbul, where the meetings were held from 1998 onwards. Later, as international journalists and intellectuals started to participate, some of the meetings were held in cities like Washington D.C., Brussels, Cairo, and Erbil. Among the issues discussed in these meetings were church-state separation, Islam and democracy, laicism, the conflict between East and West, etc.

CHAPTER 3

WESTERN CIVILIZATION

Western Civilization

Due to its geographic position, Turkey's relations with Europe has been more intense than any other Muslim-majority country has ever had. The Ottoman territories included all of the Balkans and stretched to the gates of Vienna. Istanbul, Turkey's mega-city with a population over an estimated 15 million, is split in two, one half in Asia and the other half in Europe. It symbolizes Turkey's location connecting two continents. Thus, Turkey is as much an Eastern country as it is a European one.

Turkey's relations with the West have always remained a hot topic, at least for the last three hundred years. The highest goal in the minds of Turks has always been Europe, the ultimate target to reach.

The Ottomans looked to Europe when it felt the need to reform itself to survive. The first constitutional movements, in the Western sense, took place in 1839, when the Tanzimat Reforms were declared by the secretary of state. These reforms basically emphasized that the rule of law and the right to property were ensured for every individual. The Tanzimat Reforms are considered to be the first of the "Westernization" movements, after which the process of adopting Western institutions began to modernize the state.

The first constitution was put into effect in 1876, which was followed by a Constitutional Monarchy in 1908, which gave rise to political parties. None of these efforts, however, were sufficient to keep the Ottoman Empire intact – after the First World War, the Empire collapsed altogether.

Relations with the West remained on the agenda after the establishment of the Turkish Republic. As a matter of fact, the Westernization issue has never been out of agenda in Turkey. Should Turkey be facing the West or the East? Is it possible to become a Westerner while remaining an Easterner? While such questions remained, Turkey's journey to the West has never ended, becoming an issue of friction and polarization among different groups in the society. In 1987, Turkey applied to enter the European Economic Community, which later became European Union.

Fethullah Gülen has always supported Turkey's accession to the European Union. When he visited Turkish immigrants in Germany in

1977, he encouraged them to integrate with Europe, and have their kids study at German schools and colleges. In those years, Turks used to live in isolated ghettos. They would not learn German and they would even send their deceased to be buried in Turkey.

Gülen asked for the Pope's support when he went to the Vatican to meet with John Paul II. Gülen's pro-EU position had made him a target for radical Islamists in Turkey. The government assigned security to him for a while after he started receiving threats. Gülen spoke of this in his interview with *Die Zeit*:

"At the very beginning, when I argued for EU membership, Erdoğan's supporters condemned me as un-Islamic. Then, Erdoğan changed his mind" (*Die Zeit*, October 2, 2016).

As Gülen said, at first Erdoğan was against the European Union, but then he changed his mind and supported the EU; now he's back to opposing it. During his term, Turkey has pulled back from all the reforms they had realized en route to Europe, bringing Turkey's accession process to a full stop. On many occasions, Erdoğan has openly threatened to freeze all relations with Europe. He's made real overtures to Russia and China.

One might say that one of the permanent central items on Turkey's agenda has been the issue of Turkey's relations with the West and Westernization. Of course, the issue of Westernization has a history dating back to the Ottomans. In the Republican period, the issue of the West and Western civilization did not lose popularity, and also split society into two. It has become a major point of polarization in Turkish society.

Naturally, this has been one of the topics most frequently addressed to Gülen in the interviews he has given. In what direction would the Turkey of the 1900s and 2000s be facing? What were the views of the religiously-minded toward the West, the European Union, and the United States? Was integration with the Western world possible?

I was not concerned the West would assimilate us

In an interview broadcast on *Star* TV on July 6, 1995, Gülen was asked, "What are your thoughts concerning integration with the West?"

He gave the following response:

"Now, there are some things that are inevitable, that we too cannot avoid either. To a certain extent since the Tanzimat Reforms,[7] there was this dream of being a part of the West. Turkish society has lived with a longing for a union. The Turkish intellectual, especially, felt this keenly, both back then, and now.

"We took one step with the First Constitutional Era (1876), and another move with the Second Constitutional Era (1908). We began a separate process with the Republican era, which surfaced after a certain time. Certain things were done after 1963, like the signing of the Ankara Treaty. At one point, the European Common Market, and later the European Community, was brought into question. And now, a customs union is the subject of discussion. In good faith and worried that our society has not been properly nurtured in terms of national and religious values, some people have been concerned about the assimilation of Turkish society in the event of such an integration."

Turkish society will protect its identity under any conditions

"Do you have such a concern?"

Gülen: "I have never had any such concern, even during the earliest time when this was first being debated. That is, I did not have such a concern in 1965-66, when the matter was on the agenda. I believed then, as now, that Turkish society would be prudent, that it would protect its own identity, and that even if it were to be Europeanized and – to echo the late [Mehmet] Akif's words – take what it needed to take from Europe, it would essentially put across to Europe what we would expect it to put across. There may have been certain concerns at the time.

"As I personally witnessed in 1977 when I traveled to some countries in Europe – having been sent there by Religious Affairs to deliver sermons – our workers travelling in Europe, the Turkish community there, had already veered off its course 98 percent by then. Those in the Netherlands had completely come under Dutch tutelage, and those in Germany had come under German tutelage. About 4-5 years later, I saw

---

7   The Tanzimat Reforms were a series of modernization efforts in the Ottoman Empire, which started in 1839 and continued for several decades. The reforms included reforming institutions, granting civil liberties, a reorganization of the army and the finance system, etc.

that these people who were working for the Germans and Dutch had now opened their own businesses, established their own corporations, and were employing German and Dutch workers.

"This goes to show that maybe an indirect assimilation took place during a certain period, but the Turkish community is rediscovering and returning to its own essence. They are no longer raising their own children as workers. They are seeking to be among the respective country's elite by opening university preparatory courses. Thus, neither the European Common Market, nor the European Community, nor the customs union would give rise to such an assimilation as would warrant such concern."

The Turkish people aspire to the European Union

Nine years after this interview on *Star* TV, Gülen reiterated his views on the European Union, this time on Samanyolu TV, on July 14, 2004:

"The reality is this: Turkey has been living in the process of entering the EU since 1960. I have always been for entering the EU. Even when some called it a Christian club, I said, 'Let those who question their own belief and religiosity worry.' I can have close relations with Europe. I can explain my culture to them and express myself. I can share my feelings and thoughts with them. Perhaps they will get to know us better and become more closely acquainted with us. But if there are some who have doubts about their religion and piety, they may well fear becoming Christian if they join them. I never had such a fear. I have supported the European Union from the very beginning. European Union, joining Europe, being European, being on the same course with Europe have always been a dream of the free generations of Turkey since the establishment of the Turkish Republic. This dream is to some extent becoming a reality.

"My views on the subject have not changed since the beginning. Turkey is making progress. I think the European Union is something the Turkish people aspire to. I hope that it becomes a reality."

Believers support integration with the West

Gülen has had a very clear stance on the issue of the European Union from the beginning, and he has always maintained two things:

1. He sees integration with the West as necessary.

2. It is inconceivable for a believer to be against integration with the West.

He explained why he views integration with the West as necessary in an interview published in *Yeni Yüzyıl* newspaper on July 27, 1997: "We have been deprived of many aspects of the West that can be considered as being to our advantage. We are deprived of the advantages America can invest us with. We are speaking of an abstract, dry East. That's right, the East should be maintained alongside the West, but frankly speaking, there seems to be nothing much to praise coming from the East in our times... I can say loud and clear that I view integration with Europe as necessary. If there is to be more serious cooperation in the future, it would be to our advantage to enter into this in a planned and programmed fashion..."

In an interview with *Zaman* newspaper dated September 4, 1999, Gülen explained why a believer cannot be against integration with the West:

"What makes the West what it is today is its painstaking research into the nature and natural phenomena, its interpretation of the universe, and its giving symphonious expression to the melody of the book of the universe, which we call the laws of creation arising from God's power and will. This is the wellspring of physics, chemistry, and astronomy.

"I believe that this [studying the universe] is a duty upon the Muslims, too. This is what they should have done. Doing so is a service to our nation and people.

"In this sense, it is absolutely unthinkable for a Muslim to be against the West, against integration with the West, and against integration with America. But of course it is important that we protect our own interests, our national honor and dignity, our own hue, and our own identity. We are not going to immediately dissolve within that pool like a snowflake that has fallen in, but are going to retain our selfhood... "

Gülen voiced the same views in an interview published in *Sabah* newspaper on January 28, 1995, in his answer to the question, "So you are not concerned, in this case, of Turkey's entry into the European Community giving rise to assimilation?":

"Indeed, our people there [in Europe] should rise out of their for-

mer position and establish themselves at various levels in the upper ech-
elons. They should live in certain regions, and strive to study at such
schools that which can enable them to become bureaucrats, instead of
vocational schools. They must carry the richness of their own beliefs and
views, values that they believe lead to true happiness, to the European
Community. These individuals will form the lobbies that our nation so
needs in the European countries they reside in."

There are many good things to be taken from the West

One of the questions Gülen was asked in his twenty-two part *Milliyet*
interview, and which was published January 9, 2005, was this: *"Are we
going to lose religion as a consequence of the EU-Turkey relationship?*
Gülen answered as follows:

"Some people perceive joining of Turkey into the EU as an inva-
sion. The foreigners will come and invade our lands... If such thoughts
arise from national concerns, we may argue that our national values have
blended with our soul to the extent that we cannot tolerate any compromises. As long as they (Europe) accept us as we are, then we can be
together; we respect them as they are with their values. If the concern
is that our religious values will be devastated, [we must remember that]
our nation has overcome so many obstacles. We have suffered more than
any other nation in the region... poverty, remaining aloof to our values,
lost identity...

"Despite all these, thankfully today, we can see that 80-90% of our
nation is still firmly attached to its history and the roots of our soul and
meaning. During the time of the Common Market and the later the Customs Union, I was always sure, and am still sure, that our nation would
not compromise either its national or their religious values. I am not
worried that we are about to lose our lands."

Seeking the good and the beautiful is part of human nature

In the views he expressed during a *Zaman* interview dated August 15,
1995, Gülen said:

"Of course, it is vital to keep our essence, our color, and identity,
but isn't it necessary to also develop different policies with various nations in the world, which is being globalized? We have to be open to the

changes experienced in the fields of science and technology. But unfortunately, up until today, we've recently experienced a period of interregnum in this area. Things like the common heritage of humanity and the globalization were not sufficiently thought out. Our dynamics should be reviewed one more time and should be appropriated by the society. By adding the things promised by this new age, we can realize the Anatolian proverb, 'If everyone brings and pitches in from the things cooked at home, a rich table can be prepared. "

Echoing Mehmet Akif's belief that Turkey should, "import the science of the West," Gülen said, "In this sense, I do not see any objection to becoming 'Western.'"

"There is no reason for objecting to unification with the Westerners and the Western thought, specifically on certain necessary points. This is inevitable, anyway. If we have found our true self, the things we would be taking from them can only be good and beautiful things. And there are many good things to be taken from the West. Mehmet Akif had expressed it succinctly: 'Take the science of the West.' In this sense, I do not see any objection to becoming 'Western'" (*Zaman*, August 15, 1995).

The West was not halfhearted at all when taking from the East

Gülen drew attention to one particular facet of Western civilization. He said, "The foundations of the Renaissance in the West were laid in Asia." Suggesting that the West was never conservative or halfhearted when benefiting from the East, he highlighted that today, the East needs to exhibit the same stance regarding what it takes from the West:

"I think, an absolute and unconditional animosity toward the West would push us to a point to lose touch with the age. And [if this happens] you will be eliminated over time. There remains the fact that, they did not hesitate to borrow from us what they thought they needed. Those who read a little history of science would submit that before the Renaissance occurred in the West, in a real sense, a Renaissance took place in Asia in the fifth Islamic century AH (twelfth century CE). From Biruni and Khawarizmi, to Ibn Sina [Avicenna]... In Andalusia, in Asia, to the extent that their voices were heard all around, and ... they had become the breath of a great civilization. And again, according to many historians of science, the foundations of the Renaissance in Europe were laid in Asia.

"Considering the age in which we live, it is inescapable for the Turkish people to integrate with the West. I am convinced that if Turkey enters into this affair, by reviewing once more time on this way with its own reasoning and logic, its own dynamics, and its own values, we are not going to lose anything" (*Zaman*, August 15, 1995).

Gülen has always attached great importance to integration with the West. He believes it is essential for Turkey's survival in the global village. Taking the strength of Asia behind it... In his 1997 interview with *Yeni Yüzyıl*, he said:

"Integration with the West, in one way or another, is crucial. Integration with the West will have its separate advantages. Following and evaluating America closely in matters that we find convenient is important. We can raise a golden generation through this way. A young generation representing science and technology on the world stage. I give credence to this from a psycho-sociological standpoint also... A Turkic world not at loggerheads with the United States and with Europe, but one which adopts and appraises Western thought in line with contemporary realities, and which also respects those values that are not averse to its own spiritual roots, and a very unique, vast world which can simultaneously facilitate ongoing peace with the rest of the world" (*Yeni Yüzyıl*, July 25-27, 1997).

In describing why he encouraged the transition from the Cyrillic alphabet to the Latin alphabet, Gülen connected this to Central Asia's integration, along with Turkey, to the Western world:

"This does not imply that the letters of the Qur'an, the Qur'anic alphabet would not be taught. But it does not seem possible for a nation to survive as a nation, in a world rich in scientific and technological terms, with the Cyrillic alphabet" (*Yeni Yüzyıl*, July 28, 1997).

For Gülen, Turkey's accession to the European Union has added importance due to the country serving as a bridge to the Middle East and the Far East:

"Turkey can be a bridge across the Middle East and the Far East. Europe is in need of Turkey's profound and rich heritage of insight into the Middle East. They have accepted Cyprus, but Turkey is a much more important country, and Europe has to make a proper assessment of this" (*Milliyet*, January 8, 2005).

Turkey has both a Western and an Eastern side

Gülen does not agree with those who want to see Turkey turned away from Europe, and as the leader of the Muslim world in the East. For those people, Turkey is not European. Gülen thinks this argument is erroneous:

"I can't accept that, either. We have one side in common with Europe and one side in common with the Muslim world. If we are required to be a leader in the world of Islam, European integration will facilitate it. If those who voice [forgetting about Europe] do so consciously, then this is mistaken" (*Yeni Yüzyıl*, July 21, 1997).

When he gave an interview on Dutch television on October 19, 1995, Gülen was asked the following question: "It has been 35 years since the Turks' immigration to Europe. Were they to return today, they would do so having left no cultural imprints on the mind of Europe. What do you see as being the cause of this situation?"

Gülen gave the following answer to this question:

"It was out of need that those Turks emigrated to Europe. They planned to go, save a penny or two, and come back to Turkey to achieve the standard of living they sought. Their purpose was not to practice their religion or lead a life according to their spiritual roots. This was not out of respect for their religious dynamics. Perhaps their goal was only to earn some wealth and then return.

"In fact, people are guided with their purposes. Whereas those who emigrated from here were deprived of any credible purpose. There was, on the other hand, ignorance and a lack of knowledge. There was also the inability to hold Islam up as an example and duly represent it. Whereas Islamic culture needed to be represented for it to leave a mark. Islam had to be lived in practice for it to leave a mark. We went there with lack of knowledge on the one hand, and perhaps a thought of division on the other. Yet still, we were impoverished and our abject poverty had blinded us. We were unable to see anything else. We found ourselves in a world we didn't know.

"Far from setting an example, it might even be said that we did certain things that were a cause of shame to our nation and our material and spiritual roots."

Possibility of a European Muslim identity

In 1997 Gülen was asked a question that was relevant at the time, and has only grown more relevant since: "Can Turkey's Europeanization, or its Westernization, be in question? And in a corresponding manner, is a European Muslim identity possible?"

His answer was hopeful, though it has not yet been realized:

"If both Europe and Turkey could come to a mutually acceptable agreement, the future could be promising. In this sense, there is actually nothing wrong with accepting Europe and Europeanization, and this can, to such a degree, be called a European Muslim identity" (Yeni Yüzyıl, 1997).

When people in Turkey think of the Western world, they often think of America. The US has become one of the most hotly debated topics in Turkey in relation to the Western world and Western civilization.

Turkey has always had close relations with America – closer than with any other Western state, in fact. The relationship started in the 1950s, when Turkish and American troops fought side-by-side in Korea. It was immediately followed by Turkey's entry into NATO, which allowed Turkish-American relations to gain a broader scope.

And this America phenomenon from the beginning paved the way for intense and deep debate within Turkish political and cultural life. Some governments and politicians were accused of Americanism. There were politicians and servicemen who said that Turkey should leave NATO. The slogans 'Americanism' and 'servants of America' featured prominently in student demonstrations from the 1960s onwards.

The USA upholds democracy like ancient Babylon

Gülen's comments in 1997 concerning his view of the United States of America deserve particular attention, because at this time he had not yet begun living in America, and any possibility of his residence in the US State of Pennsylvania was not on the agenda. At precisely such a time, Gülen said, "America is the name of a nation that still sits at the helm of the world ship," and described the Unites States as follows:

"Democracy and certain national traditions are well established in the US. The social mosaic perhaps necessitates this. The US is like ancient Babylon. If there weren't a democracy of the kind that Americans understand, establish, and sanctify, its national unity could not be protected. The soft air of democracy shelters everyone. America remains in its current position in the world; it is not sliding into the Atlantic as some have long been expecting. Many things can be achieved in the US.

"Another dimension of the issue of anti-Americanism is this: Being an enemy to people or to countries is not something that brings much benefit. I am not talking about taking refuge in the NATO pact as opposed to the Warsaw Pact. The world needs the United States at present also" (*Yeni Yüzyıl*, July 23, 1997).

Located to the south of Baghdad, Babylon was a major city in ancient Mesopotamian history. Built on the banks of the Euphrates River, Babylon became known as a center of power. Babylon stretched across forty kilometers and was marked by glorious palaces and fortresses; its hanging gardens were among the seven wonders of the ancient world. The Tower of Babylon is recognized as the symbol of the diversification of nations and languages. For Gülen, the US today represents the strength and diversity of Babylon.

Does Islam threaten Europe?

The journalist interviewing Gülen for Dutch television then asked him a question that many people have asked: "It is said that at the end of time the sun will rise from the West. As far as we can see now, the West is not sympathetic towards Islam. How do you assess the situation?"

Gülen's response was expansive and insightful on the contentious topic of Islam and Europe. He also didn't mince words about the harsh stance the West has often taken towards the Islamic world. Despite this, as he always has, he urged reconciliation and compassion:

"The West's lack of sympathy for Islam is not new. Since time immemorial, it has not looked favorably on Islam and has taken no interest in it. In fact, during the first days of Islam's emergence, I think the West was more in need of Islam than it is today. But due to its lack of good guides and leaders, instead of getting along with Islam, it brought antiquity forward to challenge it. It took refuge in its glorious, honored, and grandiose past. With it, it stood against Islam and thus missed an opportunity.

"The West still does not approach Islam in a positive way. Of course there are reasons for this. One of these is Christian fanaticism; it has taken an extreme position against Islam. In other words, there may be differences between religions and denominations. These differences can give rise to some disputes and conflicts, but Christianity's attitude towards Islam has been very harsh. This constantly kept the Westerner in a negative tension against Islam. They could not analyze Islam rationally. This is why they do not now look favorably upon Islam...

"When they saw the Muslims [who had immigrated to Europe] before them, they saw Islam in them – exceedingly poor, slovenly, utterly uninformed, ill-bred ... and divided. They were groups at each other's throats... such an image did not lend itself to the view that Islam was something worth researching and thinking about.

"Muslims' failure to live up to the virtues of Islam seems to have further fueled the anti-Islamic sentiment Westerners inherited from their past. They could not regard Islam with sympathy. Sympathy necessitates approaching [someone or something] with sound thoughts and contemplation.

"Just as Muslims are not enemies to the West, Muslims are exceedingly offended by hostilities against them. The toll of these hostilities has been extremely high. However, it would be naïve to expect the world to become suddenly agreeable to Islam.

"Of course, such transformations between countries take a long time. The opportunity has not been missed. Time has not run out. Let us wait a half-century, a quarter of a century more, and see what happens. We can talk after that."

Terror and radicalism have been ascribed to Islam

The interviewer's next question was in the same vein: the threat the West ascribes to Islam.

"According to the West, while the 'red threat is over' with the fall of the Berlin Wall and developments in Russia, there is now the 'green threat' (in reference to Islam). What is your opinion on this?"

Gülen: "Perhaps an answer to this question can be offered through connection with the previous question. There is an enmity that has been inherited. Unfortunately, there have also been seemingly-radical movements that have fostered this idea. Some Muslims in different parts of the world erroneously took part in terrorist acts. These were ascribed to Islam.... They justified every means to the end. They were very pragmatist in their actions. [Again] all of this was ascribed to Islam. Without looking at the Islam in the Qur'an and as it was lived in the Era of Happiness (the age of the Prophet), they [the West] looked at the Islam, practiced by today's weak and slovenly Muslims. And this was the way in which they made judgements about Islam. This was exactly how some people wanted it to be. They did not want Islam to appear as it truly is, in its original form. They wanted it to appear in the manner they wanted it to appear, so that this would forever frighten the people and put them off. In this respect, indeed, the Berlin Wall fell, and a lot of things changed in the world, but new formations began. The contribution of Islam to these formations, having been an age-old religion enduring for 1400 years, would be significant. Islam's leaven role in the enlivening of these new formations across the world could have substantial contributions. But the world turned its back on Islam. I think that was mainly due to our inability to duly represent Islam.

"We could not represent it as it should have been represented. On the basis of the frightening image presented in some places, the disgust this caused, and the resultant misrepresentation, they invented a 'green threat.' And they will carry on doing this. If a community that represents tolerance and acceptance and overcomes these negative actions and currents against all the odds, and if they can then represent Islam in its own original fashion, or the way in which it was lived during the Era of Happiness, then these negative images will be dispelled..."

"Do you view radicalism as enmity toward Islam?"

"They may be unaware of it; actually, these are marginal groups. They are few in number, and weak, but have their voice heard through the power of destruction. Due to the relative ease of the destruction, they utilize it, and thus have their voice heard. They are more recognized and better known across the globe than those people who live Islam in its original form. I don't want to name names. But it seems to me that we would encounter many of them were we to take a mental journey to different parts of the world. These acts have induced a negative image. They are unwittingly doing harm to Islam, and it is my humble opinion that they are preventing the West from benefiting from the light of the Qur'an.

There are religiously-minded people who suppose hostility against the West jihad

"Why is the West portraying Islam so negatively?"

"It seems to me that like the various misconceptions on our side, people of the church were also misled. I mean, just Jesus was misunderstood for a long period of time, Islam faced the same kind of jealousy and resentment on various platforms, especially at its emergence. To begin with, such misconceptions are inherited.

"In the past, when Muslims had the opportunity to use reason, logic, and our humane qualities to develop positive relations, we all too often resorted to the use of force. Force eliminated and destroyed everything afforded by reason and logic. We gave precedence to might over right. We still see the negative effects of this in the West. It cannot be said that all the armies Muslims formed against the West in the past were established upon, and acted with, justice. Even if notions of establishing justice existed in essence, it cannot be said that it was always maintained. This gave rise to a negative image. In later periods, Muslims suffered under the oppression of the West, and the Muslim world was torn to pieces. And this brought about an antipathy in the Islamic world. But we can establish a dialogue with these people in the future, even within such antipathy. A globalizing world will bring us together. [We will be so close as neighbors that] they will be able to sit on one side of the wall, and us on the other. Telecommunications and transportation have contracted and shrunk the world, and have turned it into a global village. Ignoring projections that we will, by necessity, feel the need to come together, we have begun to harbor hostility on the basis of things we hear at the present time. And we have externalized this enmity.

"As you can see, some people in Turkey who claim to represent pure Islam suppose railing the West to be a dimension of jihad. They deem reviling a virtue. By contrast, some in the West seem to continue their historical animosity, and even by further aggravating it. This is why they speak of a 'green threat.' This is the reason for their harsh, intolerant attitude. But it is my belief that a community of tolerance, a community of vision following in the footsteps of Rumis, Yunus Emres, and Ahmet Yesevis, who are able to overcome all these odds will surmount the obstacles surrounding their lofty ideals, and will introduce Islam in all its universality to the world."

We are the descendants of a "soldier nation," and individual identity requires great effort

A fundamental criticism leveled at Islam and Eastern societies is that individualism and independent thought remain undeveloped. Gülen made very important observations about this in his *Yeni Yüzyıl* interview, in 1997:

"Changing people's habits is not that easy. People want to take refuge in something without much thought. This is because individual blossoming or development is a hard task, a difficult job. It requires much effort. Taking refuge in something is much easier. Generally, this is what is preferred.

"I am asking out of curiosity: In Turkish society, how much of this ability and inclination that gives rise to this exists? For we are the descendants of a militaristic society. It was inherited this way from our ancestors. I even put some of my concerns about this issue to friends who work in genetics. I wonder if certain things can be inherited. I was genuinely curious. I asked but could not find a satisfactory answer.

"However, one can always speak of genetics. This is reflected in parliament in one way and in the presidency in another. The way it is reflected in the military is totally different. Other parts of society remain under the influence of the same effect. If this is not a matter of genes, which would be difficult to shed, then I think we need to change this. That is, thinking freely, openly, and gaining an independent identity are very important" (*Yeni Yüzyıl*, July 27, 1997).

In the same interview Gülen described the importance, from an Islamic perspective, of individual development and a person's self-realization. In doing so, he iterated the Qur'an's approach to this matter and underscored that the Qur'an accepts every individual as a "species" unto themselves, as it were:

"After the world wars, following the periods when mass killings were widespread, the birth of existentialism spoke to this issue. The individual was lost, was being destroyed. Existentialists are certainly right in their rebellion against the destruction of the individual, but it could be said that at certain points they went too far and gave rise to another mistake.

"Just like on any issue, one has to be balanced on this one, too. One should not be worried about individual development, about the development of individuals with the motivation of other individuals. For in Islam, each individual is viewed as a species with regard to other individuals. The important thing is the mental and emotional sources nourishing them, the source of the understanding maintaining them. That is to say, when the individual reaches a certain level of thought and understanding, a certain horizon, just like trees making up the forest, they will understand the fact that they have to live in a society.

"For this reason, an individual who has completed their individual development will see the necessity of being with other people, the necessity of not being alone. On the one hand, they will understand the fact that they cannot be on their own, and on the other, they will not harm the other segments of society. An individual who uses their own rights and freedoms to not harm others, and even in the consciousness of preferring others to their own self, and who is educated within this framework, must be given extraordinary opportunities to develop.

"Otherwise, there is always going to be both hegemony and submissiveness; there will always be oppressors and an oppressed. This is one aspect of the sad situation in Turkey" (*Yeni Yüzyıl*, July 27, 1997).

Let's be a breakwater against the clash of civilizations

In an interview with *Sabah* newspaper on January 28, 1995, Gülen was asked, "If you were to speak with the Pope, what would you say to him?"

He replied:

"A globalization is being experienced all over the world. In response to the almost instantaneous transmission of anything happening in the world, whether good or bad, to other places across the globe via means of communication and transportation, I think there needs to be more tolerance and acceptance. Interreligious dialogue needs to be further developed...

"I would raise the fact that engagement among civilized people should be through persuasion – in the words of Bediüzzaman – not through force, as is the case among the uncivilized. I would share my thoughts with him that when Islam first emerged, equipped with a system of thought, belief, and worship, Christianity could have benefited from it. Yet instead, it sought refuge in antiquity, Roman paganism, and

Hellenism. It could have taken some of the dynamics of Islam and imparted vigor to its existence. Such an opportunity was missed. I would say that such an opportunity ought not be missed once more."

All knowledge belongs to God and religion is from God

In his meeting with the Pope, in 1998, Gülen handed to him an invitation letter to Turkey, courtesy of President Süleyman Demirel, and said:

"Mankind, from time to time, has denied religion in the name of science and denied science in the name of religion, arguing that the two present conflicting views. All knowledge belongs to God and religion is from God. How could the two then be in conflict? We can, by coming together, stand up against those misguided souls and skeptics. We can act as breakers, barriers if you will, against those who wish to see the so-called clash of civilizations become a reality..."

The possibility of a large-scale clash of civilizations in the future was first articulated in the 1990s. It was two Americans who first articulated this thesis: Bernard Lewis and Samuel Huntington.

Gülen explained how he views the clash of civilizations thesis:

"I don't believe there's going to be a clash between cultures or civilizations. If some people are planning such a thing based on their current dreams and making claims on this subject, and if such a wave has risen and is on its way, then before we live such a clash, let's put a bigger breakwater in front of it and break their wave" (*Yeni Yüzyıl*, 21 July 21, 1997).

American political scientist Samuel Huntington's article "The Clash of Civilizations?" published in 1993 in the respected journal *Foreign Affairs*, proposed that a clash between the East and the West was inevitable in the near future. For Gülen, however, such a clash is not the world's fate. He believes that peaceful coexistence is possible.

Finally, let us provide an excerpt from Gülen's interview with *New York Times*. Brian Knowlton asked:

"What, in your view, is the greatest challenge for Muslims in reconciling traditional religious beliefs with modern society and life? Is there any hope for an end to the conflict between extremist fundamentalists on the fringe of the Islamic world and Western countries?"

Gülen offered the following answer to this question:

"There are three essential foundations to the soul of Islam. If you neglect any one of them, it's going to affect the other dynamics and paralyze that soul. These foundations could be summarized as:

"1) Interpreting the religion according to the core sources of the Qur'an and the Sunnah of the Prophet, while also understanding the times we live in.

"2) Just as the Qur'an is a manifestation of God's Word, the universe is a manifestation of God's Power and Will. We must study the commands in this 'universal book' along with the Qur'an.

"3) Keeping the balance by being conscious of substance as much as form, the spiritual as much as the material, the hereafter as much as the world, the metaphysical as much as the physical, and vice versa.

"I believe that up until the five centuries after the Hijra, there were Muslims who established philosophical, spiritual, mystical, and Sufi systems because they had a love of truth and an enthusiasm for science. However, in later times they couldn't interpret well the times they were in and so lost that level of intellectual rigor. As a result, a certain mentality developed in some quarters, and from this mentality an attitude surfaced toward the West. This was not because of the fundamentals of faith but because of the flawed mentality. And maybe, it's possible that some of the actions of Westerners gave support to this negative attitude. As far as ending the clash mentioned in the second part of your question – it's all up to people being able to get together and talk and enlighten themselves and view each other with tolerance.

"If we can form a strong diplomacy that is tied to universal human values instead of pressure and hard power, if we can seek the good will of others instead of coming down like a hammer over their heads, probably, the situation with fundamentalists will be diminished. For example, if your aim is to help a country develop and democratize, instead of entering a country with hard power, you could try to open the doors of people's hearts with the way of love, perhaps by using humanitarian aid. If there is a sincere intention to help, and I believe it should be based on compassion. And if we could act with the philosophy of Rumi, the thoughts of Yunus Emre, and the way of Yesevi – then I think we can alleviate the fundamentalist ideology. Otherwise, using hard power will likely generate a backlash.

"With hard power, all the hatred and rancor will be inherited by upcoming generations and will even spread from the people at the top all the way down into every level of society. From this angle, the world needs to develop a new diplomacy to counteract the negativity, and this can only be accomplished by leading countries like the US and established institutions like the United Nations and NATO" (A section of this interview by Brian Knowlton was published in the *New York Times* on June 11, 2010).

CHAPTER 4

POLITICS

Politics

In a series of interviews conducted with Gülen in the aftermath of the coup attempt on July 15, 2016, almost all of the press asked the same question: "You supported Erdoğan in the past. Why did your relationship fall apart?"

In a similar vein, the first question the *Die Zeit* reporter asked was, "Why did you support Recep Tayyip Erdoğan and his AKP, which was born out of an Islamic movement?"

Gülen's response is important:

"Because he promised to pave the way for our country to the EU. At the very beginning, when I argued for EU membership, Erdoğan's supporters condemned me as un-Islamic. Then the President changed his mind. He hoped that Hizmet would praise him as the leader of all Muslims, to promote him worldwide."

Die Zeit's second question was, "What was it that connected you to him personally?"

Gülen's response explained the developments of recent years:

"Neither I nor my friends were ever really close to Erdoğan, even though there are such claims now. I met him only a few times before he became the Prime Minister in 2003. When he was founding the AKP, he promised democracy, to uphold human rights, and to curb the army's political influence. This was why Hizmet supported him. Nevertheless, he did not keep these promises after they won for a third time in the 2011 elections. They made a U-turn from a constitutional government to an executive presidency" (*Die Zeit*, October 2, 2016).

As Gülen explained, during his first years in the office, Erdoğan promised to follow up on the reforms initiated by former governments for EU accession. He even took some steps in that direction. He gave the impression that he stood against the "deep state" elements within the army, which was known as the "Turkish Gladio."

However, he took a sharp turn after the constitutional referendum on September 12, 2010, which consolidated the civilian authority over the army. This turn became sharper after his victory in the 2011 general elections. He aspired to fill in the vacuum left by the generals and become the sole authority in Turkey. He sought this authority as an executive president.

This ambition started his aggression against Gülen. Erdoğan gave directives to find out ways to shut down schools and tutoring centers affiliated with the Hizmet Movement and ordered the Turkish Intelligence Agency (MIT) to blacklist and fire every public servant who was sympathetic to Gülen and Hizmet. In order to undermine Gülen's influence in society, Erdoğan blamed him as the power behind all unfavorable things that happened in the country.

The latest piece of scapegoating came after the coup attempt on July 15, 2016. Erdoğan claimed that it was Gülen who gave the orders for the coup. The President declared a state of emergency, and only days after the coup, he purged tens of thousands of public servants based on the profiling MIT had been conducting over the last few years. Before this book was sent to the press, the number of purged individuals was over 130,000 from all government institutions. Among the purged are members of the Supreme Court, governors, professors, teachers, generals, doctors, police officers, and businessmen. Over 160,000 people have been detained and 50,000 have been arrested. To open space for the arrested, the government released about 30,000 convicted criminals from jails nationwide. Hundreds of women have been put behind bars; some have been arrested simply because their husbands were abroad.

The New York Times foreign affairs columnist Thomas L. Friedman referred to Erdoğan's witch-hunt as follows: "A day after the failed coup, Erdogan dismissed 2,745 judges and prosecutors. How did he know exactly who to fire in one day? Did he already have an enemies list?"

This is a fair question. These people were already blacklisted and Erdoğan was waiting for an opportunity to fire them. The July 15th coup attempt gave him this opportunity – and Erdoğan gladly took it. He even said, "This attempt is a gift of God for us."

Erdoğan made the best out of the coup attempt: he shut down thousands of schools, dormitories, and 17 universities opened by members and supporters of the Hizmet Movement. Banning hundreds of foundations and civil society organizations, Erdoğan had hundreds of businessmen arrested and took over more than 800 leading companies. Even the apartments owned by jailed journalists have been confiscated.

Erdoğan's primary target was Fethullah Gülen, but he gradually expanded his purge to include other oppositional groups, too. Police arrested thousands of Kurdish politicians and dismissed many others from public service. The leader of the Kurdish HDP party and many members of parliament have been arrested. All mayors elected from the HDP have been removed from their positions. Purges against Kurds were followed by purges against secularists. Many journalists from the most secularist newspaper, *Cumhuriyet*, including the editor-in-chief and many columnists, have been arrested. The former editor-in-chief, Can Dündar, survived an assassination attempt after he was released from jail. He fled to Germany when Erdoğan ordered him to be arrested again.

Erdoğan has been accusing Gülen and his supporters of infiltrating government institutions and establishing a "parallel state." This is in fact what he himself has done: he has been filling all state institutions, primarily the judiciary, with his loyalists. Kemal Kılıçdaroğlu, the leader of CHP, the main opposition party, said courts take decisions according to orders coming from Erdoğan's palace.

All critics of Erdoğan have been labeled terrorists. A few thousand people who were courageous enough to speak their mind were arrested at dawn raids in their homes. Their alleged crime? Insulting Erdoğan.

Erdoğan has taken steps to suspend the rule of law. He extended the maximum length of detentions without charge to 30 days. Charges of torture are rampant, and there are tens of suspicious deaths that have taken place in police stations and jails.

In this section, Gülen's perspectives on politics have been compiled from his interviews since the 1990s.

***

"I have never been involved in any political pursuit or activity."

This was Gülen's answer when, on January 25, 1995, *Hürriyet* editor-in-chief Ertuğrul Özkök asked, "Those who are observing you from outside feel as if you are pursuing political ambitions. Have you ever engaged in political activities?"

In almost all the interviews conducted with Gülen in the 1990s, two topics necessarily came to the fore. The first of these was the relationship between Islam and democracy, and the question of their compatibility. The second issue was the relationship between Gülen himself and politics.

For example, in his TRT interview, in July 3 1995, Gülen said:

"I am just a person who has taken it upon himself to help people know God. I aspire to tell people about Him and to join the hearts of the people around belief in Him with experiential knowledge of the divine, love, and spiritual joy. I have forever shared the same vision with those such as Mevlana [Jalal al-Din al-Rumi], Ahmet Yesevi, Yunus Emre, Hacı Bektaşi Veli, and Bediüzzaman. I believe that this is an important principle binding people together. Thus, I deem mixing other considerations into this pure, lucid notion as muddying my relationship with my Lord, as bargaining with Him. As disrespect to Him. I view the interference of politics, trying to get somewhere with politics, as tarnishing my relationship with my Lord and as irreverence to Him.

"I even say in my own way – if this is to be called a mission – if nothing remains for me to do in this mission of promoting divine knowledge, love, and spiritual joy by encouraging others to strengthen themselves in their heart, in their willpower, and to bring them together to collaborate in their work, then, my remaining on earth is meaningless."

We are sworn never to enter politics

Following these statements, the program proceeded as follows:

Question: "So you are not going to enter into politics in any way?"

Gülen: "The thought has never even crossed my mind. As I see it, for a person who has found God, has formed a connection with Him, and who has seeped through the door opening to Yunus [Emre]'s valleys, well, to become involved in such things is to take several steps back."

Question: "What if those from your close circle, those influenced by you, enter into politics?"

Gülen: "If someone should enter politics and consult me beforehand, I will tell them exactly the same things. Indeed, I often repeat the same thing to friends who are frequently in my circle. We are sworn in this regard, and God willing, we will continue this affair to the very end with such an understanding. For my part, politics is so trivial compared to what we are endeavoring to do so earnestly. I have used the good opinion of my friends about me as credit to advocate education and culture, and to try to solve our problems by starting from the individual, as Goethe illustrates in his *Faust*. Frankly, I cannot at all understand how it is that some people regard it as possible for us to become involved in mundane matters while we are engaged with such things."

When interviewed by Brian Knowlton in June of 2010 for the *New York Times*, Gülen said:

"First of all, I must state that I have always been equally close to the representatives of all the political parties, and I have always shared my views that I thought beneficial with everyone. I have supported those who are respectful to our values and who give attention to the essence of the heart and spirit and at the same time have a message for the worldly and eternal longings of human beings. This is regardless of whatever party they happen to be in. Accordingly, it cannot be said that any one party is 'close' and the other is 'far'; I stand at an equal proximity to all of them" (Brian Knowlton, *New York Times*, June 11, 2010).

What relationship do you have with governments?

When Knowlton asked, "What relationship, if any, do you have with the current Turkish government? What, if anything, would you like to see it do differently?" Gülen replied with the following:

"In my opinion, the worst state and the worst government are far better than statelessness and chaos – because there is anarchy in the latter and it leads to nihilism. From that perspective, if someone were to have a positive interest in the state, I would consider it a duty of citizenship, and at the same time an expression against anarchy. I always believe in being on the side of the rule of law, and I also believe in the importance of sharing useful ideas, ideas that can clear the path for the country, with the officials of the state. Accordingly, irrespective of whoever is in the office, I try to be respectful of those state officials, keep a reasonable level of closeness, and keep a positive attitude toward them. With this line of thinking, we would be on good terms with whoever is in charge.

"Of course, we would approve the positive actions of those individuals who happen to share some of the ideas and feelings that we have. We would applaud their efforts to strengthen democracy, establish the supremacy of the rule of law, take freedom and independence and elevate them to universal standards in the country – but that does not mean we in any way make policy recommendations to them, nor do we ever act under their influence. So, if we were to speak of a 'relationship,' it is a relationship based on Rumi's spirit to have a chair for everyone in our heart."

Was Socrates justified in saying political power makes man great?

Joe Lauria, from *Wall Street Journal* who interviewed Gülen in 2010, asked him a political question on the basis of Socrates' thoughts. Lauria asks whether or not Gülen agreed with Socrates' contention that those seeking political power without a philosophical base become tyrants and that those seeking philosophy without political power remain unimportant and small.

Gülen's response is still meaningful and it is worth looking at it in its entirety:

"Let Socrates forgive me for saying so, but while I concur with the first part of the great philosopher's words, I do not agree with the second part. You know that philosophy has its distinct subject-matter. Philosophy concerns itself with those matters such as belief, the meaning and purpose of existence and life, the existence of a Supreme Being, the nature of knowledge, beauty, or aesthetics, and morality and religion, which have nothing to do with politics. The great philosopher possibly used the philosophy in the second part of the argument in question in a narrower sense and may have implied political philosophy."

Everybody is free in their political preferences

The importance Gülen has attached to remaining above politics is just as strong as the stress he has placed on the need for people to be free in their political preferences when they go to the polls. He explained this during an interview broadcast on Star television on July 6, 1995:

"Now, I deem it useful to serve the unity of my nation, my religion, and my belief above any political considerations. No group would object to this position. It is my belief that the nation will benefit greatly [when I stay] above politics for its unity and solidarity. I aim to draw upon the esteem and regard of our people in way while pursuing educational and cultural activities. But this does not obligate them in the matter when it comes to their political preferences; I do not want to lead them in a certain direction or to put pressure on them. And I cannot, in any case."

Gülen affirms that voting in elections is a civic duty and encourages going to the ballot box:

"I have always told the people from the pulpit of the mosque to go and vote. This is a civic right. You must put forth your preference on any account; even bring patients on stretchers so that they can do so, too. Vote for whomever you will, but you must vote. The people of this nation should get used to this. They should get used to democracy" (January 25, 1995, *Hürriyet*).

An examination of Gülen's responses to questions about politics over the years reveals that his focus has always been the same. For example, looking at an answer he gave to a question in 1995 and one he gave in 2005 makes this saliently evident. On January 25, 1995, *Hürriyet* editor-in-chief Ertuğrul Özkök asked, "So, do you have any political ambitions or expectations from this point on?"

He responded unequivocally:

"No, absolutely not. After this point, I do not even have any expectation with regard to my life, let alone with regard to politics. I have a different character. I have met with people like yourselves and have made many friends. Even the crowd here in this room is too much for me. I now say that either my cloistered corner or the next world is better for me. For example, I went on the Pilgrimage one last time in 1986, with somebody's financial support. As many people had heard about *Hizmet* before I received maybe twenty separate invitations by friends who left Turkey to settle there. But I felt very distressed because of this much interest in me. In other words, 'Fethullah Hoca' is too much for me... [who is merely] a preacher of the mosque, an imam. Because a Fethullah Hoca of such magnitude far exceeds that Fethullah Hoca of the mosque, this is way over my head.... And I am greatly distressed by this.

"Especially politics, or involvement in it in this or that way – these are not things I think about. If I have an opinion on matters concerning the fate of this nation, I will not refrain from making this opinion manifest. I would think about confronting any harm to come to it, together with my people and my State. For as long as I live, of course, I would deem this one of the responsibilities conferred by God upon each and every individual. Otherwise, I would consider myself accountable before God."

Making religion subservient to politics is sacrilege

Let us now look at Gülen's comments in an interview with *Milliyet* published on January 20, 2005:

"When the religion is made servant to politics, the religious feelings of people are manipulated; the religion has been approached disrespectfully, and such attempts have brought about no result."

Gülen is neither for "statelessness" via political chaos nor does he seek any personal engagement in politics. He has also rejected claims that he is "statist." Gülen states that he is far from such accusations and from sanctifying the state. The latter can be seen in his comments to *Zaman* on September 4, 1999:

"We are as far from the reprehensible statist approach that sacrifices the individual to the state, as the distance between east and west... Statism is one thing, while being against the state is something else. 'Statist' generally implies the way in which statist regimes around the world conduct themselves, and how the notion of the personal freedom and rights of the individual are brushed aside. It is a reprehensible statism if the survival of the state is the only concern and individuals are forsaken.

"We are as far from such an understanding as the distance between east and west. But every nation has a state. This state governs that nation. The American state has its own policies. And the state is the ground, the project through which governments come and exercise sovereign authority over the people. I don't recall saying I am statist.

"But I have always said this: In being opposed to governments, we may think we are performing a healing surgery, but we may accidentally apply extra pressure with the scalpel and this may harm the state. This may even damage the state at its core. The collapse of the Turkish State, or even just the State being shaken, would spell disaster for Turkey.

"Those who take this approach for statism, they are once again mistaken. I support free thought, free enterprise, personal gain, liberalism; but I may also be critical to some of the present social attitudes of all of these. I have offered examples of the Prophet Muhammad, peace be upon him, in this regard.

"He engaged in trade in the marketplace. We are speaking of a market economy one thousand four hundred years later. And he taught this to his people. He encouraged them to participate [as in a liberal economy] and assume leading roles in the markets of Qaynuqa, Nadir, and Qurayza, the competitive markets of the Jewish community in Medina who as a nation were awakened very early to life, very astute people who governed the world. He gave them this opportunity."

Statism eliminates freedom of thought

In his 2005 *Milliyet* interview, which spanned 22 days, Gülen provided very sophisticated explanations on questions like the sanctity of the state, statism, whether there are aspirations to take over of the state, and his reasons for staying out of the state or politics. One of the key points to which he gives emphasized is that statism eliminates freedom of thought, freedom of religion and conscience, and respect for rights:

"I have always stipulated that 'even the worst State is better than no State,' and 'the State is necessary, and should not be worn down.' But I have never sanctified the State as some people have done. This preference is a necessity for me, because if the State were not to occupy a certain place, it is certain that anarchy, chaos, and disorder would dominate. Then, there would be no respect for ideas, freedom of religion, and our consciences would be violated; justice would be out of question.

"In the past there were times when our nation suffered from the absence of the State. Therefore, I regard supporting the State also as a duty of citizenship. If a person is admired by people and his words are regarded highly, then this person is bound by a responsibility not to lead those people into error and to prevent them from extremism.

"But one point must not be overlooked here. We try to see the bright side and interpret in that direction; there is no use into basing arguments upon permanent criticism, harm, opposition, revenge, hostility, and hatred, as some people do. Therefore, this is our preference and we act accordingly, despite being aware of the State's certain mistakes, which we endure in our hearts. I have never had thoughts as, 'the State is innocent; it is as infallible as a Prophet..., whatever it does it is always to the point, it is never mistaken.' The State too can be mistaken (like anyone else).

"The path for those who desire the State is evident. I could head along the same path as a member of this nation, if I had had such a yearning. At this point, I feel the need to mention an issue which is not directly related [to the question]: I have always told my friends—sometimes openly, sometimes indirectly, but consistently—to cut off our connections with this world, to devote ourselves to earning the pleasure of God, and to allow ourselves no other goal but to make the names of God and His Messenger heard everywhere. If I were to prefer this world, to prefer to be at the top of the State, I would have looked for a position in certain places where such preferences could be realized. My preferences are clear.

"What could a man have had in mind, a man who spent his youth, a slice of his lifetime when youthful desires were at their peak, in the niche of a mosque and in a wooden cabin? Yes, some proposals were made on behalf of those who admired and sympathized with us. There were proposals for political purposes as well as proposals for different purposes; these were far above my head and I could never become engaged in them. I am sorry: I find such accounts vex me so I don't want to go into further detail. If I refused all the opportunities that came to my doorstep back then and rather I spent my youth in a wooden cabin, and I now spend every night as if it is my last; how could I have such desires today?

"My heart is filled and my vision is decorated by other things. I prefer to live as Ahmad Sirhindi, Ghazali, Harrani, or Aqil Mubanji lived – to follow their traces in order to reach the lifestyle of the Prophet and thus reach the pleasure of my Lord.

"Turkish citizens with the right mindset, conscience, mind and heart who wish to be in office can step forward and govern the State. And we will support them with our ideas. We will present at their disposal whatever we can that is of any use. This is how I believe it must be... What we care about is that the reputation of our State is protected, our religion is not harmed, and that we are provided with services to live our faith."

Claim that I will enter politics is the biggest insult

In September of 1999, during a discussion with a group of journalists in the United States, Gülen was asked about rumors that he would establish a political party. He responded that he found such rumors insulting:

"I have my own point of view. I say this because it may look as though I am making light of those who engage in politics. I have considered claims that I am establishing a political party, entering politics, or becoming involved in politics as the biggest insult against my person in my entire life. I am trying, in my own way, to be a traveler on a certain path. This is the path of seeking God. I believe my efforts on this path are inadequate. I say this in all sincerity.

"I even felt this when I was visiting Medina. 'O God's Messenger,' I said, 'had I a heart that yearned for you, I would have been like Majnun here before you.'

"It is not right that a person who has found something in their own way be considered as someone who is still in searching. One who has found God has found everything. And any quest other than this is meaningless. Of course there will be politicians in this country, and they will run the country. There are already so many of them and everyone knows much better than us [how to run the country]. In this country, there are things that are being neglected. There are our values, which should be uplifted in our lives and be carried out in our actions. This is being neglected.

"I am of the view that more organizations must come out and translate into action these issues that have been relegated to the sidelines, like our culture, our past, the values we have to offer humanity to be used as cement in a world to be rebuilt anew.

"This covers my horizon entirely; this is the path I am on..." (*Zaman*, September 4, 1999).

An end to the alliance with AKP?

Following the Turkish government's nationwide closure of preparatory schools, some of which were associated with Hizmet, and the corruption investigations launched in December 2013, Gülen was frequently asked about his relationship with the ruling AKP. Journalists Joe Parkinson and Jay Solomon, writing for the *Wall Street Journal*, interviewed him on January 21, 2014.

Gülen was asked, "*The Prime Minister has repeatedly attacked you and Hizmet in recent weeks. Do you believe that your alliance with his faction of the AKP is now definitively at an end?*"

He replied, "If we can talk about an alliance, it was around shared values of democracy, universal human rights, and freedoms — never for political parties or candidates. In 2010 constitutional referendum I said that if these democratic reforms, which are in line with the European Union's requirements for membership, were done by CHP [the main opposition People's Republican Party], I would have supported them. A broad spectrum of Turkish people, including Hizmet participants, supported AKP for its democratizing reforms, for ending the military tutelage over politics, and for moving Turkey forward in the EU accession process. We have always supported what we believed to be right and in line with democratic principles.

"But we have also criticized what we saw as wrong and contrary to those principles. Our values or stance have not changed. We will continue to advocate for democracy. Whether the stance or actions of the political actors are consistent with their earlier record should be decided by the Turkish people and unbiased observers... Throughout the AKP period, we supported democratizing reforms and criticized and opposed anti-democratic actions.

"For instance, in 2005 we criticized the draft anti-terror law that defined terror crimes too broadly and risked harming freedoms. During the period between 2003 and 2010, the overall trend was toward democratic reforms and a broad spectrum of the Turkish population supported them. This was evident in the constitutional referendum of 2010, which received 58% approval.

"Indeed Turkey has made economic and democratic progress over the last 15 years. But we would like these democratizing reforms to continue. A new, civilian-drafted, democratic constitution would consolidate the democratic gains and would anchor Turkey with the democratic values of the EU. Unfortunately, that effort has now been abandoned."

I have only ever voted once in my life

One of the questions directed to Gülen in an interview with BBC television on January 27, 2014, was the following:

"Isn't it also true though that once upon a time you did see a common cause with the AK Party and Recep Tayyip Erdoğan? Now, you have your profound differences of opinion over relations with the Muslim Brotherhood, which maybe you think have been too close with Turkey, relations with Israel, which maybe you think have deteriorated under this government, and also the relationship with the Kurds. Would you say that on those three issues you have now diverged from the AK Party and Recep Tayyip Erdoğan?"

Gülen gave the following response to this question:

"We have never been completely aligned with one political party, whatever party it might be. This could be the MHP, the CHP, the AK Party, the DYP, ANAP – the last two no longer exist. Instead, we always considered it a part of our human responsibility to support the good works of these parties. As a result of this thinking, I said something that I had never said before. I said that people should vote 'yes' during the 2010 Turkish referendum in support of further democratic reforms. The Supreme Board of Judges and Prosecutors, the HSYK, should have been shaped within a democratic framework.

"Indeed, I did not just say this now: when twenty years ago I said that democracy was an irreversible course and process, those who are critical of me today raised bedlam then also, too, saying, 'What do you mean? What does democracy have to do with Islam?'

"We have never been completely aligned with one political party; our relations with parties were not beyond casting a vote at the ballot box.... Having said that, it may be that one or two sympathetic people have joined one particular party of their own accord. Had we wanted, others could have been directed to this party also, and they would have constituted the backbone of the party today. There would have been very different voices representing these parties. But we never had such a [political] desire."

Another question of the BBC correspondent was as follows: *"Would you vote for the AK Party?, Would you vote for Mr. Erdoğan to become the next president of Turkey?"*

Gülen replies: "I have only ever been able to vote once in my life. I was either in custody, on the run, or I was deprived of such a right, and so I went to the polls only once. After this, I was not able to. I have never been against going to the polls, and have not refrained from voting. This is a democratic right, one that I would want everyone to exercise.

"Now, I do not intend to say anything on this issue as I did for the referendum. That was different. If I say something, it will be this: Vote for whoever stands for the rule of law and rights, is upright and sound, whoever is respectful of democracy. [Vote for], whoever gets along with those around him... Other than that, I would consider it an insult to people's foresight and intelligence to tell them which party to vote for. Everyone sees all that is going on. I would not push people to choose one party over another."

Gülen had an article in the *Financial Times* during this time, dated March 10, 2014. Entitled, "Turkey needs a new constitution to save its democracy," the article contained these striking statements:

"Hizmet participants – and I consider myself one of them – are not political players and have no interest in the privileges of power. This is evident from their personal and financial commitment to humanitarian aid, education, and dialogue, as well as their purposeful absence from political office. Apart from encouraging citizens to vote, I have never endorsed or opposed a political party or candidate, and will refrain from doing so in the future. I trust the wisdom of the Turkish people and believe they will preserve democracy and hold the interests of the nation above partisan political concerns."

We are not a political party and will never be ...

During the corruption investigations and the debate over preparatory courses, *Zaman* editor-in-chief Ekrem Dumanlı's interview with Gülen was published, in a five-part series, dated March 18-22, 2014. Part of what Gülen had to say about politics in this interview is as follows:

"We are not and will not be a political party. Therefore, we are not a rival of any political party. We stand at an equal distance from everyone. Nevertheless, we make public our hopes and concerns about the future of our country. I think this is one of our most natural and democratic rights. I don't understand why some people do not like us enjoying this democratic right of ours. Telling the people at the helm of the country 'I have such and such ideas,' should not be a crime. In advanced democracies, individuals and civil society organizations freely disseminate their views and criticisms about the country's political issues, and no one expresses any concern about this.

"We have never established cooperation with any specific party based on the recognition of interests. We have abstained from doing this because this is the lesson we draw from the Qur'an and the Sunna. I have always seen the pursuit of strong and influential positions as a betrayal of our values. I would never say anything about choices other people make. But I have always viewed the pursuit of worldly and material gains as detrimental to my afterlife. This is also the case with my friends. We have never asked for a position such as general manager, governor, district governor, or minister.

"If someone has done so in the past – and I do not remember such a thing happening – they either had nothing to do with us or are no longer linked to us. I have forwarded this sentiment of mine to State officials. We have tried to extend support on such issues as the improvement of democracy and fundamental rights and freedoms. We would support any party to make sure anti-democratic practices come to an end and that the culture of a pluralistic democracy becomes permanent. Unconditional partisanship is one thing, and lending support to democratic practices is another.

"We now stand where we were before. We should look at who is moving away from this standpoint. A political party which has, up until recently, taken steps to expand the sphere of fundamental rights and freedoms is now considering censoring the Internet and introducing bills that would make this country an intelligence state. Is it possible to think of us as supporting attempts to do harm to social cohesion through strong and insulting discourse and to shelving democratic customs?

"If the whole issue is restricted to the Hizmet movement, you may try tolerating the repressive measures. However, the ongoing developments should be analyzed from a broader perspective. Unfortunately, Turkey is being alienated from the world. A Turkey which becomes isolated on the global stage and loses its democratic richness will hurt not only the people in this country but also everyone who takes Turkey as a model for themselves."

Our support for the referendum was not appreciated

Gülen was asked, "There are debates on what party the movement will support."

He again responded at length:

"I cannot see it as proper for Muslims to talk about this all the time and think that the ballot box is the real meaning of life. Of course the ballot box holds a crucial importance for the future of this country; but it is not everything. It is impossible not to become upset realizing that focusing on the ballot box only makes some people comfortable in telling lies.

"As for the debate on who we should vote for, I have always asked my friends to cast their votes based on their personal conviction. I believe that asking them to vote for a certain party is a type of pressure; in addition, I also consider engagement with a certain party isolation from other segments of society. Our clear and plain stance in the referendum was not for a certain party; it was for the introduction of democratic steps.

"It appears that this stance is not being appreciated... Everyone will consider their own situation and analyze the mayoral candidates (he refers to the municipality elections on March 30, 2014). In the end, this is not a general election. The candidates are more important than the parties; there are many valuable candidates in all parties. Whatever party you vote for, you will not have committed a sin."

Held on September 12, 2010, a Constitutional referendum passed with an approval of 58%. Before the referendum, Gülen called on the nation to support this referendum, which would expand human rights and institute reforms for more democracy and judicial independence.

In an interview with one of the leading papers in the Arab world *Asharq Al-Awsat*, published on March 24, 2014, he was asked, "You have always denied having political ambitions, but you have followers within the state apparatus. Do you think this works to your advantage in Turkey?"

Gülen:

"First of all, I must note that this Movement aims to serve humanity through educational, social, and cultural activities, not through politics. It invests all its time and energy in these services. It aims to solve social problems by focusing on individuals. In my sermons, I have stated that we have enough mosques but not enough schools. I have encouraged the congregation to try to open schools instead of mosques—many of which were empty at the time.

"If we nurtured any political aims, such as establishing a political party, various signs would have become manifest during the past 40 to 50 years. Over time, various political positions and ranks have been offered to me and my friends, but we rejected them all. If the Movement had political aspirations, it would have established a political party in 2001, when the political scene was quite suitable, for such an initiative as the parties of the time were collapsing; but we did not [establish a party].

"Likewise, if we really wanted to, we would have ensured that we had many supporters in the ruling parties that have come to office to date, but we did not. Until very recently, there had been only two members of Parliament associated with the Hizmet movement in the ruling party, which was known to everyone.[8]

"I have never approved of the instrumentalization of religion or religious values to attain political ends. I disapprove the abuse of religion by political motives, or the use of religious slogans in political contexts. Of course, it is legitimate for people to engage in political activities, and although we are not involved in politics—such as by establishing a political party—we do not preclude others from doing so. Indeed, political parties are essential constituents of any democratic system. Of course, the Hizmet movement does not seek to establish a political party.

"Yet the Movement's fundamental dynamics and common universal values, which I tried to elucidate in response to an earlier question of yours, do have political implications. Individually or collectively, participants in this Movement who are engaged in educational, social, and charitable projects may have demands from politics and politicians. But these legitimate demands are always sought through legitimate means and, in this process, unlawful, illegitimate, or unethical methods are strictly avoided and counseled against.

"Participants in and supporters of the Hizmet movement naturally expect its administrators to promote the rule of law, human rights, freedoms, peace, freedom of thought and enterprise, and stability and order in the country, [and they also expect] that they [the political leaders] work to eliminate chaos and anarchy and ensure that everyone is accepted as they are. Such participants resort to civilian and democratic means available to them to raise their voices about shortcomings in this regard. Raising public awareness is both a civic duty and one of the goals of civil society.

"No one can be forced to establish a political party in order to do this, and those who raise public awareness about these shortcomings cannot be accused of pursuing political goals, trying to partner with the ruling party, or meddling with democratically elected representatives. This is how it works in any true democracy. Political parties and free

---

8   Editor's note: Only two individuals Gülen was acquainted with were nominated and elected as deputies: Izmir deputy İlhan İşbilen and Istanbul deputy Muhammed Çetin.

elections are prerequisites of a democratic system, but they are not sufficient on their own. The effective and smooth functioning of civil society is important as well. It is wrong to say that elections are the only way to hold politicians accountable to the public.

"With its media, organized structure, legal activities, petitions, and social media messages, civil society continuously supervises the ruling party and checks by ensuring it fulfills its promises. Those who sympathize with Hizmet movement tend to refrain from involvement in partisan politics and from seeking political careers. But this does not mean that, as members of civil society, we relinquish our responsibility to hold politicians to account."

Claims of a parallel state

Recently, in an effort to shift attention from its own failings and corruption, the ruling AK Party and its supporters in the media have claimed a "parallel state" exists within the bureaucracy. According to the government, this faction is loyal to Hizmet and has been working to undermine the government. In responding to questions about this conspiracy theory, Gülen has drawn attention to several important points.

A *Wall Street Journal* correspondent asked, "What is your reaction to the PM's moves to purge the leadership of the police force?"

Gülen:

"If the members of the police force or any other government agency have breached the laws of the country or the rules of their institutions, nobody can defend such actions and they should be subjected to legal or institutional investigation. If, however, they have not done anything illegal and they have not violated their institutional rules, and they are simply being profiled based on their worldviews or affinities, and subjected to discriminatory treatment, then such treatment cannot be reconciled with democracy, rule of law and universal human rights.

"Shuffles and purges based on ideology, sympathy, or worldviews was a practice of the past. The present ruling party promised to stop these illegal actions while campaigning before elections. It is ironic that members of the police force and judiciary who were applauded as heroes a few months ago are now being shuffled in the middle of winter without any investigation" (January 21, 2014).

Another question the correspondent later asked was, "What is the reason that Hizmet actively encouraged their students to choose a career path in the police and the judiciary?"

Gülen's response was direct and to the point:

"First of all let's correct the premise in the question. I can only speak about my personal advocacy, which was addressed to the Turkish public in general. I have always believed that education is the best way to nurture individuals and build a solid foundation for a society. Every social problem starts with the individual and can be solved in the long term at the level of the individual. Systemic, institutional, or policy-level solutions are destined for failure when the individual is neglected.

"Therefore my first and foremost advocacy was for education. It is also why many people who agreed with my ideas have established various types of educational institutions such as dormitories, exam prep centers, private schools, and free tutoring centers. These institutions provided a wider segment of the society access to quality education, which were hitherto available only to a privileged few.

"I have encouraged Turkish people to be represented in all facets of the Turkish society and in every institution in the country, because it is important that these institutions reflect the society's diversity. But the choices that are made by students and their parents are shaped by many factors such as employment opportunities and the expected likelihood of upward mobility. As far as the institutions established by Hizmet participants, I don't have an accurate assessment of the career choices of their graduates" (January 21, 2014).

There is no single political view in the Hizmet movement

Gülen said the following to *Asharq Al-Awsat, in 2014,* on the subject:

"The Hizmet movement does not have a homogenous composition and it does not have a central or hierarchical structure, so its participants do not have a single political view. Therefore, it is unreasonable for it to closely support any specific political party. The Hizmet's participants have their personal political views, and the Movement does not impose any specific view on its participants. The Movement is not focused on elections or political developments, but on projects that promote common universal values...

"If it is true that there are people who are sympathetic to the values and projects of the Movement working in various positions within the Turkish state but whose identities are not readily obvious—it is both unlawful and unethical to attempt to profile them through various methods. Public servants who are said to be sympathetic to the Movement are bound by the laws, by-laws and the code of conduct of the authorities they work for, and they are strictly subordinated to their superiors and their duties are defined by the relevant laws. Let me repeat a point: In any state there may be those who feel affection towards me or towards another person or who sympathize with an intellectual or ideological movement. This is quite normal. No one should or can meddle with the personal convictions, beliefs, or worldviews of another person.

"The people who graduate from schools associated with the Movement or who sympathize with the ideals promoted by the Movement are expected to act in a way that is honest and respectful of the rule of law, human rights, and democratic principles, [regardless of] whatever positions they assume in public office. If there are people within the state bureaucracy who take orders from an ideological or other group instead of obeying the orders of their superiors or the provisions of laws and regulations, they must be found and punished, even if they claim to be acting on my behalf.

"If there are public servants who claim to sympathize with the Hizmet movement [who] commit crimes, investigations should be swiftly launched against them; they must be brought to justice. The Movement's stance regarding transparency and accountability is clear and will remain so" (March 24, 2014).

CHAPTER 5

FUNDAMENTAL RIGHTS AND FREEDOMS

Fundamental Rights and Freedoms

In Turkey, debates on fundamental rights and freedoms or human rights have always been multidimensional in nature. These can roughly be outlined as follows:

1. State-imposed restrictions on fundamental rights;
2. Barriers to freedom of thought and expression;
3. The State's approach to different lifestyles, different identities, and different ethnic groups;
4. Demands upon the State made by religious groups hoping to live in accordance with their beliefs...

There are still complaints voiced by the religious, as well as of the secular, socialists, and social democrats. It is very difficult to say that in Turkey there currently exists one particular group that has been fully satisfied in terms of human rights.

The recent political turmoil in Turkey has wiped away much of the progress the country had made in its efforts to protect human rights. When this edition of the book was being edited, there was a nationwide state of emergency rule in the country. A majority of basic human rights are suspended. As mentioned, the detention period has been extended to 30 days, and a detainee's access to his or her lawyer has been restricted. Public servants are being dismissed from their jobs by an executive order of the President, and with no need for a court decision. Legal options to appeal the dismissal are no longer valid. With another executive order of the President, hundreds of civil society organizations and foundations have been closed.

Freedom of speech is no more in Turkey, which has become the top jailer of journalist in the world. Currently, there are more than 200 journalists behind bars. While many critical journalists and writers have fled the country, those who have stayed behind have either lost their jobs or been arrested.

In remarks that were published in *Aksiyon* magazine in 1996, Gülen referred to the need for everyone to be afforded basic human rights. This was a basic requirement of living together:

"Respecting the fundamental rights and freedoms of all people guaranteed by law and observing the responsibilities this respect requires is an essential condition of coexistence" (November 22, 1996, *Aksiyon*).

In 1997 he was asked, "Can the government impose limitations on human rights and freedoms?"

He responded: "One may perhaps find worth debating some aspects of an argument like, 'This Constitution is rather too broad for us, it needs to be narrowed'; but no limitations on human rights and freedoms can be approved" (*Yeni Yüzyıl*, July 22, 1997).

I am for free thought and free enterprise

Gülen objects to a conception of "statism" which impairs fundamental rights and freedoms:

"In the essence of Islam lies the aim of freeing the world from disorder and corruption, and integrating this world – which has been left to the disposal of human beings with their free will, albeit within the framework of Divine Principles – with the other regions of the universe where a complete order, balance, and harmony prevail. Thus, Islam is always on the side of security, peace, welfare, concord, and stability. The pivotal role of the state in achieving, or at least maintaining this, is undeniable. But the state assuming a rigid bureaucratic structure, as in the case of fascist or communist state, [is] a very different thing. I ought to say that I am by no means interested in such a state or statism" (August 11, 1997 *Milliyet*).

Echoing Turkey's eighth president, Turgut Özal's triad, "Freedom of thought, freedom of belief, and freedom of enterprise," Gülen has said, "I am for free thought, free enterprise, and to a certain extent, liberalism": "Statism is one thing, while being against the State is something else altogether. I have always said that in being against governments, it may be that we apply extra pressure to the scalpel and shake the State at its core. The collapse of the state, the state being shaken would spell disaster for a nation. If they are taking such an approach as statism, they are once again mistaken. I am for free thought, free enterprise, personal gain, and to a certain extent, liberalism. I can criticize its excessive attitudes to some extent" (*Milliyet*, September 2, 1997).

Statism was one of the six principles that was adopted to shape the new Republic of Turkey. This principle presumed the dominance of the state in social and economic life, just as in socialist countries. The government established industries for dairy and meat products, as well as textiles. Turkey started adopting reforms for a more liberal economy after 1980. Beforehand, there were heavy restrictions on foreign currency, preventing businessmen from carrying with them sufficient funds to do business abroad.

Islam does not constrain art and free thought

Gülen has succinctly articulated Islam's approach to art and free thought: "Islam does not chain art and free thought with shackles." Likewise, he's indicated that Islam does not shackle freedom of belief, either:

"It is unthinkable for Sunni Islam to be against aesthetics, art, beauty, and the expression of beauty. If there was such a thing, the civilizations in Asia would not have come into existence. That period is the one in which the best efforts were made for [the compilation of] the works of *tafsir*, *hadith*, and *fiqh*. If there was a system of thought which would shackle the free thinking and art, it could only be through the way of *fiqh*. But if you make a little research, you will find that the period in which *fiqh* was highly developed, was the same period when Islamic society was most forward in terms of art and aesthetic thought and free thinking. In this matter, Andalusia is the land of wonders.

"These days, the authors of the Islamic history of science cannot help but reveal their admiration and adoration for that period. A civilization was established; a civilization in the chest of which was molded the aesthetic, free thought, and faith together, and where the peace, tolerance, and love were represented. The yeast of this civilization is Islam" (August 20, 1995, *Zaman*).

The minority is as valuable as the majority

Gülen has always stressed that Islam is not a despotic or repressive religion when it comes to human rights:

"Unfortunately, Islam has been wrongly portrayed as a despotic religion. Whereas Islam has such an expansiveness and flexibility regarding individual rights and freedoms... This is why the harshness of some people in the name of religion works against the religion" (*Zaman*, August 21, 1995).

In his interview for *Asharq Al-Awsat* in May 2014, Gülen enumerated the common values upon which members of the Hizmet movement converge. He underlined basic human rights in the following words:

"[Those values include] freedom, human rights, respect for beliefs, accepting everyone for who they are, openness to dialogue, dislike for abuse of religion for political ends, respect for laws, refraining from the abuse of state resources, asserting that there is no turning back from democracy, rejecting the use of the state privileges for coercion to transform individuals or societies or impose certain religious beliefs on people, trust in civil society, and promoting peace through educational activities. [It also includes more religious values such as] seeking the consent of the Creator in every act or word, loving the created for the sake of the Creator, reinforcing the moral values of individuals irrespective of their religious or other values" (March 24, 2014, *Asharq Al-Awsat*).

Accepting every person as a dignified creature demonstrates respect for free will

One of the themes Gülen underscored in his *Financial Times* article dated March 10, 2014, was the establishment of a legal order that would ensure the greatest degree of democratic rights and pluralism:

"The only way for the Turkish government to restore trust at home and regain respect abroad is by renewing its commitment to universal human rights, the rule of law and accountable governance. This commitment must include a new, democratic constitution, drafted by civilians. Democracy does not conflict with Islamic principles of governance.

"Indeed, the ethical goals of Islam, such as protection of life and religious freedom, are best served in a democracy where citizens participate in government. We also need to embrace certain values that form the fabric of a thriving nation. One such value is respect for diversity of all kinds – religious, cultural, social and political. This does not mean compromising on our beliefs.

"On the contrary, accepting every person – regardless of color or creed – as a dignified creature of God demonstrates respect for the free will God has given all human beings. Freedom of thought and expression are indispensable ingredients of democracy. Turkey's poor showing in rankings of transparency and media freedom is disappointing. Mature people welcome criticism – which, if true, helps us improve." (*Financial Times*, March 10, 2014).

Protection of the human being, not glorification of the state

While responding to *Asharq Al-Awsat*'s question, in 2014, concerning which understanding of Islam he represents, Gülen referred to a system where the basic rights of the individual prevail over the glorification of the state:

"[My understanding of Islam refers to a system where] protection of life, mind, property, family and religion prevails over the glorification of the state. People's freedom of choice and enterprise is stressed; the role of reason, public interest and even social experience is acknowledged in addition to transmitted knowledge as a way of understanding Divine revelations; the use of *ijtihad*—that is, interpretive reasoning—is encouraged in areas of the religion that are open to interpretation, reasoning and explanation; and the freedom to enjoin the good and forbid the evil is sought. [Furthermore], the freedom of practitioners of any religion to cherish their religion not only individually, but also [in] the public sphere, is recognized; the respect for laws, public order, and peace is fostered; terror and the murder of innocent people are recognized as crimes against humanity; and reasoning with others is promoted as a method to be employed instead of coercion. [It is an understating in which] religion is defined as mainly consisting of spirituality, morality, belief in the Hereafter, worshiping God, perfection, empathetic understanding, representation, and good counseling.

"As a matter of fact, from a sociological perspective, this is how Islam has been accepted and interpreted in Anatolia for thousands of years. This perception of Islam defies all forms of violence, extremism and the politicization of religion, but promotes love, tolerance, mutual acceptance, humility, humbleness and inclusiveness. In the social and public sphere, this perception of Islam prioritizes rights, freedoms, justice and peace. That is, it seeks to create a social texture open in all respects" (March 24, 2014, *Asharq Al-Awsat*).

In an interview published in the *Zaman* newspaper during the same period, he said that to achieve these goals, Turkey needed a new constitution guaranteeing democratic rights for all:

"In order to overcome the current turmoil, this country needs a new climate. A new constitution is a must to guarantee fundamental rights and freedoms. I believe there should be growing popular demand

and pressure by the relevant figures and institutions so that a democratic constitution based on the recognition of universal legal principles can be made. Unfortunately, norms for democratic rule of law appear impaired. Many intellectuals offer similar analyses. A Turkey which moves away from its own values and people will also move away from the world. Today, individuals and societies have greater importance than their states. It is impossible to implement a project that is imposed on the people" (*Zaman*, March 21, 2014).

If the masses are suppressed, fault lines will break

In the same interview, Gülen spoke of the key criteria for a pluralistic society:

"There are public servants from diverse ideological groups in every public institution. A public servant may be rightist, leftist, Alevi, Sunni, non-Muslim, a Kurd, a Turk, what have you, but he or she is supposed to perform their duties properly. What matters is their compliance with the laws and regulations when performing their duties. If public servants are profiled or face unfounded charges, this is a breach of their fundamental rights and freedoms...

"In a democratic order, if you are not allowed to express your views, then even the minimal requirements of being a democracy are not fulfilled. Imposing a type of rule with reference to religious notions will have serious political and legal repercussions... While the views of the majority certainly deserve respect, the views of minority groups should be treated with the same level of respect as well.

"If you suppress the masses, this will cause friction along social fault lines. And this is such a big risk that no political party can take, even for whatever political gain.

"Unfortunately, this is what happened during the Gezi Park protests. The people voiced democratic demands and, initially, there were innocent protests. These protests could have been tolerated. Officials could have visited the protesters and learned about their demands. Instead, the protests were violently suppressed. Is the shopping center that was to be built there worth a single drop of blood [shed during the protests]? Is it worth a single human life?" (*Zaman*, March 19-21, 2014).

Gülen echoed these same views in his article for the *Financial Times*:

"Every segment of Turkish society has a right to be represented in government. But the Turkish state has long discriminated against citizens and public servants on the basis of their views. Democratic inclusion will encourage people to disclose personal beliefs without fear of persecution." (*Financial Times*, March 10, 2014).

Theocracy and Islam

Gülen has maintained that there is no theocracy in Islam, and no class like the "church fathers" is present:

"As some people might abuse anything, they may misuse Islam, and they may exploit the religious in order to establish a regime of dictatorship. But this does not mean that there is a tyrannical side of Islam. To say this would be somewhat ignorant. Until today they criticized Islam with theocracy, but in actual fact, Islam has nothing to do with theocracy. Theocracy is a system of government which came into existence through the interpretations and implementations of the church fathers. In Islam there is neither the church nor are the church fathers" (*Zaman*, August 22, 1995).

A person who kills a single human being deserves eternal punishment in the Hereafter

In his 1995 interview with Dutch television, Gülen was asked, "What can you tell us about human rights in Islam?"

In his response, he made reference to the five basic human rights that Islam protects. These are the protection of life, property, progeny, religion, and the mind:

"As is well known, Islam is a universal religion, having come with not only human rights, but the rights of animals also. Remember the upset of God's Messenger when someone agitated a bird by taking her young. A compassion that embraces everything to such an extent does not exist in any of those systems that are the product of the human mind, nor among those systems that claim to be Divinely-inspired. This is how boundless it is.

"To begin with, the Qur'an approaches the issue of murdering a single person as a crime committed against all people. It is clear.

"Rising against the state and the nation, killing people: [again], Islam says "Killing one person is like killing all people." I have not seen this phrase in any religion, modern system of law, or in any other system. Today, we have human rights. There are various legal meetings held intergovernmentally. There are communities and associations. I have not encountered this level of expression in any of them.

"Why? Because the killing of a single human being suggests the wrong idea that a human being can be killed. One of Adam's two sons was not pleased with his own lot, and so he killed the other. The Qur'an does not specify their names, but the Qur'anic narrative in relation to this murder is most compelling.

"The Messenger of God states in authentic narrations that if a person dies for the sake of protecting their own life, mind, property, and religion, they become a martyr. And struggling in the protection of these fundamental rights is deemed jihad. These five principles form the essential basis of legal systems around the world and are thus protected. These are also in the books of methodology (*usul*) that form the basis of our works of jurisprudence.

"Islam thus approaches issues of human rights from the perspective of these fundamental principles. It cannot be said that human rights are neglected in such a religion" (from transcript of an interview with Dutch television, November 19, 1995).

The Medina Charter is a guarantee of human rights

Responding to German reporter Rainer Hermann's questions on human rights in 2012, Gülen offered the Medina Charter, signed during the time of Prophet Muhammad (pbuh), as a demonstration of the way in which Islam guarantees human rights:

"Islam affirms five fundamental principles in this regard: Life, property, religion, mind and progeny... These principles are taken as a measure of human rights. Almost all of the Qur'anic verses, Prophetic Traditions, and established judgements determine human rights and ensure their protection. The Medina Charter instituted by God's Messenger constitutes a precedent.

"Therein can be seen the guaranteed responsibilities, rights, and freedoms of Muslims and non-Muslims alike. Islam has declared each of these five universals as vital principles. Islamic law and the lives of Muslims have been organized around these principles" (*Frankfurter Allgemeine Zeitung*, Rainer Hermann, December 6, 2012).

For many political scientists, sociologists, and Islamic scholars, the Medina Charter (or the Constitution of Medina) was one of the earliest declarations of human rights in history. The Medina Charter was a deal made by the Prophet Muhammad (pbuh) with different pagan and Jewish tribes living in Medina. The Charter safeguarded the basic human rights of each tribe, including rights that pertain to their safety and the protection of their properties. In the same interview, Gülen indicated that human rights are the "shared values" of Islam and democracy:

"Justice, freedom of religion, protection of the rights of individuals and minorities, the people's say in the election of those who will govern them (and the latter being held accountable for their actions), and prevention of the majority oppressing the minority, can be cited as examples of the values and principles espoused by both Islam and democracy" (*Frankfurter Allgemeine Zeitung* interview transcript, December 6, 2012*).*

Jamie Tarabay of *The Atlantic* magazine, directed the following question to Gülen in 2013:

"You said earlier if you live in a democracy where you have full freedom of expression as a Muslim, then there's no need for any other kind of government. What is an example of being a Muslim without that freedom of expression, and what should they do in that situation?"

Gülen: "Today, some Muslims face oppression, and in response, certain individuals commit suicide attacks. Religion doesn't condone or justify responding to those who oppress with oppression. Today, Muslims face oppressive conditions in some places, and Christians in others. Some things take time. All humanity should embrace a peaceful attitude, but this can only be achieved in the long term through the rehabilitation of society. Can we achieve this? We will achieve whatever we can, and for our unrealized goals, we will be rewarded for our intention" (*The Atlantic* magazine's August 2013 issue).

A faith and way of life cannot be imposed on others

Does Islam really accept pluralism? Does it guarantee the freedom of belief for other religious traditions? Or does Islam command domination over members of other faith traditions? When answering these questions, which were put to him by Rainer Hermann, Gülen stated that just as no belief system can be imposed on another in Islam, no one can be scorned or looked down upon because of their religious identity:

"The essence of Islam is comprised of the following principles: Accepting everyone as they are; ensuring that everybody is able to enjoy their rights and freedoms as equal citizens before the law, as long as they do not violate the rights and freedoms of others; not imposing a certain belief system or way of life on others via political means; and not holding anybody in contempt or discriminating against them on ethnic, cultural, religious, or similar grounds. Freedom of belief is fundamental in Islam. Providing an example from the history of Islam can prove helpful in elucidating the matter further. When the Messenger of God emigrated from Mecca to Medina, Medina had its Jewish tribes, and a small number of Christians, in addition to its Arab population. As the Jews and Christians were People of the Book, or possessed Divine scripture, the polytheistic Arabs respected them.

"Among these Arabs, especially women or families whose children did not survive, would vow to make them Jewish or Christian if they lived. ...When God's Messenger emigrated to Medina, there were Arab children who had become Jewish or Christian in this way. When their fathers and mothers embraced Islam, they tried to force these children to become Muslim also. Upon this, the Qur'anic verse declaring that there could be no compulsion in religion, that religion was a Divine invitation that people needed to accept or reject with their own free will, was revealed, and prohibited these particular Arabs from putting pressure on their children. The different applications throughout history should be considered within their own historicity, and every event should be assessed within its own particular political, social, and economic conditions and positions.

"Pluralism and acceptance of the other, equality before the law as human beings, freedom to choose one's faith and live, learn and teach by it, and the like, are Islamic principles. These principles are valid to [the extent that others' rights are not violated]. When some verses in the Qur'an that may at first glance appear to be contrary to these principles are considered in light of the reasons for their revelation (*asbab al-nuzul*), and their textual and contextual integrity, their basis can be more readily understood. The most general comment that can be made about this is that these verses are aimed not at a generalization of individuals and groups, but at their attitudes and actions.

"Islam has predicated its treatment and relations concerning Christians, Jews or polytheists not on religious differences, but on their attitudes and behavior. The Qur'an and Sunna have put forth the principles of coexistence" (Rainer Hermann, *Frankfurter Allgemeine Zeitung*, December 6, 2012).

Private life and personal dignity are protected

In his interview with Gülen in May of 2010, *Wall Street Journal* reporter Joe Lauria asked him very important questions about the Hizmet movement's contribution to democracy, the place of privacy in a democratic state, a person's individual rights in a democratic system, and their relationship with other individuals on the basis of equality.

In the interview, one part of which was published in the *Wall Street Journal* on June 4, 2010, Gülen responded to the question of how he personally and his "followers" contribute to Turkey's democratization process:

"I do not consider myself someone who has followers. There may be those who concur with my views, or some of them, or who do not. I do not and have never had any connection with any movement with a political purpose. I merely express my views on a matter, should I have any knowledge concerning it, generally when asked. I have declared time and time again that there can be no going back from democracy."

When the journalist asked what he thought the role of privacy in a democratic state out to be, Gülen suggested that people cannot be monitored without conclusive evidence, and that according to Islam, everyone has a private life that must be protected:

"Islam prohibits derision, belittlement and insult, and playing with people's dignity and honor. It also prohibits suspicion against people, spying on and backbiting about their actions. Islam also forbids revealing and proclaiming people's flaws, misconduct and private affairs. Everybody has their own private world that needs to be respected and protected. No one can be monitored without material evidence and on suspicion of a crime that is not based on evidence."

Citing a Prophetic Tradition, Gülen affirmed that human beings are as equal before the law as the teeth on a comb, and that Muslims don a single type of garb at the Pilgrimage, without any discrimination on the basis of color or race:

"Any claim to justice that is not based on giving everyone his or her due is a false claim. God commands everyone to stand side-by-side in His presence during the prayer, without discrimination on the basis of status, position, color, or race, and we Muslims all wear the same type of clothing on the Pilgrimage. Prophet Muhammad, upon him be blessings and peace, stated that all human beings are as equal (before the law) as the teeth of a comb; moreover, he said, 'All of you are of Adam, and Adam is of earth. O people, be brothers.'"

"Islam gives people an assurance of protection for their lives, homes, and private lives, and has forbidden breaching, for whatever reason, the inviolability of individuals and engaging in behavior that compromises family privacy.

"It is declared in the Qur'an, 'O you who believe! Avoid much suspicion, for some suspicion is a grave sin (liable to God's punishment); and do not spy (on one another)' (49:12). With this verse, investigating the faults of others, revealing their wrongdoings and sins, and divulging the secrets pertaining to their private lives have been forbidden. The believers have been warned against hunting defects, errors, mistakes and sins as if engaging in espionage, accepting dubious information as though it were absolute truth, attributing offense to others, and the zealous pursuit to expose what God has concealed.

"But unfortunately, these delicate measures of our faith are not being observed. And it cannot be said that deterrent measures are being taken and stronger sanctions imposed for abuses."

Education is not just dressing students in uniforms

According to Fethullah Gülen, education is another basic human right and freedom. Every person, regardless of creed, ethnicity, or gender should have access to a quality education.

Unfortunately, many people do not. One of the problems is that education is often just a means of "dressing students in uniforms." Noting the need to promote individual differences, Gülen has frequently pointed to the importance of students being exposed to diverse ideas in taste, art, thought, and literature.

"I would like to stress that we never conceive education as dressing the students in uniforms; on the contrary, a great importance is given to individual differences, and I would like to express that these differences are even encouraged. However, we have to qualify that due to the circumstances of our time, today's students are directed more to the physical sciences. They cannot find an opportunity and possibility to display individual differences through art and literature.

"The reason for this is not the schools and the education they impart, but the circumstances dictated by this age. Nevertheless, when these students are contacted, I am sure; it can be observed that there are among them many different ideas, tastes, and shades of colors and tones in the fields of art and literature" (*Milliyet*, August 13, 1998).

Abu Hanifa deliberated with his students

During a 2004 interview in the United States with *Zaman*, Gülen referred to Abu Hanifa, the founder of one of the four main schools of Sunni law. He examined his relationship with his students and his view that truth comes from the collision of ideas:

"Abu Hanifa had always discussed issues with his students, and then took decisions accordingly. Decisions would sometimes be in the favor of his preference, and at other times they would be more in line with Abu Yusuf's, Imam Muhammad's, or Shaybani's. Sometimes, when a decision was made in the direction of Abu Hanifa's view, he would later revise it and said: 'I reviewed the sources one more time. Not what I said, but what you said is correct.'

"My horizons of thought are not as broad as Abu Hanifa's in that matter... But I believe the truth is born from the confrontation of ideas" (*Zaman*, March 31, 2004).

Preserving the ecological balance is a requirement of Islam

Finally, let us look at some of Gülen's views concerning ecology. According to Islam, the planet has its rights, too; all life should be respected. During a camp with his students in the 1960s, a student by the name of Davut caught a snake and killed it by shaking it. Gülen said to him,

"What right did you have to kill that animal?" He did not talk with this student for some time, as a punishment.

Again at another campsite, when insecticide was going to be used to kill certain insect that had swarmed the place, he changed the location of the camp saying, "We have no right to kill these animals." Relocating the camp meant dismantling the tents, re-pitching them, and re-digging the toilet pits. In other words, despite all the challenges of a new campsite, Gülen gave priority to the survival of those insects and flies.

In the 1990s, he took steps to replant trees in burnt forests across Turkey, saying, "Protecting the environment and the ecological balance are among the major duties of a Muslim. This is a religious, national, and civic duty." He continued:

"Planting trees is for me a longing which reaches the point of suffering. It grieves me deeply to see the fertile lands of this country [Turkey] so barren and I have difficulty finding the words to express my sorrow... The solution is to ensure that each and every individual of this nation plants a tree. Every couple who marries, every young man enlisting in the army, every student graduating from high school and getting into university, every public servant beginning their employment, every person starting a new job, every person who retires should be encouraged to plant a tree and this should become ingrained in the community. If only everyone planted at least ten trees in their life."

In his interview with Dutch television, Gülen was asked, "Why have Islam's unique views on ecology and human rights not been explained to the Western world? Could you explain these views?"

"Once again, it seems to me that Islam's views on ecology have fallen victim to our ignorance. In fact, we now have experts examining the issue with its primary sources. There are *hadith* and *tafsir* experts. It seems to me that we have not been able to understand the issue [ourselves]. Were we to approach the matter in terms of the illustrious life of God's Messenger, we would see, to begin with, that he turns the desert and arid region of Mecca into a protected area. He says that its grass cannot be cut, as this town was sanctified by God in His Qur'an. In a sense, he inspires people with an idea and direction towards saving nature. Otherwise, drought and aridity spell death.

"Nature, ecology, must necessarily be protected within its own balance. Although Mecca being a sanctuary is completely a religious thing, this does not stop us from taking it as an example. For the Prophet said upon arriving in Medina that God had made Mecca a sanctuary and that he himself made Medina a sanctuary. He thus incorporated it within a protected area, not allowing its grass or trees to be touched. Such violations are serious offenses when in a ritual state of *ihram* in the sacred precincts in Mecca, as well as at other times.

"This is one aspect of the matter. If this is God's Messenger, then it seems to me that were the whole world to be placed in the palm of his hand, he would extend this to exhort people to the establishment of large parks and gardens across the globe.

"When looked at from this perspective, it can be said that the sensitivity of Islam in preserving the ecological balance is equal to its sensitivity and universality in the matter of protecting the human being. For example, the Messenger of God says that if you hold a sapling in your hand when the Hour is upon you, then plant it. If you are to plant a tree even when the world is coming to an end, then you are required to forest the world when you still have hope in it.

"There are people who, while they identify themselves as the followers of a religion that commands this, followers of God's Messenger... they cut down trees and turn the place into a desert; the question of the connection of such people to God's Messenger is forever open to debate..."

CHAPTER 6

ISLAM AND WOMEN

Islam and Women

"**C**an women be administrators?"

Gülen was asked this question in 1995. The following is his answer:

"There's no reason why a woman can't be an administrator. In fact, Hanafi jurisprudence says that a woman can be a judge" (from an interview published in *Sabah* newspaper on January 23, 1995).

In speaking of women and women's rights in particular, the issue is of course not just whether or not women can be administrators. Innumerable topics, including women's place in society, their status, the extent of their inclusion in state affairs and working life, male-female relations, and manner of dress have been debated.

Turkish law did not allow female students to wear headscarves at universities. The Turkish tradition of wearing the headscarf is a bit different from the *niqab* or *burqa*, which are debated in the West. With minor exceptions, the *niqab* and *burqa* are not traditionally worn by Turkish women. Turkish women wear the headscarf to cover their hair, while their faces are fully exposed.

Perhaps it would prove useful to look at where Gülen places the woman in male-female relations, before going on to discuss all the other issues. He states the following in an interview published in *Hürriyet* newspaper in 1995:

"That man cannot be without woman, and woman without man came to light at their first creation. Adam's suffering in Paradise because he had no partner, and the Paradisial bliss he experienced upon finding Eve, is contingent upon the togetherness of these two beings, of this couple. If we are to approach the matter from an Islamic perspective, the Messenger of God, the Qur'an, and Qur'anic teachings do not differentiate between men and women as separate creatures.

"While 14 centuries ago the West gave women no place in society, and even in the 5-6 centuries afterwards debated whether or not women had a soul or whether they were devil or human, women were full participants in every aspect of life in Islam. 'A'isha, the wife of God's Messenger, led armies. In fact, in stark contrast to our day, there were no women's galleries in the mosques and women used to pray in the mosques together with the men" (Interview published in *Hürriyet* on January 27, 1995).

In an interview with *Aksiyon* magazine in June of 1998, Gülen talked about the exalted role women have held in Islam:

"The Qur'an, which gives the name "'The Women'" to one of its three longest chapters, exalts such women as Mary and Asiya, the wife of the Pharaoh, discussing them at length. Furthermore, the blessed lineage of the greatest of all humanity, the Messenger of God, has continued to our day with a daughter (Fatima), not a son. 'A'isha's distinguished position in Islam is widely known" (June 6, 1998, *Aksiyon*).

In 2012, Rainer Hermann asked, "Are men and women equal?"

Gülen's response was long and unequivocal:

"Yes, a woman is free and independent before the law. Her femaleness does not limit or invalidate any of her eligibilities. Whenever any of the rights belonging to her is violated, just like a man, she can address the grievances. If someone takes her possessions wrongly, she has all rights of reclamation. Muslims from diverse nationalities have tended to give their own historical repertoires of customs and traditions an Islamic appearance and advertise their specific traditions as provisions of the perspicuous religion of Islam. They have even based their religious rulings (*ijtihad*) on their customs and traditions, and the breach of rights of women has started this way, with women being forced to live in ever-narrowing confines and being completely isolated from social life in some places. Yet they never pondered about the dire of this tendency.

"In the fundamental principles of Islam, a woman has no difference from a man in enjoying the rights of freedom of religion, freedom of expression, freedom to own and use property as they like, equality before the law, right to marry and establish a family, and confidentiality and immunity of their private lives... Just like those of men, her property, life, and honor are under protection and for those who infringe on them there is a proper punishment" (Rainer Hermann, *Frankfurter Allgemeine Zeitung*, December 6, 2012).

Islam does not prevent women from working

On Dutch television in 1995, Gülen was asked about women's rights and the place of women in Islam. Gülen's answer was as follows:

"In Islam, women and men are like the two faces of a single truth.

In terms of complementing one another, certain things that are negative in one manifest themselves as a positive in the other. They constitute a whole in coming together. It would be more useful to view them as the cogs on a wheel. As a result, they will produce a perfectly running system through mutual agreement, support, and division of labor" (interview with Dutch television on November 19, 1995).

Women can be rulers

In his 1997 interview with *Yeni Yüzyıl* in New York, Gülen expanded his comments on the issue of women's rights, saying: "According to our religion, a woman is not even obliged to suckle her child." The relevant section in the interview reads as follows:

"In ancient times there were goddesses because women held power, then gods emerged when power passed into the hands of men. Sadly, no equilibrium was established. Rather than the other side acquiring rights, by which I mean a just and balanced order, reactions were born. In essence, what applies between men and women is not a question of superiority but a division of labor.

"According to our religion, a woman is not even obliged to suckle her child. People like Yasawi, Mawlana, and Yunus [Emre] interpreted this in an excellent way. As did Abu Hanifa, who said that women could be rulers. It was we who invented the[se false] divisions in this causal, vicious cycle" (July 21, 1997, *Yeni Yüzyıl*).

As a female journalist, Nevval Sevindi asked Gülen about the veiling of women. In his reply, he affirmed that Islam and the Qur'an do not prescribe a single manner of covering:

"The covering of women is mentioned in the Qur'an, but there is no specification as to how and in what form this is to be done. Dwelling on the form would amount to narrowing Islam's broad horizon and a lack of consideration of an aesthetic dimension. In fact, it would even wrongly reduce the religion of Islam to a mere costume religion. Likewise, the headscarf is not one of the essentials of belief or main principles and conditions of Islam (*usul*). It goes against the spirit of Islam to regard people to be outside the folds of religion because of these factors. Imposition and insistence in this regard is excessiveness and compulsion, even a cause for resentment."

Headscarf

In 1997, with the prohibition of students wearing a headscarf studying at universities in Turkey, Gülen explained the place of the headscarf in the religion and said that whether to wear it or not is a decision students who are wishing to study have to make on the basis of their own personal conscience. He explains his stance as follows in an interview published in the *Milliyet* daily in 2005:

"Some time ago, when there were attempts to prevent children from studying, I had expressed my views about the headscarf by approaching the matter from the *usul* (essentials) and *furu'* (issues connected with the essentials but relatively secondary in status) of the religion. I then said that wearing headscarves was not as crucial as the essentials of belief and the five fundamentals of Islam, and people should decide for themselves to choose between the headscarf and the school. My opinion on that issue then was to choose studying. I thought this approach was important to comfort people from diverse walks of life and for the future of Turkey.

"It is my wish that women's rights are considered together with freedom of thought and expression, as in Western countries.

"I wish people could observe all their religious duties, including the secondary topics, provided that there is no intervention with the administration, and that they were free as far as their conscience and religion were concerned. Instead of expanding the public sphere—which is limiting people's field of activity—why don't we highlight the rights of individuals and the freedom of conscience so that we can prepare opportunities for people to live both the essentials and secondary topics of their religion" (*Milliyet*, January 25, 2005).

Gülen related his use of the term *furu'at* for the headscarf in 1997 in an interview with *Radikal*:

"In the case of our young girls having difficulty, I would wish them to make their choices on the side of education. Of course, I am against the interference in the education of those who cover their hair for religious purposes. I am being saddened for them to be forced to make a choice between education and a matter which is in a sense of secondary value in religion" (June 21, 1998, *Radikal* newspaper).

Exactly seven years after Nevval Sevindi, Nuriye Akman from *Zaman* interviewed Gülen and she asked him once more about the place of women in Islam, as well as women's rights. He said the following in this interview published across eleven days in *Zaman* in 2004:

"Within the measures set forth by the religion, women and men can sit together and meet each other, as it is mostly the case. Women were also visiting our Prophet. They had matters. They had questions to ask. Sometimes, without going to another member of the household or to his wife 'A'isha, they asked him directly. If there was something related to private issues for women, they entrusted it to 'A'isha. There are similar subjects in such sources of authentic hadith as Bukhari and Muslim.

"On the subject of praying, women were praying with men. However, they usually were forming a line behind the men. In particular, everyone would participate in the supplications during a lunar or solar eclipse, or for rain (whether or not they offered prayer is a separate issue and there are differing opinions among jurists). They would be together. In my opinion, women and men can sit together side by side on sofas. One can sit in one sofa and the other on another. I personally do not see anything wrong with this. They get into cars together, walk around in shopping malls, study at the same schools, and can be together while going to and from school. They can sit together when they convene for an important subject " (*Zaman*, March 24, 2004).

Polygamy is not a religious injunction

In the part of *Yeni Yüzyıl*'s interview with Gülen dated July 28, 1997, he responded at great length to a question on polygamy. The question sparking such a lengthy response was this:

"There is another subject I would like to talk to you about: polygamy. Islamist groups maintain that having more than one wife is in the Qur'an, for which reason there can be no question of rejecting it. They claim that it is something moral. or have maintained that when on the defensive. They defend polygamy on the basis that the 'others,' secularists have affairs with more than one woman. What I find odd here is that they are using the same criteria in the name of Islam for which they criticize. the secular part of society. Do we have no shared moral values?"

"Nowhere in the Qur'an or in the hadith it is stipulated that a man would be rewarded of practicing a Prophetic tradition (*sunna*) if he arranges an imam and marries more than one woman. We can only argue that there is permission or approval only under certain circumstances to marry more than one woman in *Surat an-Nisa*, and marriage with only one woman is actively encouraged to such an extent as if it is a must. Nobody can therefore think that marrying four women is fulfilling a religious obligation, or claim that such is a religious commandment.

"The marriages of our Prophet were an ordeal, a burden for him, and they were unique to him. The Prophet began having more than one wife after the age of fifty-five. As for other people, the rule is marriage with one woman, and if circumstances call for marriage to more than one, then the basis is to observe justice among the women. The Qur'an says it is better to marry one woman for fear of inability to observe exact fairness. Therefore, having more than one wife is not Islamic law, and is not a religious obligation, let alone an act of worship. Nobody should dress their own weaknesses in a religious garb and then present it as a meritorious deed. This is the exploitation of religion. Those who permit polygamy in religion have regarded this as a special dispensation under pressing conditions of necessity, like wars happen, and many women are left unprotected."

Customs cannot be ascribed to Islam

In an interview, part of which was published in *Milliyet* on January 25, 2005, Gülen was asked to comment on the statement, "Some economic experts relate growth to female participation in production." His response was as follows:

"The contribution of women in certain fields of life is not banned in Islam, provided that physical conditions have been taken into consideration and their working conditions are suitable. Women have indeed contributed in every field of life (throughout history). For instance, they were allowed to participate in battles; their education was not only desired, but also actively sought and encouraged. Mothers of the Believers 'A'isha, Hafsa, and Umm Salama were among the jurists and *mujtahids* (the highest rank of scholarship and learning) of the Companions. Moreover, the women who were among the household of the Prophet were a source of information [not only for other women but also] for men learning religion.

"Many people from the Tabiin (the next generation after the Companions) consulted the Prophet's wives. This situation was not only restricted to the Prophet's wives; in the periods that followed, qualified women were teachers to many people. In Islam there is no such thing as limiting the life of women or narrowing their fields of activity. Things that appear negative to us today must be analyzed with respect to the conditions of the time in which they were experienced and to the policy of the respective states in which they happened.

"What really matters is the consideration of women's physical abilities and working conditions; for instance, should they be employed in heavy labor like coal mines? Should it be compulsory for them to perform military service like men? Should they undergo heavy military training? If these are considered as being necessary and feasible, I do not think that there would be anyone who would disagree."

There are many customs and rites that continue to be a part of societies around the world, which are not only wrong, but also against human rights. Yet, since culture and religion bond with each other over time, neither the followers of a certain faith, nor observers from outside, can tell where these two are separate. Religions, but especially Islam, have been unfairly blamed for many such customs that in fact have nothing to do with religion, nor are they approved by it. Female circumcision is one such example. Not allowing girls to go to school is another one. If we remember the fact that pagans in pre-Islamic Arabia buried their daughters out of shame, Islam was an enormous improvement for women's rights. Islam does not discriminate between women and men, and enjoins all believers, men and women alike, to seek knowledge and explore the mysteries of the universe.

Women can serve as heads of state

Gülen touches upon the same issue in his answer to the question put to him by *Frankfurter Allgemeine Zeitung* journalist Rainer Hermann, "How do you view the role of women? What should be her position in society and in your movement?"

"Women can assume different roles, including being magistrates and heads of state, provided these do not go against her nature and on the condition that she conforms to religious sensitivities. The woman's role is not restricted solely to preoccupation with household affairs and raising children. Today, Islam and women in particular are among the most negatively portrayed issues in the Western world. The reason for this is the many anti-Islamic practices that Muslims have unfortunately undertaken.

"Whereas the prevailing conditions of the period in which some seemingly negative things took place need to be taken into account and evaluated accordingly, including the practices of the states, governments. Moreover, the fact that the customs and traditions in some regions and societies continued after the people's acceptance of Islam has to be taken into consideration also. It would be wrong to hold Islam responsible for these. Limiting the role of women in society and narrowing their sphere of activity is not Islamic.

"Unfortunately, Muslims ignore this fact. A heavy-handed approach and coarse understanding has thrown into disarray this system, which is based on the mutual support between men and women and their sharing their lives with each other. With its breakdown, both the family and the social order have been disrupted" (Rainer Hermann, *Frankfurter Allgemeine Zeitung*, December 6, 2012).

New York Times journalist Brian Knowlton asked a similar question to Gülen in 2010, "What, for you, is the proper place for women in society, and what sort of roles do they have within the movement associated with your name?"

He replies: "In Islam, there is absolutely no such thing as putting limits on a woman's life or restricting her sphere of action. The role of a woman in the world is not restricted to housework and to raising her children.

"As a matter of fact, she has a responsibility to carry out all tasks corresponding to her in every realm of society, provided that doing so conforms to religious sensitivities and does not contradict her innate character (*fitra*). However, unfortunately, over time this reality has been ignored, even among Muslims, and instead, a rude way of understanding and an insensitive way of thinking has ruined the natural system that is based on the notions of man and woman helping one another and sharing a life together. Consequently, the order of the family as well as that of society has been spoiled. The tendency of different nations/communities to consider and portray their own traditions and cultural characteristics as the essentials of Islam, and their interpretations of Islam on the basis of their cultures, have led to a further violation of women's rights, and in some cases to women's total isolation from society.

"These practices, [many of which] that are imbedded in society, have been gradually changing. I hope that significant progress will be made in this field, in both the short and long term. [Women] too are carrying out important functions in service to humanity. Just like men, they too are using every opportunity they can seize and setting good examples to others through their attitude and conduct. When necessary, they too set out to every corner of the world to become teachers and role models."

Secular women fear Islam the most

Le Monde correspondent Nicole Pope directed the following comment to Gülen on April 28, 1998: "Today, those who fear Islam the most appear to be women among secularists."

Gülen's response illustrates how customs and traditions excluding women from society gradually came to be attributed to Islam:

"At one time, I strove to explain at length the issue of women in my sermons. Islam does not have a problem regarding women. If today there is seemingly one, it was produced in later times by those who had hardened Islam, narrowed its possibilities of entrance, those who produced impossibility within the possibilities, allotting a narrow sphere for women. During the Age of Happiness, namely the times of the Prophet and the Rightly Guided Caliphs following him, women were inside life; there was no problem whatsoever."

In 2005, Gülen was asked about what kind of jobs women can undertake today in what is called the "public sphere." Can they, for instance, become judges, prosecutors, or soldiers? Gülen responds to these questions:

"Women can assume any role. Women can be anything, a soldier or a doctor. The most important thing is to make sure they can fulfill their faith.

"There may be some women who can fulfill their faith while employed in the public service, while others at home may fail in observing the faith fully" (*Milliyet*, January 25, 2005).

Gülen offers the following response to the question put to him by Jamie Tarabay for *The Atlantic* in August of 2013, "According to Islamic tradition, is the role of women limited to motherhood?":

"No, it is not. The noble position of motherhood aside, our general opinion about women is that, while taking into account their specific needs, it should be made possible for them to take on every role, including the jobs of physician, military officer, judge and president of a country. As a matter of fact, in every aspect of life throughout history Muslim women made contributions to their societies.

"In the golden age (referring to the years during [the Prophet] Muhammad's lifetime), starting with 'A'isha, Hafsa, and Umm Salama (the Prophet's wives), women had their places among the jurists and they taught men. When these examples are taken into consideration, it would be clearly understood that it is out of the question to restrict the lives of women by narrowing down their activities. Unfortunately, the isolation of women from social activities in some places today, a practice that stems from the misinterpretation of Islamic sources, has been a subject of a worldwide propaganda campaign against Islam."

The Qur'an invites spouses to be respectful to each other

Let us turn once again to the interview conducted by Professor Zeki Sarıtoprak and journalist-writer Ali Ünal for the *Muslim World*. Sarıtoprak and Ünal asked, "The relationship between men and women in Islam is one of the controversial topics currently debated in the modern day. What are your thoughts of the place of women in society?"

Gülen offered a lengthy response. One of the most important issues he drew attention to is that, there is no difference between women and men in such matters as freedom of belief and thought, the right to life, ownership, and control of property and money, the right to be treated with equality and justice before the law, the right to marry and establish a family, and the right to privacy and the inviolability of private life. Her property, life, and dignity are protected like that of men. Violation of any of these rights results in severe punishment. She is free and independent before the law. Let us now turn to Gülen's response:

"The Qur'an invites people to form a family life and points out many wisdoms and benefits of marriage. The Qur'an views marriage as a serious commitment on the part of the husband and wife; it is a covenant between them. It speaks of the rights of the husband and the wife. In addition to this, the Holy Book in principle emphasizes what is good and consistently declares that spouses should do what is good towards each other.

'In order to strengthen the ties of marriage, the Qur'an places more responsibility upon the husband's shoulders. It also imposes part of the responsibility upon the community, in the case of a disagreement between spouses. It views divorce, which God dislikes, as the last resort when reconciliation becomes impossible.

"In addition to reminding spouses about their duties towards one another, the Qur'an emphasizes the main principles of human morality, and invites individuals to be respectful of God and virtuous towards each other. Such an atmosphere of respect is necessary for the continuation of humane and legal relations. Islam addresses women and men equally and raises women, with their remarkable breath, to a blessed position.

"After the emergence of Islam she would not be treated as property; she could not be accused of impurity. Such an accusation would result in a severe punishment on the part of the accuser. Female children would not be looked down upon. Infanticide would be prohibited.

"Even if she is physically different, this is not a reason to be looked down upon. In the Qur'anic view of creation, Adam is created first and Eve is created from the same leaven (7:189). This Qur'anic picture reminds us that men and women are both equally human. They are two entities that complete one another, as the Qur'an presents. The difference between both is based on certain purposes and designs and is not ontological.

"With regard to humanity and human relationships with God, there is no difference between women and men. They are equals concerning their rights and responsibilities. Woman is equal to man in the rights of freedom of religion, freedom of expression, freedom to live a decent life, and freedom of finance. Equality before the law, just treatment, marriage and founding a family life, personal life, privacy and protection are all among the rights of women.

"Her possessions, life and dignity are assured, like that of men. Yes, woman is free and independent before the law. Her femaleness does not limit or invalidate any of her eligibilities. Whenever any of the rights belonging to her is violated, just like man, she can address the grievances. If someone takes her possessions wrongly, she has all rights of reclamation. Considering some qualities of women and men, Islam has developed certain legal prescriptions: for example, women are exempted from certain charges such as military service, going to war, taking care of the financial obligations of a family and herself, etc.

"As for testimony, yes, the Qur'an says that when you cannot find two men to testify, find one trustworthy man and two women, for if one forgets, the other will remind her (2:282). It is not acceptable to deduce any meaning from this verse to indicate the superiority of men over women in humanity and in value.

"The fundamental issue here is the realization of justice. This is not a matter unique to women. The testimony of some male Bedouins has been rejected when the matter is related to the rights and realization of justice. The issue of testimony is related to a strong commitment to communal life. It is much better for those who are expected to testify on a certain issue that they are involved with that issue in their lives.

"This issue of testimony in the Qur'an relates to oral testimony with regard to financial matters and loans. Otherwise, the testimony of women in writing, when needed, is accepted as equal by some scholars of Islamic law" (*Muslim World*, July 2005 issue).

Domestic violence is another serious problem, threatening the safety of individuals, especially women. Gülen categorically rejects any approach that legitimizes violence against women. It is a global problem, including in many Islamic countries, as well as Turkey. Gülen explained in the strongest possible terms that such violence has no place nor approval in Islam. Gülen said that abused women have every right to defend themselves. He even suggested that women should physically resist when they have no access to law enforcement and have no other choice at the moment of violence, and possibly learn martial arts to be able to do so.

CHAPTER 7

DIALOGUE AND COEXISTENCE

Dialogue and Coexistence

"Putting pressure on people is not Islam. Those who wish to dress according to their faith, cover their head accordingly, and comply with all the injunctions of Islam, can do so. While another person who does not believe in Islam, if he is an atheist and does not believe in anything, they must be left to their own way of life."

These statements were taken from Fethullah Gülen's six-day interview published in *Hürriyet* newspaper in January 1995.

There was tremendous polarization in Turkey at the time. Society had virtually been divided into camps: Alevi and Sunni, secular and religious, Turk and Kurd, believer and non-believer, Muslim and non-Muslim. This polarization even moved out of the country, affecting the Turkish diaspora in Europe, especially in Germany, where the biggest Turkish population lives. Huntington's theory of the clash of civilizations has, in a sense, become real among Turks. The 1990s were a time of high-profile assassinations of journalists and writers known for their secularist identities.

But according to Gülen, Turkey possessed the historical references needed for living together, and Islam also demanded it. It was thus necessary to set aside differences. So he launched what was virtually a campaign of conversations and meetings. He met with members of the media, opinion leaders, leading figures of religious communities, and politicians, and to all who would listen, he expressed these views.

Discrimination goes against the value God places upon the human being

During 1995, in Istanbul, many people visited Gülen, including over 90 journalists and writers. He himself visited journalists, artists, and businessmen, going to the major papers in Istanbul and meeting with their owners and writers. For example, he visited *Milliyet* newspaper on October 18, 1995, and met with its journalists and columnists. One of the writers at the meeting, Taha Akyol, relayed in his column on October 19, how Gülen responded his question concerning the Turkish schools abroad:

"Turkey is surrounded on all sides by troubles. It must furnish its surroundings with commitments of friendship. Graduates from these schools will in the future, God willing, assume important posts in their respective countries, as friends of Turkey. Syria, Iraq, Iran, Saudi Arabia, and Armenia do not allow for them.[9] Should they grant such permission, schools should be opened in these places also. In Greece, too... How good would it be if people from Turkey opened schools there? Foreigners have been opening schools in our country since the Tanzimat. Opening private schools around the world with high educational quality and making the education of our own country attractive is the only way. Brute hostility is not the answer..."

To achieve these goals, and for Turkey to assume better standing in the global community, the country needed to heal its wounds. Turkey's becoming a country with its surroundings furnished with commitments of friendship was contingent, first of all, to putting an end to the fighting and conflict inside, between its different societal segments. It was impossible for such a country to make friends around it.

Gülen told the writers, "We have to come together on matters concerning the nation and think about Turkey's present and future."

When another writer, Altan Öymen, asked him about the rift between "believers and non-believers," which was high on the nation's agenda at the time, Gülen responded:

"There's a unique value that God attaches to the human being. Discrimination goes against this. A person must act like a prosecutor for himself, but like a lawyer to others. Otherwise, this is bigotry, arrogance, and mental disturbance. There are things that even those people who do not unite on belief in God can come together and talk about. We must talk not about divisions, but about those things we need to talk about."

Going on to discuss the political infighting, Gülen continued with a reference to a Prophetic tradition:

"Be restrained in your love for another, for it may be that you may one day see something in them that you do not love and feel shame. And be restrained in your anger for another, for that person may someday become one you love."

On the evening of July 3, 1995, when he was a guest on TRT, Gülen indicated that peaceful coexistence based on tolerance is a requirement of Islam:

---

9 This interview was conducted in 1995. These countries might have later allowed schools to be opened.

"It is my belief that peace and security will only be realized in this country on the basis of tolerance. I am deriving this from the Book (the Qur'an) we believe to have descended from the Heavens. I am deriving this from the Sunna, the life of the Messenger of God. If others think differently in this matter, theirs do not represent my view of the Qur'an, my view of the Prophetic Practice. This is what I understand from the Qur'an and the Sunna, this is what I understand from the Turkish peoples' interpretation of Islam for the past nine centuries. I act on the premise that if there is a point of dialogue with everyone in this country, whatever the circumstances, then we must make the best out of it, coming to agreement with everyone approaching each other with understanding. When we have so many things we share, we ought not be mutual scapegoats for our differences. Our God is one, our Book is one, our faith one, our nation one, and now, our suffering one, our oppression one, and our condemnation one."

People of faith have been deprived of democracy, even one tenth of it

The meeting at which Gülen made his, "There is no going back from democracy" speech was the inaugural meeting of the Journalists and Writers Foundation, held in Istanbul on June 29, 1994. Excerpts from Gülen's speech as honorary chairman of the Foundation are below:

"A process has been entered into in Turkey from which there is no going back – the process of democratization. Thus far, certain groups have lived with one tenth of democracy. There is no longer a question of a returning from democracy in the world. Within this democratization process, religious people will also enjoy democratic rights and freedoms pertaining to their faith and religious practice. They will thus have a greater opportunity to serve. A human-oriented crisis can only be resolved by giving priority to the human being and human culture. A series of crises that may lead society to various kinds of disaster are being experienced. There is an attempt to polarize the people into different factions along secular/antisecular and democratic/antidemocratic lines. I believe that tensions will soften with the coming together of moderate people by means of this Foundation, at a time when the crisis has deepened."

When he said, "Thus far, certain groups have lived with one tenth of democracy," Gülen was talking about the religiously-minded. This was a reproach to all those who until this time had deprived religious people of the fruits of democracy. The demand of the faithful for democratic rights and freedoms was carried to Turkey's agenda for the very first time by Gülen himself.

Let us talk, not quarrel

The social solidarity events and activities of the Journalists and Writers Foundation were not limited to this first meeting. Gülen attended the Foundation's Ramadan iftar dinner on the evening of February 11, 1995, in Istanbul. In his speech on the night, he said, "Let us come together not fighting, but talking."

He continued:

"I pray that God allow the Journalists and Writers Foundation, along with many of its counterparts, to bring together the different segments of our society in Turkey that have come apart like the pieces of a crystal chandelier, to reestablish the dialogue that has been lost, and to realize the ideal of having the atmosphere of acceptance permeate the nation once again. Indeed, society is more in need of coming together, conciliation, and agreement of all its diverse segments than it has ever been before. If we are able to achieve this, then we will have solved a very important matter indeed.

"In fact, our noble nation is open to this in terms of its spiritual makeup. But it falls on the shoulders of the media to undertake this job. The media will do so by accepting everyone as they are. Nobody will accuse anyone because of their faith; likewise, nobody will disparage others on account of their religion or irreligion. I believe the media will do this.

"Not only among the members of our own society, in this time and circumstances, we must also explore ways of coming together for dialogue with Christian spiritual leaders by temporarily putting aside certain matters that are bones of contention, as one scholar had suggested.

"Forgive my use of the expression, but savage people realize their aims through fighting, through conflict. Cultivated and intellectual souls believe that they will attain their aims through thought and discussion.

I am of the view that we left the period of savagery far behind. In the civilized world, triumph and winning people over will be through persuasion. This is precisely what I believe the visual and print media will do."

In a talk he gave to writers after a Ramadan iftar dinner, Gülen called the politicians of the day to conciliation and said, "Turkey is waiting for such sacrifice today."

In 1996, the Journalists and Writers Foundation presented Tolerance Awards during a special ceremony. Gülen attended not only the Foundation's programs in Istanbul, but also some of its programs in Ankara. These included an iftar dinner in Istanbul on January 27, 1996, and in Ankara on February 2 of the same year.

On the evening of January 4, 1996, Tolerance Awards were presented at Çırağan Palace, at which Gülen was also present. In his speech at the program in Istanbul, Gülen for the first time spoke of those who were trying to ambush tolerance in Turkey and who sought to destroy the bridges between various segments of society:

"I am concerned that a marginal group will continue to disquiet society, by way of concealing their own weaknesses and hoping to appear strong through wreaking havoc. Thereafter, they will lie in ambush against tolerance and try to destroy the bridges. And it seems that after this we will be tested with things much more serious. Our nation will withstand this severe trial through tolerance. We will grit our teeth in this trial. We will be without hands against those who strike us, without words against those who curse us, and even without taking [these strikes and curses] to heart, and we will walk to tomorrow embracing everything and each other with love and compassion..."

On August 16, 1996, in Istanbul, Gülen met with journalists, writers, and academics. These statements are excerpted from his answers to questions addressed to him during the meeting:

"Understanding, agreement, and coming together depend somewhat on our accepting one another as we are, with our own respective views and positions. If everyone deems their own position the most true, the most right position and, for that matter, if an esteemed teacher at a university somewhere, or even a shepherd at the top of a mountain, does not accept these positions, it seems to me that while a reconciliation process is underway, we would have begun losing once again while on the path to success.

"…The Messenger of God advises us to keep from disobedience to God through reverent piety, and not to underestimate even the smallest act of goodness for His sake. And he then enumerates them, like: removing a thing that will cause harm to the people, or removing something unsightly from a road or path, or something on which someone can trip. These are good deeds, and you can go to Paradise as a result of them.

"In the past, water used to be drawn from wells and cisterns. God's Messenger says that drawing water from a well and then emptying it into the bucket of another is an act of charity. If you cannot do anything else, then smile, he says.

"I would like to add that he also says that offering a morsel of food to your wife's mouth is charity. This is the gist of charity in Islam. It is a mark of being true to God and also denotes giving someone a gift, as the Arabic word for charity, *sadaqa*, is derived from the same root as *siddiq* (truthful), and *sadaqat* (faithfulness). Now if this is how the religion approaches the issue, then I should like to think that religion be investigated in reference to its own sources. No act of goodness or kindness should ever be underestimated, or disparaged. And this is the essence of the matter. If we cast these aside and look for Islam in the ways of life of some others, then we will not be able to escape contradictions."

Whoever we have taken one step towards has come running to us

Let us now turn to the speech Gülen delivered on the third anniversary of the Journalists and Writers Foundation, on October 1, 1996, at Istanbul's Lütfi Kırdar Convention and Exhibition Center:

"For the past couple of centuries, we have quarreled with one another. We were unable to accept each other and ultimately lost our own unity and our own paradise. And regaining all that we have lost so far lies in our accepting one another. This is what our people need most today. These past three years, we have seen that our society is really open to dialogue and understanding.

"Whoever we have taken the right steps towards in this dialogue has come running to us. As people of tolerance and understanding, we await the day when all the segments of our society, will embrace one another, and when the media and our intellectuals will lead the way. We also expect that our leaders will review their manner once more and take understanding as a basis in their thinking and mutual relations. And we call for walking hand in hand, in understanding, towards the future. If there are those who make murderous plans for our future and seek to turn Turkey into a bloody arena, then let their plans not be realized."

Jihad should be declared for tolerance

In 1997, three years after initiating the tolerance and dialogue process, he was asked by Nevval Sevindi, in New York, "Has 'tolerance' as your chosen method bore any fruit? How can peace be established in a Turkey where there is a cultural conflict?"

He responded as follows:

"Some fixed customs and forms of behavior can only be eliminated in the long run. Some sociologists and psychologists look for the greatness of our Prophet there. The way that he so quickly eliminated poor moral values and habits among such savage, primitive tribes is seen as miraculous. Tolerance in any case exists in the soul of the nation, but for it to emerge, everyone from various sections of society, from art to science, must insist upon it. It needs effort. A climate of conflict cannot be done away with all at once.

"The media has a very important responsibility here. Care is needed: it is easy to damage, but hard to repair. Restoration will not be instantaneous. The elevation of emotions and trust, the changing of perspectives, everything being based on proper foundations, all take time. I say that society must take responsibility for tolerance. Even if no jihad is issued for anything else, it must, if possible, be issued for tolerance. People must be made to believe in goodness and beauty through a mild struggle against bad feelings and passions, not against other human beings.

"I am not without hope. But I fear we have undertaken a very hard task. But no matter the price, it is worth paying. There is a need for a new type of human being today. A human type who can transcend the present, just as they have transcended the past."

Let's bring together these shattered crystals to form a necklace

At a program on the occasion of the 'Eid, held on the evening of February 3, 1998 and attended by artists and writers, Gülen said, "A very large task falls to our architects of thoughts and laborers of ideas (intellectuals) in order to establish an earthly paradise in our region."

Gülen later said in January 1999:

"Our nation is falling apart. These crystals should be brought together again into a necklace. I believe that it is essential. No one can oppose this. Even my closest friends have said there have been the fascist/communist, believer/unbeliever struggles for years on end, and they have questioned whether I can prevent them. Now instead of speaking like a merchant of doom, I would rather say, light a candle, take a torch in hand and walk towards unity.

"I see this as a responsibility. I believe that I am fulfilling my duty towards God. Those with such reservations temporarily remained one or two steps behind the movement, only to later return to join and lend their support" (*Aktüel* magazine, January 14, 1999).

The laudable person is one who can get along with scorpions and snakes

Gülen's statements were followed by this question:

"Let us just say they are not convinced. In a democracy, everyone doesn't necessarily have to think the same way. Then we will continue living nevertheless, but how?"

He replies: "This may well be our attitude towards persuasion. This is not a matter of necessarily convincing everyone, of drawing them to our own understanding. As I mentioned at the beginning, there is the issue of accepting everyone as they are, in their own respective positions. If I have a bright idea concerning the economy, a bright idea in the name of faith, in the name of love and enthusiasm that can give people a sense of peace, in the name of knowledge of God and spiritual pleasure, then I would endeavor to explain these. People may agree or not. I would relate them because this how I believe it to be so, because I see them to be beneficial.

"There is nothing like breaking away from others when they do not agree. At the core of the matter is the notion of accepting everyone as they are and, as such, seeking ways of dialogue with them. And my friends, those close to me, well know that, to me, the laudable person, the highest achiever, is a person who knows how to get along with scorpions and snakes. Such a person must always be able to have a coalition with everyone. And it seems to me that unfolding events and world developments are pushing us in such a direction. There is no place for conflict in an ever-globalizing world, in a building wherein we stand back to back with the Americans, in a world such as this."

One who attempts to reform the world must first reform their own self

According to Gülen, for the climate of tolerance and coexistence to spread to every segment of society, the individuals in that society must first abandon the idea of superiority over others:

"The heart is very important. A human being is human with their heart. If they see themselves as superior to another with respect to their humanity, even to one who does not believe, this means they are losing yet again. One needs to look at them like their lawyer, deeming their smallest virtues a means for their salvation in the Hereafter. But when approaching the things they do on account of their own self, a person needs to do so gathering evidence like a prosecutor. When I was growing up, there was Muhammed Lütfi of Alvar, whom I respected greatly. There was something he used to say very often. In a slightly Azeri manner, he said, 'Everyone is fair, I am poor. Everyone is wheat, I am straw.' In line with these thoughts, I too say the same thing. That is, no one can convince me of all this – what that others think concerning my person, their ascribing leadership to me, and seeing me as the head of a community" (January 30, 1995, *Sabah*).

He echoed the same thoughts on Kanal D on April 16, 1997:

"People have come to know me from the mosque pulpit. At times I had the opportunity to preach across a vast area. There are only one or two provinces to which I have not gone to preach or speak at a conference. This is why there is this exposure to wide masses when I have no such right or indeed qualification. I cannot really tell whether I have been a victim of it or blessed with it.

"As I see it, being viewed as a guide of a community and even more exaggeratedly, as its leader, as a figure who motivates and manages a community, forgive my saying so, comes to me as an insult.

"I say this most earnestly. I take these to be disrespect towards my person. I am a simple person and am most content with being so. As

'Ali puts it, 'be one of the people.' Even now, in my prayers and entreaties when I am alone with my Lord, I have oft said, these are for me too much, take back this trust and free me from this onerous burden."

In his interview for *Daily Nation*, a paper distributed in Kenya and throughout East Africa, Gülen once again stated that those who wish to reform the world must first reform themselves:

"... everyone should try to be saved from, first of all, such types of bigotry as seeing the truth always on one's own side... coming from ego-centrism, and showing no respect for the truth and goodness realized at the hands of others. They should also try to eliminate the reasons that separate people, such as egoism, self-interest, and discrimination based on race, ethnicity, and language. No one should move excited by impulses and emotional factors but everyone should move according to the requirements of a social contract.

"That will be by reviewing once again all the common points and the vital elements which necessitate unity and balancing them with factors that separate peoples, societies, and countries... Those who want to reform the world must first reform themselves. If they want to lead others to a better world, they must purify their inner worlds of hatred, rancor, and jealousy, and adorn their outer worlds with virtue. The words of those who cannot control and discipline themselves, and who have not refined their feelings, may seem attractive and insightful at first. However, even if they somehow manage to inspire others, which they sometimes do, the sentiments they arouse will soon wither.

"... we should never be hopeless. Goodness and kindness, righteousness and virtue – these form the basic essence of humanity, and humanity will rediscover this essence and build a new world on the foundations of belief, love, compassion, mercy, dialogue, acceptance of others, mutual respect, justice, and rights" (Interview for *Daily Nation*, Hezron Mogambi, July 30, 2004).

Let us declare war against the idea of a clash of civilizations

From the outset, Gülen did not just take up the issue of tolerance and conciliation on the Turkish scale. As he has always seen it, the antidote for the supposed "clash of civilizations" to take place in the world in the future is tolerance, dialogue, and conciliation across the globe. Indeed, in his interview with *Time* magazine on June 4, 1997, he described the tolerance and dialogue process as a declaration of war against a conflict of civilizations:

"We are a people who are fed up with internal and external fighting. In this respect, we are wondering how we can stop this fight for a good while, if not forever. The views of some academics on this subject have in actual fact motivated us to such an undertaking. According to the interpretations, there will be a clash of civilizations in the world of the future, and a lot of bloodshed. Looking at the future from the perspective of their commentaries and auguries, I can picture torrents of blood.

"War needs to be proclaimed against [this idea]. What kind of war? We need to counteract, in a civilized manner, these savage thoughts, these savage actions. A civilized counteraction is through meeting, communicating, talking, consulting, and coming to an agreement. As declared by the Messenger of God, we are all from Adam, and Adam is created from the dust of the earth. That is, we are all the living sculptures of the same dough, the same clay. If there is to be any message to be offered to the world, then I would say that I have never lost my belief that we can share the world in relations of mutual fellowship. Moreover, despite all the spine-chilling predictions of forecasters and augurs in this matter, I have always thought as I do now, both within the country and abroad."

According to Gülen, what needs to be done in the face of a potential clash of civilizations is to form "islands of peace," which are to act as a breakwater against these clashes:

"There were those people who made such predictions of fighting and conflict. Even very important figures said such things. I think that what needs to be done is the formation of islands of peace. If waves are going to rise and crash onto humanity, it would be wise to set up those breakwaters ahead of time. It seems to me that the tolerance and dialogue process will fulfil this mission, God willing" (Telephone interview with Samanyolu TV, July 14, 2004).

If there are gulfs in between, there can be no integration

In an interview published in the *Yeni Yüzyıl* newspaper in July of 1997, Gülen characterized tolerance and dialogue as a bridge allowing exchange between civilizations and cultures, and drew attention to one thing in particular. Tolerance requires accepting the other in their position. To do this is a process of mutual benefit:

"Tolerance means you are open to everyone, every idea. If gulfs are produced, that means you are deprived of the advantages of integration... Tolerance is such a bridge, one that can provide an exchange between people and civilizations... That is perhaps what we are trying to overcome with our spirit of tolerance. This means accepting very different positions and conceptions. Once you accept this idea, you will have the opportunity to benefit from many people's thoughts and ideas. There are many beneficial aspects to Western thinking. Take the example of systematic thinking, which is an attribute of a believer.

"While a believer is supposed to be a believer with all their attributes, this may not always be so in practice. There is a very fine point here: God accords treatment to people in this world in accordance with their attributes. So, your attributes, your behaviors, are important. I am hugely impressed by something here in the United States, there is a perfectly functioning system here. "In the hospital all the doctors, everyone, do their jobs at the same time, without hurting you. I have seen at least twenty doctors, thirty nurses in the hospital. Here they are warm, convincing, and cheerful. Now this is the attribute of a believer. If a believer elsewhere does not come out of the mosque, but is deprived of the attributes of a believer, they are deprived of the gist of the matter, and lead their entire life thus deprived. This seems to me to be very important" (*Yeni Yüzyıl*, July 27, 1997).

The schools acquaint people of different nationalities

In his interview with Gülen on November 30, 1999, Canadian journalist and author Fred A. Reed asked him what his solution is to the unfair [world] order.

In his response, Gülen indicated that at the root of the crises experienced across the globe lies the failure of different peoples to know one another. He then pointed to the schools opened around the world as the solution. Gülen stressed that these schools will enable such an acquaintance:

"When the world has only just begun to take on a globalized form, new styles and systems need to be found and implemented to remove the artificial barriers between people. In this way, people will be able to come together and become better acquainted with each other. Perhaps much better solutions can be offered in the future, but in my opinion, all countries should establish bridges between one another and must keep themselves open to mutual investment and commercial activity. Only in this way can they become aware of the others' way of life and thinking.

"However, what appears to be more important than this is that given the results educational activities will generate in the future, they will have a much more important role and impact between nations. The schools opened all over the world can be very fruitful: for instance, Americans can open schools here [Turkey] and we can do the same thing in the United States. Similarly, Canadians can come and open schools in Turkey, and we can open schools in Canada. If laws and regulations do not allow people to open schools at the international level and do not allow them to express themselves freely, then alternative channels such as large scale student exchanges can be considered. As I see it, the fact that people are not acquainted with one another is the primary cause of the conflicts which we experience today.

"Added advantages of undertaking these educational activities here and there are that they help to solve such problems as indifference, ignorance, poverty, and social division. These problems have consequences for the whole world, and perhaps in more dangerous dimensions in the southern hemisphere.

"People are not happy with what they have, being, to a large extent, like the villagers in Czarist Russia. We cannot see anything being done to overcome these problems by these people themselves, nor by the captains steering the world ship. Conflicts in different parts of the world, therefore, continue. I repeat, the solution depends on the sincere actions of developed countries. They must come together and resolve such crises in partnership and cooperation as problems of humanity. I am a Muslim, as were 'Ali, 'Abd al-Qadir Jilani, Ahmad Yasawi, Mawlana Jalal al-Din [al-Rumi], Yunus Emre, and Bediüzzaman. Yet, they based all their affairs on love and accepting people as they are, and they embraced all people.

"Among the other Islamic issues they devoted themselves to, peace and reconciliation dominated. On the other hand, what they did was never artificial or outside the path of Islam.... For that matter, they never compromised any of Islam's injunctions or principles. On the contrary, they possessed an approach rooted in and derived from the essence of religion."

Why education?

Le Monde correspondent Nicole Pope directed the following question to Gülen on April 28, 1998:

"Why so many schools? Why do you give so much importance to education?"

Gülen affirmed that integration with the world is contingent on modern education:

"In the final analysis, everything depends on knowledge. Without knowledge nothing can be accomplished. It is even more important today. The source of all the emptiness in Turkey and in the world, the source of all the problems regardless of time and place is the neglect of an education built on a realistic, firm, and sound foundation. While the West was experiencing the Renaissance, Muslims were sleeping. While Europe was accomplishing the scientific and technological revolution, Muslims were again sleeping. These are some of the matters we have to seriously consider.

"I am sure it has been done from time to time, but the level is important. Moreover, some of the dynamics a good education requires can be sacrificed in the state machinery in the name of certain things. For instance, in democracies, compromises can even be made in certain crucial issues for the sake of votes. We have to lend a listening ear to our age, we have to comprehend it perfectly, and all the circumstances have to be understood. Education is very important for the integration with the world. Today, no country can be in isolation. The way to the integration with the world has to go through a modern education. Historically speaking, we have had very close relations with France, especially after the Tanzimat reforms. At the time, a French instructor could be found in every rich Turkish family. The British influence was considerable during the years of constitutional monarchy, and in the early period of the Republic in particular. The Germans have had influence over the administration from time to time. Since the Second World War, we have had closer ties with the United States. If we are thinking an integration with these friends of us, these institutions of education can be very important platforms, education is the platform for these integrations. I related the same thing recently to a few German friends, and to the German Ambassador. I said the same things in America also, as well as at the Vatican.

"I believe that by virtue of these institutions of education we can better know each other, and can establish good, durable, and sound relationships with the West. If the Turkish State allows, come and establish educational institutions here and thus express yourselves. Allow us the same opportunity, so that we may open schools in France, Germany, and in the United Kingdom. It will then be seen that Turkish society is open to dialogue with every nation and possess a boundlessness that can embrace people of every nation."

If only we could unite around universal values

In his interview for the *New York Times* in 2010, journalist Brian Knowlton asked a question concerning the schools operating in 160 countries. Gülen responded as follows:

"We can say that there is a desire and search for a peaceful, tranquil world. This desire is the whole reason behind the enthusiasm we have in the field for education. For many years, whether from mosque pulpits, or lecture halls, or in my writings, I have expressed that we should nurture a generation filled with love and respect for all, a generation that is open to making peace and living together with others. I have encouraged everyone who valued my views to establish educational institutions.

"I told everyone that we could only achieve peace and reconciliation within our country and across the world by raising generations who are reading, thinking, and loving other human beings; who are opening up and sharing their knowledge in the service of humanity. Many years ago, I was reading a book by Bertrand Russell when a passage about war struck me... Today, if we consider all the atomic bombs and hydrogen bombs and nuclear weapons that are in existence, and the possibility of many nations using these weapons against each other is always there. Unfortunately, it seems nearly impossible to take these weapons out of people's hands, and, once deployed it will not be possible to deflect or be shielded from their deadly effects. Even organizations like the United Nations can hardly cope with these kinds of problems.

"So I asked myself, 'If we can motivate people with the wisdom of dialogue, mutual respect and mutual understanding, and if we can gather them around universal values, and if we can form a platform on this—could it prevent such a disastrous future from befalling humanity?' This kind of thinking led me to carrying out educational activities. I continue impressing this feeling to others at every possible opportunity and encourage them toward education. People who have believed in the importance and rationality of this belief have opened many schools in different places around the world, and because of that very same understanding, passion and enthusiasm, they continue on this course... they keep education as their core and consider it the most important element of human existence, and this is only because they don't use education as a weapon of ideology, politics or religious polarization. [Just as these schools] focus on the common grounds of humanity, they are well received by people of different faiths, colors, and races in every country from different parts of the world" (June 11, 2010, *New York Times*).

What follows is an excerpt from Gülen's talk to journalists, writers, and academics in Istanbul on August 16, 1996:

"We want to open schools motivated somewhat by the idea of Turkey getting on well with its neighbors. We say, 'Let us raise tomorrow's intellectuals and architects of thought together, under the same roof.' [We do this to build] friendships for Turkey, which is, according to the old expression, beset by enemies all round.

"I said this to the Patriarch and to the Chief Rabbi. There is a possibility I will meet with the Armenian Patriarch and I will say the very same the same thing to him...

"The Armenians were the most sincere community under the Ottomans. These current enmities are so contrived, and they do not offer us anything. Let us open schools in your countries, and you come and do whatever you are doing. You already have some people here. Know that we cannot take these hostilities any further in an ever-shrinking globalized world. Let's turn these into friendships. These are the thoughts I will raise with him. As I said to the Patriarch and to the Chief Rabbi, [Turkish-Jewish businessman] Üzeyir Garih, who offered to look into the possibility of opening a school in Israel..."

These new men and women will be altruists

Gülen said the following in his interview with Hezron Mogambi, of Kenya's *Daily Nation*, in 2004:

"One of the most dangerous kinds of separatism in our time is ethnicism. During a period when the world is increasingly becoming a global village and countries come together to form unions and when universal objectives attract people from all corners of the world, such a separatism is extremely strange, baseless, and ridiculous.

"Other factors that strengthen divisions are the imbalances in the economic field, unfilled gaps in earning and distribution of income, and the absence of institutions that can serve as a bridge between groups and individuals. The reasons for the pain we are suffering can also be better understood in view of such factors as there being no established separation of powers in the administration, democracy not functioning well, and the balance of law-power-wisdom not being established at a desirable level. Other factors are partisanship and arbitrariness, many things being designed according to the impulses of individuals, and deficiencies and mistakes in the administrative and political fields.

"Thanks to rapid developments in transportation and communication, the world has become a global village. Nations are exactly like next-door neighbors. However, this does not mean that nations and national differences will disappear. On the contrary, they will continue to exist, but not as the things causing conflicts but as contributing to the beauty of a unified mosaic of nations and countries.

"Among our people there is a saying: "'A neighbor is in need of his/her neighbor's ashes.'" If you have no ashes needed by others, no one will attach any value to you. Every nation or community has things to lend others, as well things it will borrow.

"I think one of the best ways of mutually helping is education and founding educational institutions. As every problem in human life ultimately depends on human beings themselves, education is the most effective vehicle... [and] always has been the most important road of serving people.

"Now that we live in a global village, education is the best way to serve humanity and to establish dialogue with other civilizations. Through education we should aim to bring about a generation that will rely equally on reason and experience, and give as much importance to the conscience and inspiration as to reason and experience. They will unfailingly pursue the perfect in everything, establish the balance between this world and the next, and wed the heart to the intellect. They will think, investigate, believe, and overflow with spiritual pleasures. While making the fullest use of modern facilities, they will not neglect the moral and spiritual values.

"Equipped with the good morals and virtues that make one truly human, these new men and women will be altruists who embrace humanity with love and are ready to sacrifice themselves for the good of others when necessary. ... In order to have a better future, we should strive to once more remember the true human values lying in the depths of the essence of humanity" (Interview published in *Daily Nation*, July 30, 2004).

Now, let's return to Gülen's *Time* magazine interview: "We are seeking friendship with the world through the educational activities abroad. We are of the view that just as this quest for friendship can take the form of mutual trade, by also acquainting the generations we are to raise in different parts of the world in line with a certain understanding and training, we can enable the integration and unity of these mutually-acquainted people" (Interview with *Time* correspondent on June 4, 1997).

I will never lose hope

In 2010, *New York Times* reporter Brian Knowlton asked Gülen about his efforts in interfaith dialogue: "You've devoted decades to the cause of interfaith tolerance and cooperation, but given the situation around the world what hope do you have for a long-term increase in tolerance?"

Gülen: "I've never lost hope, because I've come to realize that most of the problems can be solved with time. Up until 20 to 25 years ago, there were mountains, cliffs and rivers of blood between people in Turkey—between Muslims and people viewed as minorities, between people of the same religion but different lifestyles or points of view. And with the impact of traditional culture and ingrained habits, those distances seemed impossible to bridge. But we gathered with people, and we shared similar ideas with people from all walks of life, and time and again we met around dinner tables and broke bread together. And I humbly advocated, 'Let's not create new reasons to fight by discussing the old causes of misunderstanding and animosity. Let's bury those negative incidents into history, and let's put huge rocks on top of them. Let us not revive them, and not trigger new clashes. Let us live like friends and send waves of love to the future.' Almost everyone in Turkey has received this idea very well" (Interview for the *New York Times*, Brian Knowlton, June 11, 2010).

Gülen has always believed in the importance of democratic thought. He once asserted, "We have no eyes on anybody's land or country, and no desire of dominating anyone. Those who wish can become Muslim, those who wish can remain Shamanist."

He also said, "... our eyes and hearts are fixed on every corner of the world in terms of taking what God has blessed us with, sharing them with others, to breathe into the soul of everyone, to pour the inspirations of our souls into the bosoms of others. Our hearts beat for the whole world. No place will be outside our focus...

"Our responsibility here is to take this message and to contribute to the world's economic, political, and cultural life. In the meantime, in line with a democratic approach, those who wish can become Muslim, those who wish can remain Shamanist, those who wish can prefer your thought and feeling, those who wish can choose another" (August 17, 1995, *Zaman*).

Reasonable people outnumber extremists

In his interview for *Time* magazine in 1997, Gülen talked at length about religious extremism and how it runs counter to true faith:

"While religion does not allow for conflict, the interpretation of religion draws people into conflict. One should not try to find fault with religion. Thus, the real conflict in the future according to estimates, may not be the conflict of religion, but the conflict of the misinterpretation of religion. There may be battles in the interpretation of religion. There may also be battles in interpreting one of the sayings of God's Messenger. It seems to me that there are such groups among followers of other religions too who do not favor religion in any way but favor crude behavior.

"There is no such thing as good Muslimness or bad Muslimness in terms of genuine Islam [in other words, one cannot categorize others as good Muslims or bad Muslims]. But there is a grading and categorization before God in accordance with piety, and this only God knows. Consequently, if a radical segment that we now call 'fundamentalists' call themselves good and everyone else bad, this matter has no religious basis. This is aimed somewhat at self-approbation and discrediting the opposing side, and in this is even the effort to pull the opponent to their own side. You can say so if you wish. Yes, there is no question of such a distinction according to genuine Muslims, or saying that so-and-so or such-and-such is better. Only God knows who is better. By one Qur'anic measure, 'Surely the noblest, most honorable of you in God's sight is the one best in piety, righteousness, and reverence for God.' As such, if there is a privilege, then this is to be sought in one's relationship with God. There can be extremists in every community, every nation, and in every civilization.

"In religious terms, we refer to them as extremists also. Those who go to extremes. But there are those who are really well balanced in their approach. In that regard, we are hopeful that this chaos will disappear and expect that the balance will be restored."

In a televized interview on Samanyolu TV on March 29, 1997, he expanded on these statements:

"I do not want to believe that anyone could say no to dialogue and tolerance. I say to everyone today, from the Dalai Lama to all patriarchs, come let us not wait for a world with a clash of civilizations or the clash of religions. Let's take certain initiatives and take steps in this matter. Let's try to establish a world founded on love, understanding, and acceptance. Let's try to come together to discuss this and come to a decision. ... If we want to be remembered with gratitude by future generations, then come, let's do this good for the people and be favored with their prayers.

"[I remember once] a Patriarch who embraced me, and [I remember] his assistant. The Pope's aide said to me, they were praying for me in their places of worship. I cannot claim to merit this prayer. They probably sympathized with this vision and this is why they said their prayers. And there are the upcoming generations. They will leave behind emotional spurs. While they will embrace faith on the one hand, they will also be the people of reasoning, understanding, and thought on the other.

"This generation of logic, thought, and reasoning will at the same time be the generation of tolerance and dialogue. I believe that this future world will most definitely become a reality. In fact, if the clash of civilizations has already begun, then it is my belief that we will counter these clashes like the breakwaters taking the full impact of terrifying waves."

Let us conclude this section with two short excerpts from two separate interviews from 2010 and 2014.

New York Times reporter Brian Knowlton asked Gülen, "What are the fundamental values that bind together the followers of what is known as the Gülen movement? Are they specific beliefs, or more a way of looking at the world?"

Gülen responded as follows:

"Even if it may sound somewhat lengthy, to do justice to its encompassing character, it may be also be called 'a movement of people who are gathered around high human values'... this is a movement that anyone, poor or wealthy, could say 'yes' to in terms of avoiding clashes and chaos [through] diplomacy, countering the spread of conflicts, preventing extremist attitudes, triggering the innate humane feelings in everyone, and thereby creating 'peace islands' where everyone can live up to the full potential of their humanity. That's something anyone can say yes to.

"At the core of all this understanding is being respectful to different ideas, welcoming everyone respectfully and trying to understand each other, and accepting people as they are, no matter what they believe in and what philosophy or ideology they pursue. According to our religion, genuine respect is respect to humanity because it is God's art. Yes, a human being, whoever the person is, should be respected simply for being the art of God. Rumi, with this understanding, called to all nations, 'Come, come again, whoever you are, come!'

"Maybe ours has a small difference. We call and say, 'If you'd like to come, please come, our hearts are wide open to you, but please don't burden yourself. Let us come to your countries and homes. Just listen to us for a moment and let us listen to you as well, as we may both find something beautiful and form new sentences in the poetry of human [humane] thinking.'"

In these final statements, published in *Asharq Al-Awsat*, Gülen described the character of the Hizmet movement and the broad spectrum of people taking part in it:

"While it is a movement inspired by faith, this community of volunteers develops and delivers reasonable and universally acceptable projects which are in full compliance with humanitarian values and which aim to promote individual freedoms, human rights and peaceful coexistence for all people regardless of their faith. Accordingly, people from every nation and religion have either welcomed these projects or have lent active or passive, direct or indirect, support to them in 160 countries around the world. In this sense, it is impossible to say that the composition of this movement is homogeneous. This heterogeneity applies not only to the values nurtured by the participants in the movement, but also to their sympathy toward or participation in the Movement's projects. Some work as teachers in the schools abroad, while others pay stipends or allocate part of their time to voluntary services, etc. ..." (March 24, 2014).

CHAPTER 8

TERRORISM AND JIHAD

Terrorism and Jihad

Terrorism today has no limits. ISIS has carried out terrorist attacks against the Western world in Orlando, Berlin, Paris, Nice, Brussels, and London. While a huge population of Muslims continue to live in European countries and the US, terrorists say that they attack in the name of Islam, unfortunately.

Years ago, when Osama bin Laden, the leader of Al-Qaeda, declared jihad against the entire world, Fethullah Gülen reacted against him in the strongest possible terms. Using his authority as an Islamic scholar, he said, "I hate Bin Laden. He tainted the bright face of Islam." Gülen said that according to Islam, Bin Laden had no right or authority to declare jihad.

Gülen has been warning the youth of the Islamic world about ISIS, which has replaced Al-Qaeda and has been shedding blood around the world. While ISIS promises suicide bombers will reach paradise, Gülen warns, "those who explode themselves and kill innocent people will fall into the depths of hell, not paradise."

Given Islam's incompatibility with terrorism, how then did Osama Bin Laden become one of the faces of Islam? How did Al-Qaeda wreak terror for so many years? These are two of the key questions asked of Gülen in all of his interviews since the terrorist attacks on September 11, 2001.

In virtually every interview, Gülen issued striking statements on terrorism and jihad. He said things like, "A Muslim cannot be a terrorist and a terrorist cannot be a Muslim. A person cannot go to heaven by killing." Likewise, he said, "I hate Osama bin Laden, because he has tarnished the luminous face of Islam."

He also said, "Terrorism can only lead to disaster in the world and to the fire in the Hereafter."

Lastly, regarding jihad, he said, "Individuals cannot declare jihad."

God's approval cannot be won by killing people

These statements are taken from the interview published in the *Muslim World* in July 2005:

"...today, at best we can say Islam is not known at all. Muslims should say, 'In true Islam, terror does not exist.' No person can kill another human being. No one can touch an innocent person, even in time of war. No one can give a *fatwa* (a legal pronouncement) on this matter. No one can be a suicide bomber. No one can rush into crowds with bombs tied to his or her body. Regardless of the religion of these crowds, this is not religiously permissible.

"Even in the event of war—during which it is difficult to maintain balances—this is not permitted in Islam. Islam states, 'Do not touch children or people who worship in churches.' This has not only been said once, but has been repeated over and over throughout history. What Our Master, Prophet Muhammad, said, what Abu Bakr said, and what 'Umar said, is the same as what, at later dates, Salahaddin Ayyubi, Alparslan, and Kılıçarslan also said. Later on, Sultan Mehmet the Conqueror also said the same. Thus, the disorderly city of Constantinople, became Istanbul. In this city the Greeks did not harm the Armenians, nor did the Armenians harm the Greeks. Nor did the Muslims harm any other people.

"A short time after the conquest of Constantinople, the people of the city voluntarily hung a huge portrait of the Conqueror on the wall in the place of that of the Patriarch. It is amazing that such behavior was displayed at that time. Then, history relates that the Sultan summoned the Patriarch and gave him the key to the city. Even today, the Patriarchate remembers him with respect. But today, Islam, as with every other subject, is not understood properly. Islam has always respected different ideas and this must be understood for it to be appreciated properly.

"I regret to say that in the countries Muslims live, some religious leaders and immature Muslims have no other weapon to hand than their fundamentalist interpretation of Islam. In fact, Islam is a true faith, and it should be lived truly. On the way to attaining faith one can never use untrue methods. In Islam, just as a goal must be legitimate, so must be all the means employed to reach that goal.

"From this perspective, one cannot achieve Heaven by murdering another person. A Muslim cannot say, 'I will kill a person and then go to Heaven.' God's approval cannot be won by killing people. One of the most important goals for a Muslim is to win the approval of God, another being making the name of Almighty God known to the universe" (*The Muslim World*, 2005 issue).

In a *Zaman* interview dated March 22, 2004, Gülen was asked whether those engaging in acts of terrorism in the name of Islam see this to be a war, a jihad, and whether they think that the doors to Paradise will be thus opened to them. He responded:

"The rules of Islam are clear. Individuals cannot declare war. A group or an organization cannot declare war. War is declared by the state. War cannot be declared without a president or an army first saying that there is a war. Otherwise everybody declares war as they wish. In such a case war is entered into by gathering around oneself, forgive my language, a few bandits. Another person would gather some others around himself. Some people could say, 'I declare war against such and such a person.' A person who is tolerant to Christianity could be accused of [weakening Islam]. They would say, 'We declare war against him. A war against him should be declared and he must be killed.'

"Fortunately, declaring war is not this easy. If the state does not declare a war, no one can wage war. The rules of peace and war in Islam are clearly set out."

Those who engage in acts of terrorism in the name of religion will land right in the middle of Hell

In 2012, Rainer Hermann asked Gülen about those engaging in acts of terrorism and killing in the name of Islam, to which Gülen responded that such people are committing murder and will therefore incur the punishment of Hellfire:

"This took place in the Western world also, during a certain period, in the struggle for capital, and in the name of labor and financial opportunity. Ours was supposedly in the name of religion, a possibility I rule out entirely. It is personal interest and egotism that have been instrumental. They are committing murders in the name of religion, whereas these are murders and atrocities committed against religion. A university professor who is also a priest once asked me whether it was their sound belief in the existence of Heaven and Hell that drove these people to kill, to become suicide bombers. Without even thinking, I said that those who did so would land right in the middle of Hell, not Heaven. There cannot be such a thing in the name of religion; there cannot be killing in the name of religion; murder and the flagrant disregard for justice and fairness cannot be made to look like a religious principle. This cannot be reconciled with religion" (Rainer Hermann, *Frankfurter Allgemeine Zeitung*, December 6, 2012).

Gülen echoed the same views with equal emphasis in his *New York Times* interview in 2010:

"[J]ust like I have stated many times before whenever I've had the opportunity—a real Muslim is the embodiment of peace and tranquility. There is no place for terror in true Islam. Religion does not allow killing to achieve goals. Heaven cannot be attained by killing people. An innocent person cannot be harmed, even during times of war. These facts are indisputable, and up until now and forever, have been stated" (Brian Knowlton's interview with Gülen for the *New York Times*, dated June 11, 2010).

Doesn't the Muslim world appear to be at odds with the spirit of Islam?

In 2004, Gülen was asked a critical question: "Given that the rules of war in Islam are clearly set out, and seeing that it is not possible to commit murder in the name of religion, then why is the Muslim world in the state that it is?"

Gülen's answer was arresting:

"In my opinion, an 'Islamic World' does not really exist. There are places where Muslims live. They are more Muslims in some places and fewer in others. Islam has become a way of living, a culture; it is not being followed as a faith. There are Muslims who have restructured Islam in accordance with their thoughts. I do not refer to radical, extremist Muslims, but to ordinary Muslims who live Islam as it suits them. The prerequisite for Islam is that one should 'really' believe, and live accordingly; Muslims must assume the responsibilities inherent in Islam.

"It cannot be said that any such societies [that assume these responsibilities] exist within the Islamic geography. If we say that they exist, then we are slandering Islam. If we say that Islam does not exist, then we are slandering humans. I do not think Muslims will be able to contribute much to the balance of the world in the near future. I do not see our administrators having this vision. The Islamic world is pretty ignorant, despite a measured enlightenment that is nowadays just beginning.

"We can observe this phenomenon during the hajj. We can see this displayed during conferences and panels. We can see this in their parliaments. There is serious lack of knowledge and know-how. They—these Muslims—cannot solve the problems of the world. Maybe in the future" (*Zaman*, March 22, 2004).

Islam does not look favorably upon war, let alone terrorism

The *Daily Nation*, a newspaper published in Kenya and East Africa with a circulation of 3.5 million, asked Gülen on July 30, 2004, "Some people equate Islam with terrorism and terrorism with Islam. What is your comment on such an equation?"

Gülen asserted that one of the five fundamental values that have to be protected in Islam is the right to life, and that Islam holds killing a single person as equivalent to killing all humankind. He noted in particular that terror aside, Islam even frowns upon war, and that from the early period onwards, it established rules of war. Even war is not unrestrained by law in Islam:

"First of all, I must state very clearly that any Divinely-inspired religion, whether it be Judaism, Christianity, or Islam, never orders or condones terrorism. Life is of the utmost importance for God. God, Who attaches such importance to life, decreed that life is one of the five basic values that must be protected.

"Islam treats every human individual as a species compared to other creatures. This is why it teaches that killing one person is no different from killing all people and that saving the life of one person is equal to saving the life of all humanity. Moreover, as far as the rights of humanity are concerned, based on its principle that 'rights cannot be categorized as great and small,' Islam sees the right of an individual as being equal to the right of the community. It does not sacrifice one of these to the other. Secondly, besides requiring that the goal of a Muslim's behavior and activities must be correct, Islam delicately emphasizes that the means of achieving the goal must also be legitimate. People who attempt to realize a legitimate goal by illegitimate means will find the opposite of what they aim for.

"Accordingly, we can say that terrorism can never be a method to realize an Islamic goal. It should also be borne in mind here that Islam does not treat war favorably, although it is a reality of human life... Islam, first of all, has allowed war, provided it be for self-defense, and then only in the framework of the principles of the Qur'an. The quote, 'dissension and anarchy causing everything to be upside down are worse than murder,' places war as a legitimate means only to prevent turmoil, disorder, and cruelty. It was Islam that laid down important rules and restrictions for war and introduced an international law for the first time in human history.

"Books dealing with war within the context of an international law were published 13 centuries ago. Orders such as, *'Never take the fear of God out from your hearts. Do not trample crops or orchards. Be respectful to priests, hermits and people who devote themselves to God and do not harm them. Do not kill civilians, do not behave to women inappropriately and do not hurt the feelings of the defeated. Do not accept presents from the native people, nor attempt to have your soldiers stay in their houses. Remember performing your five daily prescribed prayers'* were recorded in history as principles that almost all Islamic state leaders have reminded their commanders of when sending them to the front-lines; these orders were followed to the word. An Islamic authority can declare war only within the framework of such definite[Islamic] principles, and only a Muslim state, not certain individuals or organizations, can declare a war. So, there is no place in Islam...

"However, if terrorist incidents occur in either the Islamic world or in other places, and if these incidents continue, the cause must be diagnosed in a sound manner, and then a treatment must be found according to this diagnosis" (*Daily Nation*, July 30, 2004).

Aggression and enmity are not religious requirements

In his interview with *Yeni Yüzyıl* in 1997, Gülen connected Islam's false association with terrorism to two key reasons. The first concerns the prejudices that became ingrained in the Western subconscious due to historical reasons. The second is Muslims in different regions of the world interpreting Islam in line with their own interests, and their whims and desires took the place of religion:

"The West's perception in this regard goes back a long way. I think instead of taking the truth of Islam at the first encounter and analyze it thoroughly, those who were shaping the Western world with their ideas, not the armies, or the commanders of armies, behaved with preconceived notions about Islam. With that they declared war on Islam... If only they had examined the basic dynamics, the basic tenets of Islam. Conditions of time and place have also resulted in changes of understanding about Islam and given rise to its forms, for example, in Afghanistan, in Iran.

"No one should be trapped in these forms, [such as] its form in Saudi Arabia, its form in Syria, about Islam. In considering the subject, Western researchers and Orientalists approach it in terms of Christianity vs. Islam, us vs. them, and are ready to find fault and attach blame.

"This has prevented the West from seeing the truth and understanding the East accurately. What needs to be done? This is another question. There is also an aspect of concern to Muslims. Muslims have interpreted Islam a little according to their own feelings, a little according to their own interests, in the way that enthusiasm has replaced theology, accurate thinking has replaced accurate reflection. People believe their own feelings to be logic and judgment, and call that religion.

"They therefore even regard aggression and enmity as religious requirements. I think that feeling and emotion have partially assumed the guise of reason in the Islamic world. Many consider religion in terms of feeling and enthusiasm, in other words, not within a divine framework, or weighing it, measuring with logic.

"One excellent present-day commentator on the Qur'an says, 'The Qur'an has made the laws, principles, and rules available to mankind to [so they can use] reason. It has no rules that conflict with reason.' When you consider an issue with emotion and enthusiasm, the true path becomes lost. Everyone follows their own carnal desires, and their fight is not for anything else. On the one hand, Westerners have such a perspective, and on the other hand there are individuals who interpret the religion according to their own desires.

"Westerners approach Islam with preconceived notions. Events and notions that reinforce these ideas constantly run through their thoughts" (*Yeni Yüzyıl*, July 28, 1997).

Al-Qaeda and Bin Laden have no place in Islam

Rainer Hermann asked Gülen how Islam can be interpreted so differently by different groups. Gülen said that there are spheres within Islam that are open to interpretation, but that Islam currently suffers from a shortage of *mujtahids*, or those qualified to exercise independent reasoning (*ijtihad*):

"Many things in the religion have been left open for commentary and interpretation. This can be explained with conditions and circumstances that change with time. Alongside the clear verses of the Qur'an that are not open to interpretation, we have commentaries that can form the basis for judgments at a certain time. Needs and demands vary over time. This is what we call *ijtihad*. If there is no one, today, who can exercise independent reasoning, then this is because there is no one who is of such a capacity and competence. Otherwise, the door of *ijtihad* is wide open. There are many different points of *ijtihad* that are to be exercised taking into account time, science, technological developments, and international relations. *Ijtihad* gave rise to certain differences in the past. It is said, 'There are as many paths to God as the breaths of beings in the universe'" (Rainer Hermann, *Frankfurter Allgemeine Zeitung*, December 6, 2012).

So, how are Osama bin Laden and al-Qaeda terror to be evaluated in terms of Islam? Gülen explained that neither Bin Laden's actions nor al-Qaeda's terrorism have any place in Islam:

"Bin Laden can argue as much as he wants that he acts upon the Qur'an and the Sunna. If God Almighty would accept me as one of the small individuals among Muslims, I can also say that we have based ourselves upon Islamic scholars and that an overwhelming majority of philosophers, sociologists, and those who know Islam have come out from among the Muslims and all of us are allied in the way we think.

"If the experience of our Prophet and the four Caliphs are to be taken as the basis for Islam, then the actions of Bin Laden cannot be justified. There is no way that the Prophet's work can be seen as being in line with what Bin Laden does. When the Prophet's battles are analyzed in the larger context of his life, it can be seen that he defended his treaties by using his legitimate rights against those who were pulling him into certain schemes. At other times he took action against those who had betrayed his system or treaty; this is quite normal, and the conquest of Mecca was realized after such a betrayal.

"Taking the Prophet's actions as essentials, it is understood that Bin Laden is not viewing the matter comprehensively. He is taking as reference only some sections; he does not explore in general terms the Qur'an, the Sunna, and the understanding of the *salaf-i salihin* (prominent guides among the Companions and their followers).

"Similarly, the section in the Qur'an that states, 'kill polytheists wherever you see them,' is taken literally and out of context (by Osama Bin Laden and others like him) without looking at what precedes or what follows this verse. Such an understanding brings about misinterpretations.

"This verse means 'to punish those who have accepted you and become part of you, and who have then rebelled and betrayed the nation in hostility.' Every state protects itself from such treachery, and punishes the traitors. This verse is followed by, 'if they return, say their Daily Prayers, fast during Ramadan, and find their original paths, release them.' The interpretations of Bin Laden and others like him come out of the arguments are based upon one single word that is taken out of context...

"When we talk about Muslims, if we do not look at the Pride of Humanity (the Prophet Muhammad), the Qur'an, and the Sunna, then our crude and harsh manners are screening them and darkening their appearance, and we are not doing good, but evil" (*Milliyet*, January 18, 2005).

Buddhists saw Islam as a religion of war

Noting that the very different interpretations of Islam across the Muslim world hurt the image of Islam, Gülen referred to even Buddhist monks' describing of Islam at one time as a religion of war:

"[S]omeone stands up and says that this is right in Algeria, and does something. Someone else does the same thing in Syria. Someone else in the Moro Front in the Philippines does something according to his own lights, similar things take place in Bangladesh, in Kashmir. Westerners say, 'You see? We told you so.' The church says, 'You see?' Even Buddhists say, 'You see?'

"Some of our colleagues say that when they first met Buddhist priests, the priests' reaction to them was, 'Oh, Islam is a religion that wages war.' That is how they regard Islam. Certain conditions may lead to a point where you cannot escape war. What happens if it becomes inevitable? Then there must be rules and regulations. Since there are no such laws about war in the Bible, the Crusaders inflicted unregulated, lawless suffering. They hanged thousands of people in the forests on their way to Palestine. This is a historical fact known to everyone. Looking at the problem from this respect only and coming to a conclusion, equating Islam with war or conflict in the positive or negative sense would be wrong.

"Yet events in the world do seem to reinforce the opinions of those who wish to interpret matters in that light. Some careless people are unaware of how they should treat whom, and when. In other words, the way they do many things are so wrong; Islam is really portrayed in a bad light" (*Yeni Yüzyıl*, July 28, 1997).

Islam in Anatolia

Gülen has maintained that across the entire Muslim geography, the way Islam has been interpreted in Anatolia has a unique place in history. He stated that this interpretation can be called "Turkish Muslimness" in the cultural sense, but that such expressions as Turkish Muslimness, Kurdish Muslimness, and Arab Muslimness are not right in terms of religion. A section of the extended interview with *Le Monde* journalist Nicole Pope in 1998 is below:

"As the religion of a people who have ruled in this region for centuries, Islam has always been interpreted in a manner softer and more inclusive. Were it not for that, the Ottomans could not have ruled for so long in their vast territories, including those countries under their protection, from Vienna all the way to China (except Iran), and from the frontiers of Moscow to central Africa. They were very good to the people, and did not interfere in their religion, or religious affairs.

"In a *kanunname*, or imperial law code, attributed to Mehmet II, it was stated, 'Everyone is free to worship in their churches, and to practice their religion free from disturbance or intervention.' These are very important things. When he had conquered Constantinople, Mehmet II was still very young and he could have acted upon emotions and grudge; however, he did not, because he was guided by the Qur'an and the Prophetic practice.

"Mehmet the Conqueror did not touch any of the images in the Hagia Sophia and said nothing to those who gathered there. His behavior was eminently democratic in the modern sense. His administration looked imperial in form, but was in actual fact exceptionally democratic. The Seljuks, before the Ottomans, behaved in the same way. The same was true for the Ilkhanates, and the Karakhanids" (Nicole Pope, *Le Monde,* April 28, 1998).

CHAPTER 9

THE KURDISH QUESTION

The Kurdish Question

The Ottoman Empire was a multi-ethnic and multi-religious society. The Republic of Turkey, founded in the aftermath of the Ottoman Empire's collapse, was established on a nation-state model which did not recognize Kurds as a separate ethnic group. The definition of the citizen in the Constitution was on the basis of Turkishness. Theories were even produced arguing that Kurds were formerly Turks who lived in the mountains.

From the establishment of the Republic until 1938, many Kurdish revolts in eastern Turkey were violently suppressed by the State. Many prominent Kurdish families were pressured to move away from their homelands, to the western provinces.

In the 1970s, the Kurdish problem was once again inflamed. After the September 12, 1980 coup, the military junta took harsh measures to suppress any Kurdish resistance. All Kurdish movements were considered to be an extension of Kurdish nationalism and were banned nationwide. Many were arrested in sweeping police and military operations; the Turkish parliament even passed a law banning the Kurdish language.

The PKK (Partiya Karkeren Kurdistane), established in 1978, conducted its first terrorist attack in August, 1984. Its target was a military station and housing unit in Siirt, a city in eastern Turkey. This was the beginning of a new phase of the Kurdish issue. It is still ongoing and has been marked by bloodshed. Many Kurdish provinces have been under prolonged states of emergency.

The toll has been very high on both sides: tens of thousands have been killed since the 1980s, including police and military officers, PKK members, and civilians.

The PKK's leader Abdullah Öcalan led his group from Syria, where he stayed in hiding for nearly thirty years. He was expelled from Syria in 1998, was caught by American forces in Kenya in February, 1999, and was handed over to Turkey. After his trial, Öcalan was put behind bars for life, serving his time on an island prison in the Marmara Sea, off of Istanbul. Yet the PKK continues to exist. Following its leader's arrest, the PKK stopped its armed attacks for a while, but returned to violence in 2004, which ushered in a yet another brutal period of fighting.

Pressed by intellectuals to bring an end to this war, the government initiated the "solution process" in January, 2013. Kurdish HDP Party deputies in the parliament mediated talks between the government and the leaders of the PKK. This process helped reduce the number of armed conflicts, and this temporary period of relative peace lasted until the elections of June 7, 2015, when the Kurdish HDP party won 80 seats and representation in the parliament. This electoral success on the Kurdish side spoiled President Erdoğan's plans for a supermajority, which would allow him to enact an executive presidency. Disappointed with the results, Erdoğan declared the "solution process" over, which paved the way for new conflicts. When the process did not serve his political interests, Erdoğan abolished it.

Recently, Syrian Kurds, supported by the PKK, have taken control of some territories in northern Syria. They've declared autonomy in Kobani. Turkey does not recognize the rule of Kurds in this region. These PKK members, taking refuge in Syria, have been behind some of the recent violent bomb attacks across Turkey, which have claimed hundreds of lives. Syrian Kurds claim that the Turkish army entered Syria in an effort to prevent Kurdish autonomy.

Following the coup attempt on July 15, 2016, Erdoğan increased his pressure on the Kurds. Many Kurdish HDP members of parliament, including co-leader Selahattin Demirtaş, as well as over ten thousand Kurdish party members, have been detained and arrested.

It was October 10, 2011. There were still fifteen months until the launch of the Turkish government's "peace process," aimed at ending the violence and reaching an agreement with Kurdish separatists.

Gülen was with a few visitors in his residence in rural Pennsylvania. When the Kurdish issue came up, he said the following:

"If things continue as they are for the next few years, the state will be hard pressed to resolve the Kurdish issue."

During that talk, Gülen put forth a framework by which the Turkish state could resolve the Kurdish issue. The point he emphatically emphasized was that the human dimension of the matter be brought to the fore:

"There is a need for empathy there... The essence of the issue needs to be read properly. A robust diplomacy is necessary for its resolution. The feelings of those [Kurdish] people with whom we have lived together for centuries should not be offended. Brute force alone cannot solve the problem. The region needs to be developed rapidly, in economic terms. If the long-standing position of the region, after years of neglect, continues while Northern Iraq develops rapidly in the region, this will be the cause of separate problems. I never lost hope about the country's East and Southeast, but it should not be forgotten that there is a need there for people of compassion. We need people who carry the spirit of Yunus and Rumi... The people need to be embraced as a whole."

Insufficient government action

Gülen had already voiced these views in the media years before, in the early 1990s. The subject on which he painstakingly focused was always the same: Approaching the Kurdish issue from a humanitarian perspective.

In an interview published in the *Zaman* daily, on November 5, 1993, he indicated that as a result of the misguided policies implemented throughout the history of the Turkish Republic, antipathy had developed towards the term "Kurdish":

"Until now, and especially during the Republican era, the government policies towards the issue of the Southeast has not been approached in a serious way, consistent with our long history of state governance. Left unattended, the matter finally became gangrenous. And now, as many have said, the prevailing mood is characterized by responding to violence with violence. This approach is highly objectionable and causes unease among our citizens in the East. Just as pollens cause irritation, even the very term 'Kurdish' is enough to give rise to allergic reaction (in many Turks). As I see it, the tone needs to change and policies thus far need to be evaluated..."

There is good in peace and peace is always good

Exactly twenty years after Gülen said, "If we do not want the country to be divided, we must do things differently," the government launched the "peace process," in December of 2012.

By the end of 2012, the government was having meetings with the leader (Abdullah Öcalan) of the Kurdistan Workers' Party (or PKK) on İmralı island, where he is imprisoned.

At the time, everybody wondered how Gülen viewed the government's peace process. In a talk he gave on January 9, 2013, Gülen said, "There is good in peace and peace is always good." An excerpt from Gülen's speech, which attracted widespread attention in the media as well as in the political arena, follows:

"One must be open to coming to an agreement with everyone; or rather, one must be open to peace, even if burdensome. If a person can be thus open, they are likewise open to legitimate efforts to obtain peace... Endeavoring to ensure a general peace, whatever the context, and demonstrating the possibility of peaceful coexistence, is therefore imperative.

"In what areas are you trying to ensure such a general peace, let us say for instance, in Turkey? There are people with many different worldviews: some believe in God and some don't; some are monotheists, others are atheists, deists, and those in between. There is a need to demonstrate that coexistence is possible even among those groups who seem opposites. Plans for action need to be put forth to this end.

"However, today's issues do not seem to be following this plan. There are Alevis and Sunnis, Kurds and Turks, or Lazs and Circassians, etc. We need to establish peace between these groups. One needs to do their utmost for this to be realized. If necessary, one must even set aside their own troubles and suffering. As long as national pride and honor are not trampled on, then we must make this effort. There is good in peace and peace is always good... There may be some things we are strongly disinclined to. 'If only this meeting, this agreement, this reconciliation did not take place,' one might say, 'what about our pride and honor? If only we did not have to bow to certain demands.' But if there is the possibility that certain problems will be solved by such agreements or reconciliations, then one needs to do whatever is necessary, in view of the Treaty of Hudaybiya[10] and by means of its logic and reasoning" (January 9, 2013).

Wishing for others what we wish for ourselves

Six months after these comments, Gülen lent his support to the peace

---

10 The Treaty of Hudaybiya was signed between the Prophet Muhammad and the Meccan pagans in 628 CE. The treaty imposed certain sanctions on the Muslim side, yet the Prophet still signed it as it promised peace.

process in an interview on June 24, 2013, with Northern Iraq's Kurdish daily *Rudaw*, published in Erbil, and also aired on Rudaw television. He said the following:

"It is impossible not to support efforts that aim to stop the years of tears and bloodshed in the region. It is crucial that we be constructive and leave the pain of the past behind. I am of the belief that sincerity, mutual respect and, as mentioned in a Prophetic tradition, wishing for others what we wish for ourselves, will cut to the core of the problems at hand and will condemn them to disappear."

One of the questions put to Gülen in an interview on BBC television, which aired on January 27, 2014, was the following:

"I want to ask another question, concerning the Kurdish issue, in terms of clarifying your ideas. You said that you moved earlier for a resolution to the Kurdish issue and opened schools, but that this was not truly appreciated at the time. Later, however, especially in the last four or five years, the Kurdistan Communities Union (KCK) investigations, the issue of the leaked Oslo negotiations,[11] and later the operation against the National Intelligence Organization (MIT) on February 7, 2012, were all imputed to you. You said in an interview that the issue of Kurdish language as a native tongue should not even be debated [because it is a natural right]. What is it that you are particularly against in this matter; negotiations made with the terrorist organization?"

Gülen gave the following response:

"The Republic of Turkey is a nation of Kurds, Turks, Laz, Circassians and Abkhazians; that is, the people of Anatolia. Actually, we use that phrase often. In terms of emphasizing unity and togetherness, it is an important term. We were never against the Oslo negotiations, the discussions with Öcalan, the discussions with the PKK in Kandil. I said in a recent interview that I believe peace is essential, and agreeing with one another is essential. I believe that 80 percent of our nation agrees on these matters... I have both encouraged and told those people who have come to see me that Kurdish language should be taught on TV, that there

---

11 Oslo negotiations refer to a series of meetings between representatives of the Turkish government – including officers from the National Intelligence Service (MIT) – and representatives of the Kurdish separatists, PKK, between 2009 and 2011, reportedly to stop armed conflict.

should be a Kurdish TV channel. At the same time, I have encouraged and said that Kurdish should be taught as an elective lesson in public schools and universities. In other words, I have encouraged these reasonable and necessary steps to be taken; I have said these things. You would end up with a big volume if all the things that we have said on the subject were collected. But for some reason, to denigrate the Hizmet movement, certain media has shown us as being against the peace process. The current administration, in order to have good relations, to look good to the Kurds, and to get their support in the elections, blamed everything on what they call 'Hizmet,' the community or movement... Perhaps it has been about 10 years since we put our views and recommendations forward. We did this before they had done so... But, for whatever reason, they have tried to show me as being against the peace process. No. Absolutely not..."

The State should be fair to its citizens

In the last part of an interview in the English language newspaper *Today's Zaman*, dated March 19, 2014, Gülen was asked about the peace process. His response went as follows:

"This is something I had spoken about previously on a number of occasions. A believer always favors peace. A believer adopts the attitude required for peace. There are problems that have accumulated over time. In the past, violence was wielded to solve these problems. But this did not solve any of them; it only exacerbated them further.

"Now there is a process of peace and reconciliation. This shouldn't be disrupted. This is a good opportunity for both sides to forget about hostilities and turn back from their mistakes. A state must be fair in its dealings with its citizens. Fundamental rights and freedoms should not be seen or used as a bargaining chip. Even before the peace process began, I had expressed my perspective about education in one's mother tongue. But no step was taken to this end. This matter is still not resolved.

"Turkey must raise teachers who are capable of teaching in Kurdish. This is not something that can be done only when demanded by the public. The state must take the first step. In taking this step, we must refrain from words, attitudes, and behaviors that may give the impression that we are doing this as a favor. The region [Turkey's Southeast] was home to numerous major civilizations and great thinkers. In addition to recognizing the due rights and freedoms of its Kurdish citizens, Turkey must extend a helping hand to the Kurds in other regions. We must re-establish and reinforce our cultural and historical ties with them.

"We have three fundamental problems, which were outlined by Bediüzzaman Said Nursi almost a century ago; they are ignorance, poverty, and disunity. These problems have bred despair, deception, circumvention, mutual distrust, and so on. We need to discuss these problems on a common platform. This is not something that can be done with disdain and arrogance. If reconciliation is to be achieved, we must be all-inclusive, embracing the entirety of the region and its diverse groups. No one should be excluded from it. Common denominators should be found, so as to embrace political and non-political groups. We should let local people solve their problems with their own capabilities.

"If steps are not taken quickly, I fear the peace process may come to a halt. Focusing on stopping the bloodshed is important; but even this indicates a certain level of pragmatism. We should have objectives beyond that point. We must generate an atmosphere in which everyone -- Turks, Kurds, Sunnis, Alevis, Arabs, Syriacs, and so on -- can co-exist as members of the same family in happiness and prosperity."

Nationalism cannot replace religion

In nearly all of his speeches since the 1990s, Fethullah Gülen has painstakingly drawn attention to one particular topic:

"There is no room for racism in Islam."

In a televized interview in the Netherlands, on October 19, 1995, he was asked, "[If] there is no racism in Islam, and it does not take place in practice, from where does it originate?"

Gülen gave the following response:

"There are certain feelings with which God has vested human nature... Every person has in their nature a love for their own nation. God declares that He has created us in groups, in tribes. There are different nations, different ways of thinking. This is essential to a universal acquaintance...

"Now this feeling has been conferred upon humanity and exists within all of us. A person first favors, regards, and loves their own self, to a certain extent. Then they love their family. This is the constituent unit of society, its molecule. Then their own community. They love them because they are closest to them, most familiar, and most well-known.

"When this love is tempered with religious principles and modern, developed legal systems, it is harmless. But if it is left to its own intemperance, a terrifying racism can emerge, as was experienced in Italy and in Germany [during the 1930s and 1940s]. We can still see this racism in different parts of the world...

"It can be experienced and played out in a way which gives rise to a great deal of vice, affliction, and violence...

"I see much use in considering the issue from Said Nursi's perspective, especially when looking at Islam's approach to the issue. He refers to 'negative nationalism' and 'positive nationalism.' Negative nationalism is a nationalism that has not been tempered and softened by religion, and one which has not reached the level of accepting others in their own right. This can lead to racism and a notion of nationality based on blood or ancestry, and becomes dangerous. This is what leads to a Hitler or a Mussolini.

"But there is also a positive nationalism. Indeed, I love my own nation more than others. Just as I love my school of thought more than other schools of thought, as I love my religion more than other religions. But this does not warrant my enmity towards others. Again, in Nursi's approach, this is living with the love of one's own way without bearing enmity towards others. These are two different things. For example, nurturing love and affection for one's nation while not having hostility towards others. This is positive nationalism. This must not replace religion, but it should aid it...

"Today, many legal systems are being developed and pacts are signed to rein in racism around the globe. It seems to me that those who approach matters with racist ideas while appearing to be Muslim have not understood Islam either. It can be said that they have failed to understand the universality of Islam."

Gülen highlighted the need for state officials to consult broadly with representatives from every segment of society in bringing a solution to this multifaceted issue:

"In a world where everyone sees themselves as individually sufficient, and with no need for help; when everyone believes that they can overcome anything and plans their lives accordingly, you cannot convey to other people even the greatest truths and you cannot convince officials and those in authority of the need for certain changes. This is a major handicap; even if we were to generate very serious strategies, unfortunately today, nobody would listen. In fact, this is no longer even possible. Prophets of God were perhaps able to do it; but today, even if you were to bring messages based on divine revelation or inspirations, you would not be able to make anyone listen."

Military dimension

In a 1993 interview, Gülen maintained that the Kurdish question was, for a long time, considered merely from a military perspective. He pointed out the complications that could rise from only viewing the issue from this perspective, and from the damage a continued military presence in the Southeast could cause.

"How much longer will the State keep the military there? How much longer will the state of emergency continue? It is not clear. The State needs to have a determined policy on this matter. As I see it, the military needs to be withdrawn from the region in the very near future. This is important. It will not allow the army's name to erode and it will prevent the rise of a possible antipathy among the local population. Unfortunately, there is nothing being done in harmony and mutual agreement with the civil society in that region. Such an agreement is a must, whatever the cost" (November 5, 1993, *Zaman* newspaper).

Unfortunately, despite this interview being given in 1993, by 1997, the military was still present in Southeastern Turkey. Thus, Gülen reiterated the same thing in an interview with *Zaman* on September 3, 1997:

"In speaking of the Southeast [of Turkey], ascribing the problem to the people of the region generally would be an injustice, both to the region and to its people. I am of the opinion that this was not fully understood in the past and seems not to be fully grasped today either. The State has its armed forces there. The military does what can be done with power and force. And when you seek solutions with power, you cannot attain logical, rational, and fundamental solutions. It is very rare for those in power to utilize their reason and good judgment when they are so focused on their power. There are certainly some issues in the South-east where using force is necessary for deterrence. But any such solution should be consolidated with reason and a political formula has to follow, with solutions especially for education, which is so problematic..." (*Zaman* newspaper, September 3, 1997).

Education in one's native language is a prerequisite of State's justice

Education taught in one's mother tongue or native language is a subject that has long been discussed, especially in Turkey, and is one of the main dimensions of the Kurdish issue. As a part of the peace process, the Constitutional Reconciliation Commission that was formed under parliament and had representatives from all four parties. But they were unable to reach a consensus in either 2012 or 2013 on the issue of education in the Kurdish language. Gülen said the following in an interview with the Iraqi Kurdish newspaper *Rudaw* in June 2013:

"Being fair to all of its citizens requires a state to recognize as a primary principle their rights to be educated in their native tongue."

In this interview, Gülen definitively stated that education in one's native language is an inalienable right for every human being and that the state granting its citizens this right is not an act of grace or favor.

Part of his response to *Rudaw* correspondent Rebwar Kerim's questions is printed below:

"The rights and freedoms of human beings are not things that any power can invest them with and are therefore not to be expected from others. They are the rights and freedoms bestowed upon all of us by God our Creator and Sustainer. Every human being, without exception, including the Prophets, is equal because of the fact that they were created by God. Without prior recognition of this fact, there would be no justice, nor law. In taking this step, we must refrain from words, attitudes, and behaviors that may give the impression that we are doing this as a favor. Fundamental rights and freedoms should not be seen or used as a bargaining chip. It is essential to avoid non-legitimate means which transgress the bounds of law and which involve violence, whatever the purpose."

Turkish-Kurdish conflict

In a speech dated October 24, 2011, Gülen indicated that there are those seeking a "Turkish-Kurdish conflict" in Turkey:

"While vicious forces have long provoked certain groups and driven them into the streets, they have simultaneously incited other groups against them, instigating them to attack and bringing them into open confrontation. They are seeking to achieve their own interests.

"In similar provocations beginning before May 27th coup (1960), and continuing until the 1980 coup, and even after, the same forces divided the people into different groups, such as left or right, aroused mutual sensitivities, pit the children of the same nation against each other, and then sought to establish their own rule upon the ruins of all the bloodshed.

"A staging of the same scenario in the current circumstances appears likely, with an instigation of a Kurdish-Turkish conflict... Everybody who cares about our nation and our people, in all its colors and stripes, needs to be very careful and on the alert against provocations, and must especially avoid engaging in unjust retaliatory action. Violence or loud proclamations, such as shouting the slogan, 'Martyrs never die, the country will never be divided,' will not solve the problem.

"Those who want to stop the disorder and provocation can present their criticisms and recommendations to authorities in sound reports or statements. The issue should not be approached with screaming and shouting, destruction and killing, but with reason, sagacity, and compassion."

Kurdish notables consulted during the Ottoman period

When talking to foreign journalists in May 1998, Gülen looked to history for a possible solution to the Kurdish issue:

"During the reign of Ottoman Sultan Yavuz Selim, Kurdish notables were consulted and no problems were experienced for four centuries. They lived as *beys* (provincial princes) and were loyal citizens of their state."

Gülen believes that a group which has been wronged can seek redress, but he holds that there are various methods of seeking such redress. Under no circumstances can these methods include anarchy or shedding the blood of innocent people:

"Killing as a means to an end is not conceivable for any Prophet or any of God's friends. The Messenger of God, upon him be peace and blessings, spent thirteen years in the city of Mecca under persecution and oppression, but he did not even so much as step on an ant. He instead treated those obdurate, tyrannical, and imperious people with humanity. It is precisely this spirit that needs to be conveyed to those who might take to the mountains [to join terrorists]. Indeed, no matter what one's objectives, killing and bloodshed can never be justified and no good can come of it" (October 24, 2011).

In the same interview, Gülen provided examples from the life of Said Nursi, a great 20th-century scholar who was born and raised in the region:

"Bediüzzaman was from the region. Having voluntarily fought with his students against invading forces as the commanding officer of a regiment, Bediüzzaman had his leg broken and was taken prisoner. He was held captive in Kostroma, wherefrom he miraculously fled and returned to Turkey and supported the War of Independence. The path for his entry into Parliament was paved, but he retreated to Mount Erek (for a secluded life) when he realized that he would not be able to serve humanity through politics. He would be persecuted for years on end, under various pretexts. He faced enough pain and suffering that he said, 'I have known nothing of worldly pleasure in my life of over 80 years. All my life has passed on battlefields, in prisons, and in various places of suffering. There is no torment that I have not experienced, no oppression I have not suffered. I have been treated like a criminal at war tribunals and exiled from one place to another like a vagabond. I was barred from communication for months while in confinement. I was poisoned many times over. I was subjected to all kinds of insults. There were times when I preferred death over life. Had my religion not forbidden suicide, perhaps Said would have long become dust.' But he never once adopted a negative attitude nor did anything that would disconcert the people."

Turning the discussion to himself, Gülen added:

"I cannot even be regarded Bediüzzaman's apprentice or his servant, but I, too, have for all these years faced separation from my homeland. I remain here [in the US] voluntarily, lest my presence in Turkey cause any imbalance.

"Redressing rights through violence has never been the way, neither in the luminous lives of the Prophets, nor in the lives of certain leaders such as Zoroaster, Hermes, Buddha, or Brahman... Despite all the persecution he faced, Bediüzzaman never inflicted the slightest harm on anyone; he never asked others to take vengeance on his behalf, even responding to those who proposed as such by saying, 'The Turkish nation has acted as the standard-bearer of Islam for centuries. It has produced millions of saints and given millions of martyrs. The sword cannot be drawn against the descendants of such a nation. We are Muslims. We are their brothers and will not pit brother against brother. This is not religiously permissible. The sword is drawn against an external enemy. It may not be used internally.' Such sound thought and judgement ought to have been widely appropriated and internalized, but, regrettably, this has not been realized" (October 24, 2011).

Turkey's recent political turmoil has destroyed hopes for an immediate, peaceful solution to the Kurdish problem. Turkey missed a big opportunity during the period between 2013 and 2015. The July 2016 coup attempt was followed by oppressive measures taken by Erdoğan, who shut all Kurdish newspapers and TV networks, as well as many legal Kurdish cultural centers and foundations. Despite these actions, the headquarters of the PKK are still in the Qandil Mountains in northern Iraq, yet the Iraqi government is not allowing the Turkish army to enter their territories to fight the PKK. The Kurdish leaders in Iraq oppose Erdoğan's policies of arresting Kurdish politicians and oppressing the Kurdish populace. While Syrian Kurds have aligned with the PKK, Erdoğan's harsh stance against both groups has triggered terrorist activities in Turkey.

Erdoğan had many opportunities to achieve a real, lasting peace, but he did not take into consideration the ideas Fethullah Gülen proposed for many years. These ideas could have served as a solution. Gülen emphasized in his letter to Erdoğan in 2006 that substantial steps should have been taken to ensure Kurds had full rights. Erdoğan attempted to start a peace initiative only in 2013, after intensifying public pressure, and he brought it to an end, failed and unfinished.

Yet one single bill in parliament could have solved the two major Kurdish demands: the right to education in their mother tongue and revising the definition of citizenship in the Constitution. Erdoğan's party, the AKP, always had the power to pass such a bill in parliament. It is profoundly unfortunate that they did not take these steps, and violent attacks continue to shake Turkey, which has already paid a high price since 1984. There is no end in sight to such violence.

CHAPTER 10

ALEVI-SUNNI DIVIDE

Alevi-Sunni Divide

After the Prophet, two major currents emerged in Islam: Sunni (85% of the world's Muslims) and Shi'a (15%). While Sunnis consider the Prophet's time and the reigns of the first four successors, i.e. Caliphs, as the Age of Happiness, the Shiites believe 'Ali was the Prophet's rightful successor; as such, they do not recognize the first three Caliphs as legitimate rulers. After 'Ali was murdered, the chaos over who should rule did not settle, and in one of the most tragic incidents in human history, Husayn, 'Ali's son, and his family members were slaughtered in Kerbela, which is within the borders of today's Iraq.

The term "Alevi" literally means a follower of 'Ali. Like the Shiites in Iran and in other parts of the Middle East, Alevis in Turkey also believe 'Ali and his family (*ahl al-bayt*) were the rightful political successors to the Prophet and that their rights were violated.

Alevis constitute an important social group in Turkey. Historically, the Sunni Ottomans were in military conflict with the Shi'a Safavids, which ruled what is today Iran. The Safavid's willingness to recruit from the Alevi population in the Ottoman lands, and mutual incursions into each other's territory, led to the Battle of Chaldiran in 1514. The Ottomans won the battle decisively; however, the Alevi-Sunni cleavage in Anatolia was far from repaired.

Like the Kurds, Turkey's Alevis have long demanded the equal rights of full citizenship. One of these demands is to have their Cemevis (houses of worship) officially recognized as places of worship, given the same status as mosques. The government sponsors the utilities of a mosque, and pays salary of the imam who is a public servant. Alevis ask for the same sponsorship for their Cemevis, and demand their Dedes (spiritual leaders) to be treated as public servants.

Their second demand is to remove all negative elements about Alevism in religion classes in Turkish public schools.

But much like the Kurdish problem, the Alevi problem hasn't yet been solved.

***

"I, too, am Alevi..."

These words belong to Fethullah Gülen.

He used this expression myriad times in the 1990s.

In an interview published in the *Milliyet* newspaper on July 8, 1995, he explained his use of these words:

"Whether in the house in which I was born and grew up, the madrasa and Sufi lodge in which I was educated, or while following the way of Bediüzzaman, a love of the Prophet's noble household (*ahl al-bayt*) and Alevi Sufism was one of the most prominent elements. So much so, that due to the love of the Noble Household pervading our home, my attachment to 'Ali overshadowed the other Companions. But the greatness of all the Companions, Abu Bakr, 'Umar, and 'Uthman first and foremost, is a given. Love and attachment need to be felt for them also. I have worked over the years to not let my love of 'Ali overshadow my love for the other Companions.

"'Ali is honored with many titles, like Haydar al-Karrar ('the Charging Lion') and the son-in-law of the Prophet. He is superior to all the Companions by virtue of being ancestor to the blessed bloodline of the Prophet's descendants, and great saints will come from this bloodline to the Last Day. Hasan is superior in this respect also, as is Husayn.[12] This is what I meant when I spoke of Alevi Sufism or sainthood. Just as the Hanafi legal school to which I adhere rests to a large extent on 'Ali, there is also an important connection between Abu Hanifa and Ja'far al-Sadiq. 'Hasanism' is central to our way. Giving up the cause of caliphate against Mu'awiya, Hasan secured the unity of the Muslim community and prevented bloodshed. That is to say, he demonstrated through his own actions that he had nothing to do with politics, worldly rank, or position, and that what mattered was the unity of the Muslims. It is precisely in this sense that I am on Hasan's path and share the selfsame view. Our hearts are forever open to Alevis who say that they love 'Ali, Fatima, Hasan, and Husayn. This is how receptive and open we are to everyone. We are ready to help Alevis of all dispositions and I personally can lay myself under their feet.

"It is in this sense that I said, 'I, too, am Alevi,' during the events in Gaziosmanpaşa. This is how Alevi my mother was and how Alevi my father was, for it was my father who inculcated such an understanding in me. Indeed, he was the one who instilled in me a sense of 'Ali's heroism by constantly relating his chivalry and heroic feats."

---

12 Hasan and Husayn are the sons of 'Ali, thus the grandsons of the Prophet.

Let us not burn all bridges for the sake of one bridge

Before examining Gülen's views on the Alevi issue, it would be useful to recall the Gaziosmanpaşa events. On the night of March 12, 1995, unidentified individuals raided a coffee shop in the Gazi quarter of Istanbul's Gaziosmanpaşa district and killed an Alevi spiritual leader. Tragic incidents unfolded that night and the following day in Istanbul's Gaziosmanpaşa and Ümraniye districts. Twenty-one people were killed and dozens of people were injured.

Another incident – just like the Gaziosmanpaşa events – had drawn Alevism into Turkey's contentious political debates during the 1990s. On July 3, 1993, 37 people died when the Madımak Hotel in Sivas was set on fire. This happened following anti-Alevi provocations, and represents one of the worst anti-Alevi acts of violence in Turkey's history.

Unfortunately, the Alevi issue remains contentious nearly 20 years later. In fact, the Gezi Park protests (which broke out in Istanbul's Taksim Square in the summer of 2013), the mosque-cemevi[13] project to be constructed in Ankara's Mamak district, and the naming of the third Bosphorus bridge after Ottoman Sultan Yavuz Selim, brought Alevism to the forefront of Turkey's agenda yet again. Alevis have long disliked the Ottoman Sultan Selim I (Yavuz), who defeated Shah Ismail of the Safavids, due to oppressive policies against Alevis.

As a result of the Taksim protests, which began as a reaction against the proposed reconstruction of the Gezi Park area, the government sought a familiar scapegoat. They made the following claim:

"The ringleaders of the protests are Alevis. Most of those taken into police custody are Alevi citizens."

When it was later announced that the third Bosporous bridge would be named the "Yavuz Sultan Selim Bridge,"[14] it sparked concern and unease in the Alevi community. When tensions reached their apex, Gülen made the following remarks on June 18, 2013:

---

13 Cemevi (literally "house of gathering") is a place of worship for Alevis.

14 Yavuz Sultan Selim is not a popular figure among Alevis. Selim ruled the Ottomans from 1512 to 1520. His era was marked with his conquests in the Middle East. Despite disputes among historians on the authenticity of information and volume of losses, Alevi folklore records massacres of the Alevi community during the Ottoman-Safavid conflict in this era.

"Errors in the way something is implemented may ruin the entire procedure altogether. Great caution needs to be taken in this regard. One may enjoy practicing his or her own tradition, but when you expect others to do the same, you engender an antipathy towards them without even being aware of it. You would be mistaken in replacing the basics or fundamentals with the details, and will have destroyed the bridges in between communities. If details will drive people away, then I would say you need to back down. You can reach a consensus with others on mutually agreed points...

"For example, how is Rumi's whirling (*sema*) different from what Alevis are practicing today (*semah*)? The former is still being performed on the stage and people applaud the show. Then what is the harm of two believers participating in a *semah*? We can come together with Alevis during the month of Muharram or Ramadan. We can see the *sema* and the *semah* together. Alevis and Sunnis can break bread together. As such, we should not sacrifice essentials for the sake of a single bridge, on the basis of a detail... Our God is one, our Prophet is one, our religion is one: one, one, one... Ones up to a thousand.

"There are many bridges between us with respect to our connection with God, His Messenger, and the Qur'an. There are those bridges between us that stem from our common values such as [Sufi thinkers] Ahmad Yasawi, Mawlana [Jalal al-Din al-Rumi], and Yunus Emre.

"Naming a bridge 'Yavuz Sultan Selim,' is a detail, and when such a detail is harped on as though it were an essential matter, all those bridges are ignored... If you draw near, they will draw near; when you accept them as pleasant, they will accept you as pleasant, too. If you accept, you will gain acceptance. Never forget that what you expect from the world, the world expects from you."

Alevis and Sunnis do not know each other

An examination of Gülen's comments concerning the Alevi issue from the 1990s until Gülen's June 18, 2013, speech entitled, "Let us not burn all the bridges for the sake of a single one," reveals an emphasis on three themes:

1. Alevis and Sunnis do not know each other. Despite all the connecting bridges, there is a serious estrangement between them, and this estrangement must be brought to an end;

2. Alevism, which is based more on an oral tradition, is being exploited. Today's generation is not given the opportunity to engage with Alevism's written sources; this engagement needs to be ensured;

3. Cemevis should be opened, and for that matter, mosques and cemevis should be built side-by-side as a symbol of Alevi-Sunni solidarity.

Gülen has returned to the idea of a "mosque-cemevi" venture in both the early 1990s and 2013. His position has remained consistent across the decades, even as successive Turkish governments have been wracked by turmoil and inconsistent policy positions.

And indeed, on September 8, 2013, the foundations of a mosque and an adjacent cemevi were laid in Ankara's Mamak district. The project was named the "Mosque-Cemevi and Cultural Center Complex."

One must ask: why, for so long, was Turkey incapable of bringing a mosque and cemevi together when it had allowed mosques, synagogues, and churches to exist side-by-side for centuries? Was it not Turkey that had hosted so many different ethnicities, religions, and sects, who lived and worshipped together in peaceful coexistence for so long?

Meaning of the joint mosque and cemevi project

In an interview with *Milliyet* newspaper dated July 8, 1995, Gülen said the following about the joint mosque, cemevi, and school project. Back then, the project was going to be constructed in the Narlıdere district of Izmir, Turkey, and it would symbolize Alevi-Sunni solidarity:

"We came together and discussed certain issues with some Alevi citizens, among whom were also Alevi spiritual leaders (*dede*s), either via representatives or face to face over a meal. They proposed that we work together in the construction of a cemevi... As for what I can do to help our Alevi brothers and sisters open a cemevi, I can say this: Alevism has remained for years an oral tradition. I am of the opinion that in this age of learning, Alevism, too, needs to return to its written sources. Moreover, just as I am respectful of our fellow Alevi citizens and their cemevis, they should also respect my values... The political infighting among Muslims and certain incidents between the Prophet's Companions remain entirely a thing of the past; so it is self-evident that an Alevi-Sunni divide is irrelevant and there is at present not a single factor to substantiate such a divide."

Gülen touched upon the same issue in an interview with BBC television in January 2014. First, let's look at the question put to him by the BBC correspondent:

"You have always touched on the importance of interfaith dialogue on an international level, but there are certain tensions between Sunni and Alevi communities. As far as I remember, you indicated the necessity of joint mosque-cemevi projects. However, some Alevi groups gave their objections to the projects as well as disclosing their assimilation concerns. How would you respond to those concerns?"

Gülen's response to the question was as follows:

"The joint mosque-cemevi project, as you indicated, dates back to 1995. We believed that this was something important for establishing unity and solidarity with our Alevi brothers and sisters in Turkey. We may have been mistaken here; human beings can make mistakes. But there were many who condoned the matter. Those who objected on the basis of assimilation [of Alevis by Sunnis], I suspect, will one day regret having said so.

"The mosque-cemevi project was certainly not initiated on the basis of assimilating one group into another. However, for years, certain things were impressed upon the minds of both Sunnis and Alevis so much so that both sides have seen the other as cannibals. With the state's similar stance against them due to the Dersim incident and with all the associated trauma, the years 1938-39 saw these spurious words and thoughts gain acceptance in Turkey.

"[This project allows] those who want to go to the mosque go to the mosque and offer their prayers, and those who wish to go to the cemevi go to the cemevi and perform their *semah*. And when they come out, they will sit together in a common space, eating, drinking tea, or just sitting together in the garden, they will see that neither side is trying to consume the other. The idea that one side will annihilate the other has become embedded in the subconscious. It seems that some are really hoping for such an annihilation, and only time will tell how this will develop.

"Moreover, the joint mosque-cemevi was already realized 15-20 years ago. There was media coverage of this in Turkey. In other words, this is nothing new. Media hype about the issue was also generated, perhaps to some advantage. If this has been realized in Ankara, Izmir will follow – and so, too, will Istanbul. It will be in places with concentrated Alevi populations.

"These places should benefit from the same opportunities and resources provided to the Religious Affairs Directorate of Turkey. These were, at least, the guiding considerations. The Alevi dedes would come and head these cemevis, and they would be paid a salary by the state. There, they would live, teach, and embody their own values. The Sunnis would embody and represent their own values, too. This idea was about establishing fellowship between these two communities. No one has any intention of assimilating anybody."

Alevism is a source of richness

In a July 1997 interview, published across 10 days in the Yeni Yüzyıl newspaper, Gülen stressed the importance of the process of dialogue – especially the one initiated in 1994 in the hopes of inspiring Alevi-Sunni unity and togetherness. In the ninth part of the interview, published on July 28, 1997, he said:

"There are people we know who are engaged in research on Alevism. When you look at their observations, you see that Alevism truly is a special source of richness. As I see it, such a culture should not go to the wayside in favor of Sunnism. Instead, it should be appraised.

"Now, if we set all this aside and establish anew between us the unity and fellowship that being one nation requires, it seems to me that such a mutual flow of culture will naturally take place. In other words, we will have the opportunity to enrich each other. Becoming thus acquainted with one another is an accomplishment unto itself. Delving into the inner worlds and spiritual profundities of each other is a separate dimension of the matter with respect to mutual benefit. To attain such unity and richness, Alevis must also open themselves up to the Sunnis. As it stands, this matter still appears as though it is open to abuse by certain circles.

"In this regard, I will go back to the beginning. Perhaps there are certain vital things that tolerance and dialogue promise for different groups living in Turkey; however, it seems that they will prove much more useful in breaking the artificial icebergs between us and the Alevis."

If we are going to fight in the mosque, then let us make peace outside

In a meeting with the writers and management of *Akşam* newspaper in June 1995, Gülen said, "My efforts are aimed at a right-left, Alevi-Sunni fellowship."

In August of the same year, in an interview he gave to Cumhuriyet columnist Oral Çalışlar, Gülen offered a formula for overcoming the danger of an Alevi-Sunni conflict:

"If we can ensure one side gives up on the idea of fighting, the punch of the other side will be left hanging in the air."

Gülen said the following in a meeting with a group of journalists in March of 1995:

"Waves in Turkey are not flowing in the same direction; they move against each other. They are not completing each other. These waves should come together to strengthen instead of hitting each other and neutralizing their powers."

According to Gülen, this was the result achieved by such societal polarization – and desired by certain powers. It was why they divided people along idealogical lines, like secular vs. anti-secular or Kemalist[15] vs. religious. Gülen said in January 1997, "These divisions are attempts to sabotage the rise of Turkey."

Gülen believed that if Turkish society could break the walls separating people from different walks of life and allow different groups to know each other better, both these polarizations would end – and they would end without any bloodshed, thus avoiding any further incidents like at Madımak or Gazi.[16] He made his point succinctly:

"If we are going to fight inside the mosque, then let us make peace outside."

---

15 "Kemalist" refers to Turkish secularists who are in extreme opposition to Islamic groups. The word is derived from Mustafa Kemal Ataturk's name, the founder of Turkish Republic. His reforms were aimed at establishing a staunch secularism in the country, leaving no room for religion in the public space.

16 Madımak (1993) and Gazi (1995) are two violent incidents which were plotted to further inflame Alevi-Sunni conflict. Scores of people, mostly of Alevi origin, were killed.

For Gülen, the first task fell to the learned people. Turkey's intellectuals needed to be able to gather, regardless of ideology, and talk. After the violent right-wing vs. left-wing conflict of the 1970s dragged the country to the brink of anarchy and economical collapse, the contemporary hostility between Alevi-Sunni and secular-anti-secular can only be overcome through dialogue and non-violence. Accusing every leftist of being a totalitarian and communist, every nationalist of being a chauvinist, fascist, and Nazi, every religious person of being a reactionary and bigot will add nothing to the country.

The oral Alevi tradition should be written down

In an interview with *Yeni Yüzyıl* newspaper dated July 28, 1997, Gülen elucidated his proposal for the oral tradition on which Alevism rests to be written:

"Alevism is based on an oral, face-to-face culture. I had suggested that Alevi sources be placed in cemevis, for the textualization of this culture and for it to acquire a scientific character and identity. Knowledge transmitted orally from one generation to the next may not be transmitted verbatim. Haji Baktash Wali's *Makalat*, and the works of Rumi, Yunus Emre, and Niyazi Misri should be placed in your local meeting places, educational centers, and reading rooms. In other words, put the books of whoever, whichever individuals you love, and transform Alevi culture, a word-of-mouth culture, into a textual one so that it may be permanent. There should be certain coordinates on which you can agree when you sit down together and talk. Otherwise, the ground will be very slippery; there will be difficulties in understanding. These were my thoughts and suggestions.

"I even recommended some of my acquaintances, such as those in Tunceli, to lend their help and support to cemevis. A joint school project was under consideration for Narlıdere in Izmir. There is an Alevi dede, a former senator, there with whom I had very cordial relations. We met on the matter of building a cemevi with a mosque adjacent to it. This is the Ottoman tolerance: a mosque right beside a church, and a synagogue right beside the mosque. All of this happened, and with very pleasing results. All this is very important in breaking the harshness and severity that is not based on sound reason and logic."

The biggest danger is sectarian violence

Gülen said in a speech from August of 1993, "The most horrible terror awaiting tomorrow's Turkey is a sectarian conflict."

Gülen made this warning two years before the Gazi Incidents occurred in Istanbul.

One and a half months before the incidents in Gaziosmanpaşa, he conveyed some of his concerns and thoughts about a resolution to the Alevi issue to then-Prime Minister Tansu Çiller.

Gülen worried this conflict could lead Turkey back to the bloody events of the 1970s. The Turkish people were separated by a chasm, and vengeance lay between them. But this chasm was artificial; the Turkish people had created it themselves.

Unfortunately, despite many people's efforts, violence did erupt in Turkey between Sunnis and Alevis. The day after the Gaziosmanpaşa events, March 13, 1995, Gülen gave an interview. Relevant sections of the interview are excerpted below.

The first question read:

"New killings were added to the list of so-called unsolved murders in Istanbul's Gaziosmanpaşa yesterday. People were killed and many injured in shootings in four coffee houses frequented by Alevi citizens. What are your thoughts on these events?" Gülen offered a lengthy response:

"There is use in addressing the matter in its myriad facets. The Turkish nation is a society made up of Sunnis and Alevis. One might say that the Turkish nation is, in a sense, Alevi in its entirety. Even in places where there are more Alevis by population, no country loves 'Ali more than Turkey. Every individual believer in Turkey feels as much intense attachment and devotion to the Rightly-Guided Caliphs and 'Ali as they do to the religion of Islam. In this respect, all Muslims are Alevis when the issue concerns 'Ali. Each and every believer feels as strong an attachment to the Rightly-Guided Caliphs and 'Ali as they do to the religion of Islam. When the issue is thus associated with 'Ali, an Alevi-Sunni conflict is unsupported.

"I personally deplore this detestable attack against our Alevi citizens in Gaziosmanpaşa. Alevis are our brothers and sisters.

"As I have already stated, I am as fervently attached to 'Ali as any ardent Alevi. I have shed a world of tears for Karbala. As such, my hatred towards such an incident is only natural... And I am of the belief that my nation shares the same feeling. I believe that the nation will stifle such a development with a vengeance...

"It seems to me that these acts against the Alevis have been planned by certain groups and are easily exacerbated. They are aimed at triggering a Sunni-Alevi conflict. Rightminded individuals can respond with equanimity, and stifle such schemes with love and compassion. But the mood of the masses should not be ignored. Anarchy must not be used to oppose such anarchy. Otherwise, everyone would resort to using arms in their demand for justice, and if they insist upon self-enforcing their rights, all rights will have been violated. There is a state and there are security forces. Some may entertain different ideas about them, but they need to be trusted. The state needs to be trusted...."

If only Sultan Selim I had taken the path of diplomacy

Below is an extended excerpt from Gülen's June 2013 speech entitled, "Let us not burn bridges":

"I myself have questioned whether or not Yavuz (Selim) had the opportunity to use diplomacy instead of confrontation with Shah Ismail. If only he could have used diplomacy to the very end. If only he did not come down like a ton of bricks. If only the matter had not turned into hatred, animosity, and rancor."

Turkish Alevis objected to naming the recently built Bosporus Bridge after Sultan Selim I (Yavuz). Some Alevis even proposed Shah Ismail be the bridge's name.

Alevism in Turkey is more of a political problem than a religious one. There is no substantial reason as to why Alevis and Sunnis cannot live side by side in Turkey, where many diverse religious groups and sects coexisted for hundreds of years. Many problems inherited from the past are still leading to tensions. Turkey has to seriously consider Alevi demands and provide solutions for a fresh start. Since questions like religious sect or ethnicity are not asked during censuses in Turkey, the exact number Alevis and Kurds are not accurately known. For Alevis, estimates range from 5 to 10 million.

Alevis and Kurds are not considered minority groups in Turkey. In the Treaty of Lausanne, signed by Turkey and European countries,

Greeks, Armenians, and Jews are recognized under the minority status. In the case of Alevis and Kurds, Turkish administrations have failed to take the necessary steps to ensure their rights as equal citizens in the country.

Reha Çamuroğlu, a novelist and one of the leading Alevi intellectuals, was a consultant to Erdoğan and a member of parliament in 2007, when he helped the government form an initiative to solve the problems with the Alevi community. Many conferences and panels were organized to bring together scholars of religion, sociologists, political scientists, and Alevi community leaders. However, this initiative failed to produce any result, and Çamuroğlu left Erdoğan's party. Çamuroğlu thinks the annual cost of recognizing the Cemevis and sponsoring Dedes is not more than a couple million dollars. This huge problem, which could be solved by an insignificant amount of money, have gone unsolved for many years.

CHAPTER 11

MINORITIES AND THEIR RIGHTS

Minorities and Their Rights

Turkey has always had large minority populations, from Jews to Greeks and Armenians. The term "community" is generally used in reference to these groups. The Jewish community, the Greek community, the Armenian Community, and the like.

All the three communities were given minority status with the Treaty of Lausanne; any group not counted as a minority by the treaty do not have legal minority status in Turkey. The Treaty of Lausanne was signed by European countries and Turkey in 1923 (to be effective from 1924) in Switzerland. This treaty recognized Turkish independence and determined its current borders.

For this reason, the Assyrian community, whose numbers have fallen to several thousand today, are not counted as an official minority group. A person belonging to the Assyrian community possesses all of the rights of any other citizen of the Republic of Turkey. Likewise, Kurds and Alevis do not have official minority status.

Though there are large numbers of Kurds and Alevis in contemporary Turkey, the other groups are much smaller in number. This wasn't always the case. Up until the early years of the Republic, there were considerable Jewish, Armenian, and Greek populations in Turkey.

There was a serious decline in the Greek population due the population exchange with Greece, and in the Jewish population shrunk after the establishment of the State of Israel in 1948. After the violence directed at minorities in 1955, in Istanbul, in what has come to be known as the September 6-7 events, a further decline was seen in the population of all three communities.

Gülen's talks with leading figures in these minority communities during the dialogue, tolerance, and coexistence process he launched in 1994 have a special place in Hizmet's literature. They, as much as anything, have proven Hizmet's commitment to tolerance and dialogue.

Gülen first met with the Greek Patriarch Bartholomew, the religious leader of the Orthodox Church, in Istanbul, in April 1996. His meeting with the Pope, which attracted great attention not only in Turkey but also around the world, took place at the Vatican on February 9, 1998. During the same period, Gülen held meetings with Armenian Patriarch Mesrob Mutafyan and the leader of the Jewish community David Aseo.

Meeting with the Pope was an opportunity for dialogue

During a television program on NTV on February 27, 1998, he has discussed his visit to the Vatican:

"The Vatican's representative in Istanbul, Georges Marovitch, made serious efforts in this regard [on the meeting]. I found myself in the process. And I deemed saying no to something like this as disrespectful to the Pope, as the representative of a great religion in the Vatican. I could not reconcile it with the gentlemanliness of the Turkish nation. Such an opportunity arose and we were looking for dialogue in Turkey, so why shouldn't we take it up? But this has a beginning. Some people criticized the whole affair again after the meeting with Bartholomew. But he went to the United States and spoke of it there. Afterwards, we found the opportunity to meet with a cardinal there.

"We are meeting with the Jewish community here. We have very good dialogue. When I went to America for treatment I was staying in a modest home and due to what they too had related in America, the Jewish community came to meet with me there. They showed much interest. Let's support the schools you will open here, they said. Seeing that some people are talking about interreligious and intercivilizational clashes, we see this movement as a breakwater and we want to join you, they said. This issue was discussed in various platforms. This also brought the whole process of a meeting with the Pope our way.

"...Then they invited us, and we went. In fact, Marovitch was not going to come, but he accompanied us as an interpreter. I do not regret such a meeting. Were the opportunity to arise again, I would go once more. I even said to my friends when leaving, 'I can die, the Pope could die, but I think this process should continue.'"

We must think of good things for humanity

Three months after his meeting with the Pope at the Vatican on February 9, 1998, Gülen met with a group of Italian journalists on May 13, 1998. One journalist asked, "What is your evaluation of interreligious dialogue and the meeting with the Pope?" he responds in the following words:

"There is already a relationship between us. We visit them during religious festivals, or they visit us. We visit them on their holy days or holidays also. Coming together and eating together, these have always happened. In this respect, just as such a relationship with members of different religions has always been fostered, these kinds of relations continued before the meeting with the Pope at the Vatican also. For this reason, we agreed amongst ourselves that it would be good if the meeting took place.

"This was another step in the whole process. In other words, we essentially took steps on the path in which we have firm conviction, in the path of dialogue, and all these transpired as the requirements of this path. In the end, the meeting with the Pope at the Vatican took place so fast and so easily...

"In our contact with everyone, we meet with members of different religions on the basis of our own view that religions do not drive people away from each other, and to demonstrate that they maybe even bring people together and reconcile them."

We have to enter into dialogue with Buddhists and Brahmins

During this meeting at the Vatican, Gülen gave the Pope a letter. He explained both why he felt the need to give the Pope this letter and its contents to *Le Monde* correspondent Nicole Pope:

"The Pope is elderly, and may thus not be comfortable listening to every issue brought before him. So we decided to convey everything we wanted to discuss with him in the form of a letter, which we later presented to him... The letter focused mainly on such theories like the clash of civilizations and the clash of religions. I am of the opinion that such theories stem from misunderstandings or from certain intentions. But if there is such a thing, if this is indeed possible, then putting a set of breakwaters in place against it would not go amiss. If we come together in cooperation and join forces as those who believe, then the masses will look to us for guidance and direction.

"We could take important steps in the name of protecting the world against such potential conflict. I expressed my thoughts on this matter. I also suggested more frequent meetings. I presented joint projects in view of further enhancing mutual rapprochement. One case in point was the proposal to establish a university in Harran (Urfa, Turkey), where the major religions, especially the Abrahamic faiths Islam, Christianity, and Judaism, are taught. They received all of these very favorably.

"Furthermore, we indicated that we can lend assistance in matters where we can be of help; for instance, we said that should they wish to go to Palestine, we could go on a trip there together. I expressed these same sentiments at the Council also. I tried to express all my views, including Turkey's accession to the European Union."

In a program aired on NTV on February 27, 1998, Taha Akyol asked Gülen a question regarding his meeting with the Pope:

"The meeting with the Pope is important essentially in terms of interreligious dialogue. What do you expect from this interreligious dialogue? In other words, what would it matter if there was no interreligious dialogue, and we continued to see them as infidels, or they continued to see us as barbarians, as has been the case since the Crusades? Moreover, you were not content with interreligious dialogue, but also urged the Pope to strive for Turkey's accession to the European Union. I mean, you are such a religious leader, such a community leader, such a leader of an Islamic thought movement that you initiate a religious dialogue with the Pope and ask for Turkey's entry into the EU. Why?"

Let us now look at Gülen's response: "As it is known, there is talk recently of a clash of civilizations, which may take place in the future. And the future is being regarded as virtual bedlam. I explained this matter there too. I spoke to the Pope of those [people and ideas] behind this, their delusions, and their aspirations. When discussing these issues at the Council, before meeting the Pope, we had a longer meeting for about an hour and a half. They sent the transcript of these discussions to the Pope. We also presented these issues to the Pope himself.

"At the same time, I had a friend translate these into a letter in English from the night before, in case certain issues were forgotten. They became aware of everything and received all this with an unmatched cordiality. There have been dialogue initiatives to date, but for lack of dialogue to this extent, they found this matter novel.

"This issue of dialogue now is the dialogue between members of different faith traditions in any case. And this will be founded on the commonalities between them. There are many common aspects between us and the Old and New Testaments, and that we can come together using them. A great thinker of our age (Bediüzzaman) says that we must refrain, for the time being, from arguing over controversial issues. This bewildering time and its manifestations require this to be the case, as there are those who forever want to see the world's fate in this state of disarray and commotion. There are those who draw conclusions from their groundless fears, and to some extent wish to their desires and dreams in the shape of ideas. As a result, the People of the Book first need to come together, and this matter should then be taken to the members of other religions such as the Buddhists, Confucianists, and Brahmins.

"The Divine religions need to come first, as they tend to dominate in different parts of the world. When realizing such a dialogue within its theological dimension, and by putting forth of our common ground, and by presenting those people we respect, it will generate a centripetal force. We believe that the rest will follow naturally. I saw that they believe in this, too."

Being a leader of Muslims around the world

The Gülen-Pope meeting which made a great impact across the globe drew criticism from some circles in Turkey. There were even those who claimed that Gülen wanted to be the leader of the world's Muslims. Gülen gave the following answer to these criticisms in an interview published in *Aksiyon* magazine on June 6, 1998:

"I have no need for lobbying or behind-the-scene activities. But there is nothing more natural for me than entering, as a plain person, into dialogue with others that I believe will be beneficial to my country and mankind. There are no institutions or ranks of religious men in [Sunni] Islamic leadership like there are in Shi'ism or in some other religions.

"I have remained very far from any kind of leadership or desire for rank... a clash of civilizations, which is based on culture and religion, has been under public discussion and Turkey was mentioned as one of the central bases in this clash. During the last three or four years I have been in dialogue with representatives of other religions inside and outside of Turkey, even at the expense of occasionally receiving heavy criticisms from many radical Muslim groups at times. I've been trying to explain that Islam is not a religion of fighting, violence, and terror; to the contrary, it's based on principles of love, mercy, forgiveness, and leniency. I've been trying to show that there are the same principles in the foundation of every religion and that leaving aside the historical enmity among religions and starting a warm dialogue would make an important contribution towards realizing a better and more peaceful future for this world, which is tired of war and conflict."

In an interview published in the *Milliyet* daily on January 27, 2005, Gülen remarked: "When the Prophet came to Medina he issued the declaration of Medina, made a treaty with the people there, and took them under his protection... We can see that the Rightly Guided Caliphs followed the same path. Likewise, we know how Salahaddin Ayyubi, Zengi, and Alparslan behaved. The Ottoman Sultan, Bayezid II, brought the Jews who were persecuted in Spain to Istanbul by ship. The Foundation of the 500th Year was established in memory of this. The same tolerance was found during the Republican Era, and some of those fleeing the tyranny of the Nazis took refuge in Anatolia. This phenomenon exists within our culture. Under our rule, a mosque, a church, and a synagogue are side by side, and people lived without any problems.

"Thanks to dialogue, the process of presenting the glorious face of Islam – a face which has been darkened by suicide attacks and people who have been turned into robots through oppression – has started. And it will continue. The fact that the Prophet has been introduced as the founder of a religion whose members are terrorists is a grave injustice to his name. While there is the important duty awaiting the representatives of dialogue and tolerance of introducing God's Messenger correctly, the pursuit of different thoughts would mean destroying the positive impressions that have been created about the representatives, which is tantamount to treason.

"There were some people who visited me during the process of dialogue. We had a chance to meet in different environments. When we were together, the time for prayer came. They responded with respect when we asked them to excuse us. They said: 'Please, we will be praying here until you finish your prayer.'"

Dialogue and missionary activities

During an interview with the Italian daily *La Repubblica*, on March 28, 2014, Gülen was asked, "Some in Turkey and even around the world have regarded and interpreted your relationship with members of other religious traditions as compromising religion or as proselytizing;

they have produced many publications to this end. What do you say about this?"

Gülen responds: "Some have criticized dialogue as a vehicle of religious indoctrination, as a means for uniting all religions, or as compromising one's own religion. We have never viewed dialogue in this way and have not embarked upon it with such an intention. Far from it, we have seen it as a means for everyone to know one another as fellow human beings by adhering to their own religion first and foremost. [We also view it], as a means of searching for solutions to the common problems facing humanity, and as an opportunity to come together around lofty human values.... We have long learned about each other from others, while now by means of dialogue, we are coming face to face and learning about each other directly.

"In a world where globalization has brought us closer together, if we can seize this as an opportunity and willingly enter into human relations aimed at ensuring peace and harmony, then we can earn great rewards. There is the subconscious historical baggage, and there are the misconceptions and the prejudices. There are the pains that hang on from periods of war, colonialism, and struggles for independence. Historical events need to be left within their historical context and not carried to the present; a fresh new page needs to be opened and the past not resurrected. In response to the attempts of some to make religious differences a cause for disagreement and conflict, we seek, through dialogue, to know each other as human beings and to instill in hearts the understanding that every person needs to be held dear as a human being."

We see Gülen echoed the same views in his 2014 BBC and 2010 *New York Times* interviews. He said to the BBC, "We have met repeatedly with the Orthodox community and the Armenians in Turkey who have been pushed around and thrown aside. We have eaten at the same table with them and shared the same dishes. This door was opened for the first time, through the grace of God Almighty, by our friends" (BBC, January 27, 2014).

And while talking with the *New York Times*, he said the following:

"With Christians in all their different denominations, with Jews, Armenians and Greeks, we have developed sincere relationships, and we got to know each other on a personal level and visited each other to share ideas. Moreover, we started the dialogue initiatives and the notion of respecting people for who they are. Further down the road, state officials warmed up to the idea and even took ownership of the initiatives due to the universal appeal of the ideas. I am of the view that just as they have been emulated in Turkey, these dialogue activities will be emulated around the world over time. However, these kinds of overarching projects do not come into being in just five or ten years; it's not a simple house that you can fix in six months. Nonetheless, success is in the hands of God. We ask from Him and we wish from Him that people love each other and embrace each other" (From Brian Knowlton's interview with Gülen for the *New York Times*, June 11, 2010).

Prophet Muhammad's (pbuh) attitude towards Christians

Gülen has offered very important examples from Islam's history concerning the dialogue process with members of other religions. In his interview with *Zaman* newspaper in March of 2004, he described Prophet Muhammad's, peace be upon him, attitude towards non-Muslims in the following words:

"I have seen different people on this subject of tolerance and dialogue. There were some who had fallen into suspicion by saying, "'I wonder if I am doing good or not?'" But, at first, our Prophet behaved well towards Christians. The Caliph 'Umar had treated both Christians and Jews well when he conquered Palestine. Salah al-Din Ayyubi had treated them very well. When Fatih [Mehmed the Conqueror] conquered Istanbul, Orthodox believers and Armenians said, 'We have been freed from the barbarism that came from the West,' when they saw the tolerance and leniency of Muslims. On this subject, we have predecessors.

"After this generation, there are future generations. If you do not fill these gaps today, you will not be able to find the opportunity to express yourself, to share your right thoughts, tomorrow. Until now, with the gaps, we have always stayed at a distance from one another. We waited for them to come to us.... The matter is not so. The gaps should be filled. These are now the People of the Book. This is how the Qur'an calls them. Bediüzzaman interprets this Qur'anic description in a way that no one has done before; he calls them, 'O, People of the School.... ' 'You are educated ones. Come, let's unite around a single word: God'" (*Zaman*, March 30, 2004).

The Prophet Muhammad's (pbuh) relations with Christians and Jews show some of the best examples of peaceful engagement across faiths. A striking example was when he hosted the Christians from Najran in his mosque. Despite many such well-recorded accounts, some Muslims today do not look favorably on dialogue initiatives among Muslims and non-Muslims; they even consider it dangerous. Gülen pioneered such an initiative in the 1990s and met with all the Christian and Jewish religious leaders in Turkey. In 1998, when he went to the Vatican and met with the Pope, radical Islamists accused him of being a "secret cardinal." Despite all such attacks, Gülen did not change his approach and called on all Muslims to engage in dialogue with their non-Muslim neighbors.

'Ali: Our non-Muslim brethren in humanity

In an interview published in the Bulgarian daily *Trud* on October 15, 1996, Gülen was asked about the troubles between the Orthodox and Muslim communities in the Balkans, to which he responded:

"Religions are aimed not at dividing the people but bringing them together. There is more that is common and unifying between Islam and Orthodox Christianity than there is that separates them. Both religions speak of God, the Prophets, the angels, the Hereafter, and sacred scripture. Moral and legal concepts are the same in both religions. This is the truth. Those giving rise to conflict between the two religions are either those self-seekers who have forgotten God and are in pursuit of political benefits, or are misunderstood. It is declared clearly and unmistakably in the Qur'an: 'Come to a word common between us and you, that we worship none but God, and associate none as partner with Him.'

"This is a warning to those people who seek to make religions enemies of each other and who want to disseminate hostility. Whereas there are hundreds of bridges on which we can meet in agreement. In my opinion, the only common and effective language among people is provided through education. This is what we seek. Our stronghold is knowledge and science. We want to help people in the way of finding happiness in this fleeting world. And we would prefer this a million times more to being the sole masters of a single nation that has conquered all the others.

"'Ali, who holds an important place in our religion, said, 'The Muslims are brethren in faith, while non-Muslims are brethren in humanity.' Our humanity is exactly what the common denominator uniting us should be. To this end, the people must be educated in the spirit of respect for moral values, and their hearts should overflow with love towards their other brothers and sisters. Only in this way can we leave a happier and more prosperous world to present and future generations. This is the purpose of my life and my work."

Meeting with the Greek Orthodox Patriarch Bartholomew

Gülen described his meeting with the Fener Greek Orthodox Patriarch Bartholomew, in Istanbul in April 1996, in his interview with *Milliyet* newspaper on January 11, 2005:

"When I met him, he had the following demand: 'I am a Turkish citizen. I would like to be given the opportunity to have the Seminary re-opened, so that we can train our staff and send them off to the rest of the world from Turkey. It would be beneficial to Turkey if priests were trained in Turkey and within the Turkish culture.'

"Such a practice started with the Sultan Fatih (Mehmed II, the Conqueror) and has continued to our day; if this is going to be a solution (re-opening the Seminary) we should not make it a problem. Reacting with emotions or associating the matter with hostility is not suited to the Turkish nation, which has a mature, settled, and marvelous past. The ecumenical (universal patriarch) has been the top person of the patriarchate since the day it was established. Naturally, they are still using this title... You may disagree with their calling themselves 'ecumenical,' but this is how they have used the term up until now.

"Similarly, there are no titles like *hocaefendi* (teacher), *vaiz efendi* (preacher), or *mufti efendi*; but they are being used, as this is what people are used to. I don't ask to be called by such a title, but our people call me *hocaefendi*, too. This aspect of the matter should be taken into consideration."

In the May 13th, 1996 edition of *Zaman* newspaper, Fener Greek Orthodox Patriarch Bartholomew made the following remarks concerning his meeting with Gülen:

"We have been sending our staff members to the faculty of theology in Salonica since 1971. But nobody returns despite the fact that we grant them a scholarship. We are in a very difficult situation in this regard. We cannot raise new clergy. Until the closure of the seminary, we had students from Turkey as well as from other countries. Were we to reopen now, we would again enroll students from Turkey and abroad as we did before.

"The Patriarchate had sweeping powers until Lausanne. It had jurisdiction over education, the division of inheritance, and in family law. Its dealing only with religious issues was stipulated in Lausanne. But religious issues should not be understood as offering prayer in the church alone. Moral and spiritual problems, as well as social problems, should be addressed within the framework of our religious activity. These cannot be separated from religion. Whenever we express views on these matters, our views are misinterpreted.

"I used to watch Fethullah Hoca on television from time to time. This was the first time I had the opportunity to see him up close. Another aspect that impressed me greatly was his humility, his congeniality, and his lack of pride. He was exceedingly simple in his manner of dress, his speech, and his actions. This shows that he is a true man of religion, a man who attaches no importance to worldly values."

If schools were opened in Greece and Armenia

Gülen has made mention of schools being opened in Greece, Armenia, and Israel, all countries who have fraught relationships with Turkey. In an interview published in *Aksiyon* magazine on April 13, 1996, he expounded upon the issue:

"The road to friendship passes through here. People who know our ethos, our culture, and our history establish a ground for dialogue between the two countries. We can send students to Greece, and they can send students here. We are neighbors. We cannot become estranged. We will live side by side and share the same fate...

"On another occasion, I said that if Armenia were to soften, we could consider opening a school there too. This is how I see it... We want for us to get along without doing things that will cause mutual unease. We are all people of the same region, we are the people of Mesopotamia. According to sociologists, behind the Greek civilization and Hellenism are the Mesopotamian people, Eastern civilization."

The term "Christian" cannot be used as an insult

One of the questions put to Gülen on a Dutch television program on

October 19, 1995, was, "Were Turkey today to be a country governed in accordance with Islamic law, would the lifestyles of Muslims and non-Muslims be as they were 14 centuries ago; or in other words, would the concept of *dhimmi* be used, or would they be more in congruence with contemporary conditions?"

Gülen offered the following answer to this question:

"The use of the term or title *dhimmi* is a historical circumstance. This issue is a historical one. The principle underlying the notion is an acceptance of such people within their own legal systems, their own understandings, their own thoughts, their freedom of religion/belief/work/trade/enterprise, and their own assumptions. As an expression of such acceptance, the State, at the time, took them under protection. They were referred to as *dhimmi* due to their protected status. This is an Arabic word.

"But, if we are now to accept them with their own respective positions, whatever their own laws and system, if we are to embrace them with tolerance, and if Islam decrees this, then a name or title cannot at all be spoken of. Names and titles are historical details. Referring to them as *dhimmi*... Especially if this is being used in the form of an insult, it can never be used. For that matter, even if they were to consider using 'Christian' as an insult, then this would also be unacceptable.

"This is what Islam commands, what the Messenger of God commands. On the issue of saying unbeliever (*kafir*), an unbeliever is someone who does not accept God and, as such, an atheist is an unbeliever. If such a person regards being called an unbeliever as an insult, then we cannot call them an unbeliever. This is the attitude that we need to adopt in the name of Islam, and what such an attitude requires. This is the expression of our own education and upbringing. This is our manner and way. Thus, to some extent, perhaps contemporary conditions will be taken into consideration with the utmost sensitivity, and no one will be offended.

"If only we could live with that boundlessness as it was understood by the Messenger of God himself. If only we could live with the all-embracing disposition of the Rightly Guided Caliphs. Yes, these are things that are longed for.

"But... pertaining to the details, in two-sided matters such as this, agreements can be reached taking into account their laws and their understandings. It cannot be one-sided. In this respect, [in comparing] the Ottoman state with the thought that destroyed earlier Islamic administrations, thinkers and commentators assert from a philosophical stand-point that the former were secular. There was no breakdown for four centuries. This is not something that can be achieved with a police state or police forces."

"Whereas, previously [during the Ottoman period], getting to any incident that erupted in Timbuktu would take 3 months on horseback [but peace was established with no need to be a police state]. This goes to show how profound the human dimensions of the matter really were. Everyone was truly content with their situation. And we understand this much better today. It can be argued that the collapse of a state [the Otto-mans], in that golden age which represented truth and justice alongside strength and power in the balance of power between states, has con-founded the general harmony in this region."

Whoever hurts a non-Muslim hurts God's Messenger

In Muslim-majority countries, the term usually employed in reference to minorities is "non-Muslim," in reference to their religious identity. In the same televized interview, in the Netherlands, Gülen was asked, "What are your thoughts on non-Muslims?" His answer reads as follows:

"The Messenger of God said while on his deathbed, 'Whoever hurts a *dhimmi* (non-Muslim) hurts me.' That is to say, because they have accepted our administration, they have in a sense taken refuge in our justie and fairness. If you do an injustice to them, you would have done an injustice to me. In other words, this is not a thought or expression that the Prophet merely expressed out of his mercy and compassion [it is a matter of justice].

"In the last moments before his death 'Umar said, 'I entrust the *dhimmis* to your care and protection.' *Dhimmi*s are of the two things he entrusts his community with. Muslim conquerors came to a country and they came to an agreement and understanding. They paid *jizya*, or cap-itation tax, as a tithe; it was the same amount that the Muslims gave in the alms-tax. And they came under the protection of the Muslims. This practice was certified in the pacts signed at various times. When the Muslim conquerors came to Aleppo, for example, or Damascus and Homs, they encountered the Christians. When the Christians became acquainted with the Muslims, they accepted their protection.

"Maulana Shibli states in his extensive study of the Age of Happiness that when Heraclius came all the way to Antioch with his invincible armies, Abu 'Ubayda, who was in Damascus at the time, had taken the Christians under protection having levied the *jizya* upon them. But when he realized that he could not resist such a force, he summoned the Christian elders and told them that he could not protect them. He said that this is why he had levied the tax, proportional to the alms-tax, in the first instance – to protect them. He ordered them to come and collect it as he would have done them an injustice if they had not. He reimbursed the full amount and thus retreated. The Christians then filled the churches and wept, exclaiming, 'May God enable your return!' Here there is approval for a particular administration, there is acceptance. The same thing was experienced at the beginning of the Ottoman state. Just consider how tolerant they were.

"For example, there were great Christian figures among the *akıncı* (frontier light cavalry) beys. Evranos did not change his name and was recorded in our history as such. Then there is Zaganos Pasha. Mosques and bridges were built in their name. Those who are familiar with Edirne and Istanbul will know Ghazi Mihal, for instance. Those who fought alongside Osman Ghazi. There was such tolerance and acceptance that these people were in no way forced [to serve]. If they had been forced, there would have been no Christians remaining where the Ottomans went in the name of Islam. In this respect, it can be said that the religion really was very flexible and lenient on the subject of the *dhimma*, or pact of protection, and as it already encompasses the embracing of all humanity in its principles and universality, it embraced the Jews as well as the Christians.

"So long as they did not violate this agreement or engage in unilateral treaty violations, Islam never denounced this pact. Whatever was its stance and response when its own citizens revolted, that's exactly the stance and treatment it displayed when others violated the *dhimma* covenant, being perhaps even more tolerant."

Demolishing Istanbul's ancient walls has nothing to do with religion

In 1995, some figures from the political arena spoke of demolishing Istanbul's historic city walls. The walls that surround the old peninsular part of Istanbul are among the most prominent landmarks in the city. Erdoğan was elected mayor of Istanbul in 1994, and many of the candidates from his party came to office in local administrations. One of the topics they brought up was to uproot the city's Christian and Byzantine heritage, and that is why they proposed demolishing the walls. Unfortunately, this mindset still persists today, as we saw the destruction of Buddha statues in Afghanistan by the Taliban and the demolition of Palmyra in Syria by ISIS. This is a manifestation of intolerance. Other civilizations have a right to exist, and it is so disappointing to see that these groups think they are destroying in the name of Islam. Gülen's reaction was as follows:

"Fatih (Mehmed II, the Conqueror), who was a lot more religious than us, did not demolish the ancient city walls when he conquered Istanbul. The city walls have been standing for five centuries. There is no such custom in our nation as destroying history, or tearing down the monuments of others. Troy still stands. As concerns Hellenism, when going from here towards Salihli, the ancient ruins of Sardis are still standing.

"It would be very wrong to claim that these had anything to do with religion. I am elucidating in reference to *hadith* criteria. ... There are so many Prophetic Traditions for a restructuring. Were there to be an Ottoman tolerance in the world today, it seems to me an excellent ground for dialogue would be prepared not just for Muslims, but simultaneously for all humanity. Being thus open to such a dialogue in an increasingly globalizing world is a crucial factor" (From an interview published in *Hürriyet* newspaper on January 26, 1995).

GÜLEN'S RECENT ARTICLES ON TURKEY, THE COUP ATTEMPT, AND DENOUNCEMENT OF TERRORISM

Appendix

Turkey's Eroding Democracy

by Fethullah Gulen

The New York Times, February 3, 2015

It is deeply disappointing to see what has become of Turkey in the last few years. Not long ago, it was the envy of Muslim-majority countries: a viable candidate for the European Union on its path to becoming a functioning democracy that upholds universal human rights, gender equality, the rule of law and the rights of Kurdish and non-Muslim citizens. This historic opportunity now appears to have been squandered as Turkey's ruling party, known as the A.K.P., reverses that progress and clamps down on civil society, media, the judiciary and free enterprise.

Turkey's current leaders seem to claim an absolute mandate by virtue of winning elections. But victory doesn't grant them permission to ignore the Constitution or suppress dissent, especially when election victories are built on crony capitalism and media subservience. The A.K.P.'s leaders now depict every democratic criticism of them as an attack on the state. By viewing every critical voice as an enemy — or worse, a traitor — they are leading the country toward totalitarianism.

The latest victims of the clampdown are the staff, executives and editors of independent media organizations who were detained and are now facing charges made possible by recent changes to the laws and the court system. The director of one of the most popular TV channels, arrested in December, is still behind bars. Public officials investigating corruption charges have also been purged and jailed for simply doing their jobs. An independent judiciary, a functioning civil society and media are checks and balances against government transgressions. Such harassment sends the message that whoever stands in the way of the ruling party's agenda will be targeted by slander, sanctions and even trumped-up charges.

Turkey's rulers have not only alienated the West, they are also now losing credibility in the Middle East. Turkey's ability to assert positive influence in the region depends not only on its economy but also on the health of its own democracy.

The core tenets of a functioning democracy — the rule of law, respect for individual freedoms — are also the most basic of Islamic values bestowed upon us by God. No political or religious leader has the authority to take them away. It is disheartening to see religious scholars provide theological justification for the ruling party's oppression and corruption or simply stay silent. Those who use the language and symbols of religious observance but violate the core principles of their religion do not deserve such loyalty from religious scholars.

Speaking against oppression is a democratic right, a civic duty and for believers, a religious obligation. The Quran makes clear that people should not remain silent in the face of injustice: "O you who believe! Be upholders and standard-bearers of justice, bearing witness to the truth for God's sake, even though it be against your own selves, or parents or kindred."

For the past 50 years, I have been fortunate to take part in a civil society movement, sometimes referred to as Hizmet, whose participants and supporters include millions of Turkish citizens. These citizens have committed themselves to interfaith dialogue, community service, relief efforts and making life-changing education accessible. They have established more than 1,000 modern secular schools, tutoring centers, colleges, hospitals and relief organizations in over 150 countries. They are teachers, journalists, businessmen and ordinary citizens.

The rhetoric used by the ruling party repeatedly to crack down on Hizmet participants is nothing but a pretext to justify their own authoritarianism. Hizmet participants have never formed a political party nor have they pursued political ambitions. Their participation in the movement is driven by intrinsic rewards, not extrinsic ones.

I have spent over 50 years preaching and teaching the values of peace, mutual respect and altruism. I've advocated for education, community service and interfaith dialogue. I have always believed in seeking happiness in the happiness of others and the virtue of seeking God's pleasure in helping His people. Whatever influence is attributed to me, I have used it as a means to promote educational and social projects that help nurture virtuous individuals. I have no interest in political power.

Many Hizmet participants, including me, once supported the ruling party's agenda, including the 2005 opening of accession negotiations with the European Union. Our support then was based on principle, as is our criticism today. It is our right and duty to speak out about government policies that have a deep impact on society. Unfortunately, our democratic expression against public corruption and authoritarianism has made us victims of a witch-hunt; both the Hizmet movement and I are being targeted with hate speech, media smear campaigns and legal harassment.

Like all segments of Turkish society, Hizmet participants have a presence in government organizations and in the private sector. These citizens cannot be denied their constitutional rights or be subjected to discrimination for their sympathy to Hizmet's ideals, as long as they abide by the laws of the country, the rules of their institutions and basic ethical principles. Profiling any segment of society and viewing them as a threat is a sign of intolerance.

We are not the only victims of the A.K.P.'s crackdown. Peaceful environmental protesters, Kurds, Alevis, non-Muslim citizens and some Sunni Muslim groups not aligned with the ruling party have suffered, too. Without checks and balances, no individual or group is safe from the ruling party's wrath. Regardless of their religious observance, citizens can and should unite around universal human rights and freedoms, and democratically oppose those who violate them.

Turkey has now reached a point where democracy and human rights have almost been shelved. I hope and pray that those in power reverse their current domineering path. In the past the Turkish people have rejected elected leaders who strayed from a democratic path. I hope they will exercise their legal and democratic rights again to reclaim the future of their country.

Muslims Must Combat the Extremist Cancer

by Fethullah Gülen
Wall Street Journal, August 27, 2015

As the group that calls itself Islamic State, known as ISIS, continues to produce carnage in the Middle East, Muslims must confront the totalitarian ideology that animates it and other terrorist groups. Every terrorist act carried out in the name of Islam profoundly affects all Muslims, alienating them from fellow citizens and deepening the misperceptions about their faith's ethos.

It isn't fair to blame Islam for the atrocities of violent radicals. But when terrorists claim the Muslim mantle, then they bear this identity, if only nominally. Thus members of the faith must do whatever possible to prevent this cancer from metastasizing in our communities. If we don't, we'll be partly responsible for the smeared image of our faith.

First, we must denounce violence and not fall prey to victimhood. Having suffered oppression is no excuse for causing it or for failing to condemn terrorism. That the terrorists are committing grave sins in the name of Islam is not merely my opinion; it is the inevitable conclusion of an honest reading of primary sources: the Quran and the accounts of the life of Prophet Muhammad. The core principles of these sources—relayed over the centuries by scholars who devoted themselves to studying the Prophet's sayings and practices, and to the "author's intent" in the Holy Book—dispels any claims terrorists make of religious justification.

Second, it is important to promote a holistic understanding of Islam, as the flexibility to accommodate the diverse backgrounds of its adherents can sometimes be abused. Islam's core ethics, however, are not left to interpretation. One such principle is that taking the life of a single innocent is a crime against all humanity (Quran 5:32). Even in an act of defense in war, violence against any noncombatants, especially women, children and clergy, is specifically prohibited by the Prophet's teachings.

We must demonstrate these values by showing solidarity with people who seek peace around the world. Given the nature of human psychology and the dynamics of the news, it's obvious that mainstream voices are less likely to capture headlines than extremist ones. But instead of blaming the media, we should find innovative ways to ensure our voices are heard.

Third, Muslims must publicly promote human rights—dignity, life and liberty. These are the most basic of Islamic values and no individual, nor any political or religious leader, has the authority to snatch them away. Living the essence of our faith means respecting diversity—cultural, social, religious and political. God identifies learning from one another as the primary goal of diversity (Quran 49:13). Respecting each human being as a creation of God (17:70) is respecting God.

Fourth, Muslims must provide educational opportunities to every member of their communities, where the study of sciences, humanities and arts is embedded in a culture of respect for every living being. Governments in the Muslim world must design school curricula that nurture democratic values. Civil society has a role in promoting respect and acceptance. This is the reason participants of the Hizmet movement have set up more than 1,000 schools, tutoring centers and dialogue institutions in more than 150 countries.

Fifth, providing religious education to Muslims is critical to depriving extremists of a tool that they use to spread their twisted ideologies. When religious freedom is denied, as it has been for decades in parts of the Muslim world, faith grows in the shadows, leaving it to be interpreted by unqualified and radical figures.

Finally, it is imperative that Muslims support equal rights for women and men. Women should be given opportunity and be free from social pressures that deny their equality. Muslims have a great example in Prophet Muhammad's wife Aisha, a highly educated scholar, teacher and prominent community leader of her time.

Terrorism is a multifaceted problem, so the solutions should address the political, economic, social and religious layers. Approaches that reduce the problem to religion do a disservice to at-risk youth and the world at large. The international community would do well to realize that Muslims are the primary victims of terrorism—both literally and symbolically—and they can help marginalize terrorists and prevent recruitment. That's why governments should avoid statements and actions that result in the alienation of Muslims.

Violent extremism has no religion; there will always be people who manipulate faith texts. Just as Christians do not endorse Quran burnings or the actions of the Ku Klux Klan, and Buddhists do not endorse atrocities against Rohingya Muslims, mainstream Muslims do not endorse violence.

Muslims have historically added much to the flourishing of human civilization. Our greatest contributions were made in eras when the faith cherished mutual respect, freedom and justice. It may be immensely difficult to restore the blotted image of Islam, but Muslims can be beacons of peace and tranquility in their societies.

Muslims, We Have to Critically Review Our Understanding of Islam

by Fethullah Gülen
Le Monde, December 17, 2015

Words fall short to truly express my deep sadness and revolt in the face of the carnage perpetrated by terrorist groups such as the so-called ISIS. I share a profound frustration with a billion and a half Muslims around the world at the fact that such groups commit terror while dressing up their perverted ideologies as religion. We Muslims have a special responsibility to not only join hands with fellow human beings to save our world from the scourge of terrorism and violent extremism, but also to help repair the tarnished image of our faith.

It is easy to proclaim a certain identity in the abstract with words and symbols. The sincerity of such claims, however, can only be measured by comparing our actions with core values of our self-proclaimed identities. The true test for belief is not slogans or dressing up in a certain way; the true test of our beliefs is in living up to core principles shared by all major world faiths such as upholding the sanctity of life and respecting the dignity of all humans.

We must categorically condemn the ideology that terrorists propagate and instead promote a pluralistic mindset with clarity and confidence. After all, before our ethnic, national or religious identity comes our common humanity, which suffers a setback each time a barbaric act is committed. French citizens who lost their lives in Paris, Shiite Muslim Lebanese citizens who lost their lives in Beirut a day earlier and scores of Sunni Muslims in Iraq who lost their lives in the hands of the same terrorists are first and foremost human beings. Our civilization will not progress until we treat the suffering of humans regardless of their religious or ethnic identity as equally tragic in our empathy and respond with the same determination.

Muslims must also reject and avoid conspiracy theories, which have so far only helped us avoid facing our social problems. Instead, we must tackle the real questions: do our communities provide recruitment ground for groups with totalitarian mindsets due to unrecognized authoritarianism within ourselves, domestic physical abuse, neglect of youth, lack of balanced education? Did our failure to establish basic human rights and freedoms, supremacy of the rule of law, and pluralist mindsets in our communities lead those who are struggling to seek alternative paths?

The recent tragedy in Paris is yet another reminder for both theologians and ordinary Muslims to strongly reject and condemn barbaric acts perpetrated in the name of our religion. However, at this juncture, rejection and condemnation are not enough; terrorist recruitment within Muslim communities must be fought and countered by an effective collaboration of state authorities, religious leaders and civil society actors. We must organize community-wide efforts to address all factors that aid terrorist recruitment.

Ways of expressing support and dissent within democratic means

We need to work with our community to set up the necessary framework for identifying at-risk youth, preventing them from seeking self-destructive paths, assisting families with counseling and other support services. We must promote a proactive, positive government engagement so that engaged Muslim citizens can sit at the table where counterterrorism measures are planned and share their ideas. Our youth should be taught ways of expressing support and dissent within democratic means. Incorporation of democratic values into school curricula early on is crucial for inculcating a culture of democracy in young minds.

In the aftermath of such tragedies, historically strong reactions have surfaced. Anti-Muslim and anti-religious sentiment as well as governments' security-driven treatment of their Muslim citizens would be counter-productive. The Muslim citizens of Europe want to live in peace and tranquility. Despite the negative climate, they should strive to engage more with their local and national governments to help work toward more inclusive policies that better integrate their community into the larger society.

It is also important for us Muslims to critically review our understanding and practice of Islam, in the light of the conditions and requirements of our age and the clarifications provided by our collective historic experiences. This does not mean a rupture from the cumulative Islamic tradition but rather, an intelligent questioning so we can confirm the true teachings of the Qur'an and the Prophetic tradition that our Muslim predecessors attempted to reveal.

We must proactively marginalize de-contextualized reading of our religious sources that have been employed in the service of perverted ideologies. Muslim thinkers and intellectuals should encourage a holistic approach and reconsider jurisprudential verdicts of the Middle Ages that were issued under perpetual conflict where religious affiliation often coincided with political affiliation. Having core beliefs should be distinguished from dogmatism. It is possible, indeed absolutely necessary, to revive the spirit of freedom of thought that gave birth to a renaissance of Islam while staying true to the ethos of the religion. Only in such an atmosphere can Muslims effectively combat incivility and violent extremism.

In the aftermath of the recent events I witness, with chagrin, the revival of the thesis of the clash of civilizations. I do not know whether those who first put out such a hypothesis did so out of vision or desire. What is certain is that today, the revival of this rhetoric simply serves the recruitment efforts of the terrorist networks. I want to state clearly that what we are witnessing is not a clash of civilizations but rather the clash of our common civilization as humanity with barbarity.

Our responsibility as Muslim citizens is to be part of the solution despite our grievances. If we want to defend the life and civil liberties of Muslims around the world, and the peace and tranquility of every human regardless of their faith, we must act now to tackle the violent extremism problem in all its dimensions: political, economic, social and religious. By setting virtuous examples through our lives, by discrediting and marginalizing the extremist interpretations of religious sources, by staying vigilant toward their impact on our youth, and by incorporating democratic values early in education, we can counter violence and terrorism as well as totalitarian ideologies that lead to them.

I Condemn All Threats to Turkey's Democracy

by Fethullah Gülen
The New York Times, July 25, 2016

During the attempted military coup in Turkey this month, I condemned it in the strongest terms. "Government should be won through a process of free and fair elections, not force," I said. "I pray to God for Turkey, for Turkish citizens, and for all those currently in Turkey that this situation is resolved peacefully and quickly."

Despite my unequivocal protest, similar to statements issued by all three of the major opposition parties, Turkey's increasingly authoritarian president, Recep Tayyip Erdoğan, immediately accused me of orchestrating the putsch. He demanded that the United States extradite me from my home in Pennsylvania, where I have lived in voluntary exile since 1999.

Not only does Mr. Erdogan's suggestion run afoul of everything I believe in, it is also irresponsible and wrong.

My philosophy — inclusive and pluralist Islam, dedicated to service to human beings from every faith — is antithetical to armed rebellion. For more than 40 years, the participants in the movement that I am associated with — called Hizmet, the Turkish word for "service" — have advocated for, and demonstrated their commitment to, a form of government that derives its legitimacy from the will of the people and that respects the rights of all citizens regardless of their religious views, political affiliations or ethnic origins. Entrepreneurs and volunteers inspired by Hizmet's values have invested in modern education and community service in more than 150 countries.

At a time when Western democracies are searching for moderate Muslim voices, I and my friends in the Hizmet movement have taken a clear stance against extremist violence, from the Sept. 11 attacks by Al Qaeda to brutal executions by the Islamic State to the kidnappings by Boko Haram.

In addition to condemning mindless violence, including during the coup attempt, we have emphasized our commitment to preventing terrorists' recruitment from among Muslim youth and nurturing a peaceful, pluralist mind-set.

Throughout my life, I have publicly and privately denounced military interventions in domestic politics. In fact, I have been advocating for democracy for decades. Having suffered through four military coups in four decades in Turkey — and having been subjected by those military regimes to harassment and wrongful imprisonment — I would never want my fellow citizens to endure such an ordeal again. If somebody who appears to be a Hizmet sympathizer has been involved in an attempted coup, he betrays my ideals.

Nevertheless, Mr. Erdogan's accusation is no surprise, not for what it says about me but rather for what it reveals about his systematic and dangerous drive toward one-man rule.

Like many Turkish citizens, the Hizmet movement's participants supported Mr. Erdogan's early efforts to democratize Turkey and fulfill the requirements for membership in the European Union. But we were not silent as he turned from democracy to despotism. Even before these new purges, Mr. Erdogan in recent years has arbitrarily closed newspapers; removed thousands of judges, prosecutors, police officers and civil servants from their positions; and taken especially harsh measures against Kurdish communities. He has declared his detractors enemies of the state.

Hizmet, in particular, has been the target of the president's wrath. In 2013, Mr. Erdogan blamed Hizmet sympathizers within the Turkish bureaucracy for initiating a corruption investigation that implicated members of his cabinet and other close associates. As a result, scores of members of the judiciary and the police forces were purged or arrested for simply doing their jobs.

Since 2014, when Mr. Erdogan was elected president after 11 years as prime minister, he has sought to transform Turkey from a parliamentary democracy into an "executive presidency," essentially without checks on his power. In that context, Mr. Erdogan's recent statement that the failed coup was a "gift from God" is ominous. As he seeks to purge still more dissenters from government agencies — nearly 70,000 people have been fired so far — and to crack down further on Hizmet and other civil society organizations, he is removing many of the remaining impediments to absolute power. Amnesty International has revealed "credible" reports of torture, including rape, at detention centers. No wonder Mr. Erdogan's government suspended the European Convention on Human Rights and declared a state of emergency.

Turkey's president is blackmailing the United States by threatening to curb his country's support for the international coalition against the Islamic State. His goal: to ensure my extradition, despite a lack of credible evidence and virtually no prospect for a fair trial. The temptation to give Mr. Erdogan whatever he wants is understandable. But the United States must resist it.

Violent extremism feeds on the frustrations of those forced to live under dictators who cannot be challenged by peaceful protests and democratic politics. In Turkey, the Erdogan government's shift toward a dictatorship is polarizing the population along sectarian, political, religious and ethnic lines, fueling the fanatics.

For the sake of worldwide efforts to restore peace in turbulent times, as well as to safeguard the future of democracy in the Middle East, the United States must not accommodate an autocrat who is turning a failed putsch into a slow-motion coup of his own against constitutional government.

I Call for an International Investigation
into the Failed Putsch in Turkey

by Fethullah Gülen
Le Monde, August 10, 2016

On the night of July 15, Turkey went through the most catastrophic trag-edy in its recent history as a result of the attempted military coup. The events of that night could be called a serious terror coup.

Turkish people from all walks of life who thought the era of mil-itary coups was over showed solidarity against the coup and stood on the side of democracy. While the coup attempt was in progress, I con-demned it in the strongest terms.

Twenty minutes after the military coup attempt surfaced, before the real actors were known, President Erdogan hastily blamed me. It is troubling that an accusation was issued without waiting for the event's details and the perpetrators' motives to emerge. As someone who has suffered through four coups in the last 50 years, it is especially insult-ing to be associated with a coup attempt. I categorically reject such accusations.

I have been living a reclusive life in self-exile in a small town in the United States for the last 17 years. The assertion that I convinced the eighth largest army in the world — from 6,000 miles away — to act against its own government is not only baseless, it is false, and has not resonated throughout the world.

If there are any officers among the coup plotters who consider themselves as a sympathizer of Hizmet movement, in my opinion those people committed treason against the unity of their country by taking part in an event where their own citizens lost their lives. They also violat-ed the values that I have cherished throughout my life, and caused hun-dreds of thousands of innocent people to suffer under the government's oppressive treatment.

If there are those who acted under the influence of an interven-tionist culture that persists among some of the military officers and have put these interventionist reflexes before Hizmet values, which I believe is unlikely, then an entire movement cannot be blamed for the wrongdo-ings of those individuals. I leave them to God's judgment.

No one is above the rule of law, myself included. I would like for those who are responsible for this coup attempt, regardless of their identities, to receive the punishment they deserve if found guilty in a fair trial. The Turkish judiciary has been politicized and controlled by the government since 2014 and, consequently, the possibility of a fair trial is very small. For this reason, I have advocated several times for the establishment of an international commission to investigate the coup attempt and I have expressed my commitment to abide by the findings of such a commission.

Hizmet movement participants have not been involved in one single violent incident throughout its 50-year history. They haven't even taken to the streets to confront Turkish security forces while they have been suffering under the government's "witch hunt," to use Mr. Erdoğan's own words, for the last three years.

Despite being subjected to a smear campaign and suffering under state oppression for the last three years in the hands of a politically controlled law enforcement and the judiciary, Hizmet movement participants have complied with the law, opposed injustices through legitimate means and only defended their rights within the legal framework.

Turkey's legal and law enforcement agencies have been mobilized for the last three years to investigate and reveal an alleged "parallel state" that they claim that I run.

The administration called the 2013 public corruption probe an organized attempt by Hizmet sympathizers within the bureaucracy to bring down the government. Despite detaining 4,000 people, purging tens of thousands of government employees and unlawfully seizing hundreds of NGOs and private businesses, authorities were unable to find a single piece of credible evidence to prove their claims.

Turkey's prime minister called an opportunity to meet with me "heaven-sent" in May 2013; however, after the public corruption probe emerged in December 2013, he began using hate language such as "assassins" and "blood sucking vampires" when referring to Hizmet movement participants.

After the treasonous coup attempt of July 15, the attacks have become unbearable. Turkish government officials also began referring to me and people sympathetic to my views as a "virus" and "cancer cells that need to be wiped out." Hundreds of thousands of people that have supported institutions and organizations affiliated with the Hizmet movement have been dehumanized in one way or another.

Their private properties have been confiscated, bank accounts taken over and their passports cancelled, restricting their freedom of travel. Hundreds of thousands of families are living through a humanitarian tragedy due to this ongoing witch hunt. News reports show that nearly 90,000 individuals have been purged from their jobs and 21,000 teachers' teaching licenses have been revoked.

Is the Turkish government forcing these families to starve to death by preventing them from working and prohibiting them from leaving the country? What is the difference between this treatment and the pre-genocide practices throughout European history?

I've witnessed every single military coup in Turkey and, like many other Turkish citizens, have suffered during and after each one. I was imprisoned by the order of the junta administration after the March 12, 1971 coup. After the coup of September 12, 1980, a detention warrant was issued against me and I lived as a fugitive for six years.

Right after the February 28, 1997, post-modern military coup, a lawsuit asking for capital punishment was filed against me with the charge of "an unarmed terrorist organization consisting of one person."

During all of these oppressive, military-dominated administrations, three cases accusing me of "leading a terror organization" were opened and, in each case, I was cleared of the charges. I was targeted by the authoritarian military administrations back then, and now, I face the very same accusations projected in an even more unlawful manner by a civilian autocratic regime.

I had friendly relations with leaders from various political parties, such as Mr. Turgut Ozal, Mr. Suleyman Demirel and Mr. Bulent Ecevit, and genuinely supported their policies that I found to be beneficial to the larger community. They treated me with respect, especially when recognizing Hizmet activities that contribute to social peace and education.

Even though I distanced myself from the idea of political Islam, I praised the democratic reforms undertaken by Mr. Erdogan and AKP leaders during their first term in power.

But throughout my life, I have stood against military coups and intervention in domestic politics. When I declared 20 years ago that "there is no turning back from democracy and secularism of the state," I was accused and insulted by the same political Islamists who are close to the current administration. I still stand behind my words. More than 70 books based on my articles and sermons spanning 40 years are publicly available. Not only is there not a single expression that legitimizes the idea of a coup in these works, but, on the contrary, they discuss universal human values that are the foundation of democracy.

Emancipating Turkey from the vicious cycle of authoritarianism is possible only through the adoption of a democratic culture and a merit-based administration. Neither a military coup nor a civilian autocracy is a solution.

Unfortunately, in a country where independent media outlets are shut down or taken under government custody, a significant portion of Turkish citizens were made to believe — through relentless pro-government propaganda — that I am the actor behind the July 15 coup. However, world opinion, which is shaped by objective information, clearly sees that what is going on is a power grab by the administration under the guise of a witch-hunt.

Of course, what matters is not majority opinion but the truths that will emerge through the process of a fair trial. Tens of thousands of people, including myself, who have been the target of such gross accusations, would like to clear our names through a fair judicial process. We do not want to live with this suspicion that was cast on us. Unfortunately, the government has exerted political control over the judiciary since 2014, thereby destroying the opportunity for Hizmet sympathizers to clear their names of these accusations.

I openly call on the Turkish government to allow for an international commission to investigate the coup attempt, and promise my full cooperation in this matter. If the commission finds one-tenth of the accusations against me to be justified, I am ready to return to Turkey and receive the harshest punishment.

Participants in the Hizmet movement have been overseen by hundreds of governments, intelligence agencies, researchers or independent civil society organizations for 25 years and have never been found to be involved in illegal activity. For this reason, many countries do not take seriously the accusations of the Turkish government.

The most important characteristic of the Hizmet movement is to not to seek political power, but instead to seek long-term solutions for the problems threatening the future of their societies. At a time when

Muslim-majority societies are featured in the news for terror, bloodshed and underdevelopment, Hizmet participants have been focusing on raising educated generations who are open to dialogue and actively contributing to their societies.

Since I have always believed that the biggest problems facing these societies are ignorance, intolerance-driven conflicts and poverty, I have always encouraged those who would listen to build schools instead of mosques or Quran tutoring centers.

Hizmet participants are active in education, health care and humanitarian aid not only in Turkey, but also in more than 160 countries around the world. The most significant characteristic of these activities is that they serve people of all religions and ethnic backgrounds - not just Muslims.

Hizmet movement participants opened schools for girls in the most difficult areas of Pakistan and continued to provide education in the Central African Republic during the country's civil war. While Boko Haram took young girls hostage in Nigeria, Hizmet participants opened schools that educated girls and women. In France and the French-speaking world, I have encouraged people who share my ideas and values to fight against groups that embrace radical Islamic ideologies and to support the authorities in this struggle. In these countries, I strived for Muslims to be recognized as free and contributing members of society, and have urged them to become part of the solution rather than be associated with the problems.

Despite receiving threats, I categorically condemned numerous times terrorist groups such as Al Qaida and ISIS who taint the bright face of Islam. However, the Turkish government is trying to convince governments around the world to act against schools that have been opened by individuals who did not take part in the July 15 coup attempt, and who have always categorically rejected violence. My appeal to governments around the world is that they ignore the Turkish government's claims and reject its irrational demands.

Indeed, the Turkish government's political decision to designate the Hizmet movement as a terrorist organization resulted in the closure of institutions such as schools, hospitals and relief organizations. Those who have been jailed are teachers, entrepreneurs, doctors, academics and journalists. The government did not produce any evidence to show that the hundreds of thousands targeted in the government's witch hunt supported the coup or that they were associated with any violence.

It is impossible to justify actions such as burning down a cultural center in Paris, detaining or holding hostage family members of wanted individuals, denying detained journalists access to medical care, shutting down 35 hospitals and the humanitarian relief organization Kimse Yok Mu, or forcing 1,500 university deans to resign as part of a post-coup investigation.

It appears that, by presenting the recent purges as efforts that target only Hizmet participants, the Turkish government is in fact removing anyone from the bureaucracy who is not loyal to the ruling party, while also intimidating civil society organizations. It is dreadful to see human rights violations occurring in Turkey, including the torture detailed in recent reports by Amnesty International. This is truly a human tragedy.

The fact that the July 15 coup attempt — which was an anti-democratic intervention against an elected government — was foiled with Turkish citizens' support is historically significant. However, the coup's failure does not mean a victory for democracy. Neither the domination by a minority nor the domination of a majority that results in the oppression of a minority nor the rule of an elected autocrat is a true democracy.

One cannot speak of democracy in the absence of the rule of law, separation of powers and essential human rights and freedoms, especially the freedom of expression. True victory for democracy in Turkey is only possible by reviving these core values.